WITHDRAWN

*A Social and Economic
History of Medieval Europe*

309.14
H667s

A Social and Economic History of Medieval Europe

GERALD A. J. HODGETT

METHUEN & CO LTD
11 New Fetter Lane London EC4

First published 1972
by Methuen & Co Ltd
11 New Fetter Lane, London EC4
© 1972 Gerald A. J. Hodgett
Printed in Great Britain by
Cox and Wyman Ltd
Fakenham, Norfolk

SBN (Hardback) 416 75740 5
SBN (Paperback) 416 75750 2

This title is available in both hardbound and paperback
editions. The paperback edition is sold subject to the
condition that it shall not, by way of trade or otherwise, be lent, resold, hired out or otherwise circulated
without the publisher's prior consent in any form of binding
or cover other than that in which it is published and
without a similar condition including this condition
being imposed on the subsequent purchaser.

Distributed in the U.S.A. by
HARPER & ROW PUBLISHERS, INC.
BARNES & NOBLE IMPORT DIVISION

*To the History Department
of the University of British Columbia*

CATJan14'7?

12-4-73

204452

Contents

Preface

The writing of this book was greatly advanced by an invitation from the University of British Columbia to deliver to the Summer Session in 1967 a course of lectures on 'The Social and Economic History of the Middle Ages'. I was deeply grateful to the History Department of that University for the invitation to teach 'History 304', for in accepting the assignment I was compelled to review the recent literature in the field of medieval social and economic history, to assess its importance and to interpret it to an undergraduate audience. Moreover the stimulus which I received from teaching in Vancouver encouraged me to continue a book which had already been partially written, and the sabbatical leave granted to me by King's College in the session 1969–70 enabled me substantially to complete it.

This book is not a book of the lectures given in 1967 although parts of it are based upon them. It is obviously, having regard to the length of the period covered, not a work of original research as historians understand that term but an attempt to summarize the basic research which has been done in many sectors of the social and economic history of medieval Europe, particularly within the last twenty-five years. My aim has been to provide an introduction to some aspects of the economic and social life of man in the millennium between the fall of the Roman Empire and the discovery of America, and to suggest some reasons for such economic growth as there was at times within that lengthy period.

Apart from my gratitude to the two university institutions mentioned, I am indebted to many scholars with whom I have discussed various problems over a number of years. Dr Peter A. Wood of University College London, directed my attention to modern writing in theoretical human geography. My colleague Dr Janet L. Nelson and Dr John A. Thompson of St Catharine's College,

Cambridge, read chapter 8 in typescript and offered most helpful suggestions. Above all I owe a debt to my cousin Mrs Scott Garnet who typed each chapter as it was written and who unfailingly checked my manuscript.

King's College
London
October 1971

G.A.J.H.

CHAPTER I

A Changing Europe

In 395 when Theodosius died, the Roman Empire was still intact and the division between east and west did not imply any weakening of the Roman state. Within ninety years all traces of imperial rule in western Europe had passed away and the land from Hadrian's Wall to the Atlas mountains and from the western coast of the Iberian peninsula to the Danube, Montenegro and Libya had been parcelled out among Germanic rulers. When Theodosius's two sons, Arcadius, a young man barely eighteen, and Honorius, a boy of eleven, succeeded their father, the former to reign over the eastern part of the empire, the latter over the western, no new principle was involved for two emperors rather than one had been usual for over a century. The west, however, was more barbarized than the east. The army had long depended upon barbarian recruits (i.e. recruits from beyond the imperial frontiers) and barbarians like Arbogast, a Frank, and Stilicho, a Vandal, had influenced or even controlled imperial policy from the 380s, but from 395 emperors in the west became nominees and puppets of barbarian generals.

Until 476, however, a façade of Roman rule was maintained over the western part of the Empire. Honorius, despite the fact that Stilicho as military commander controlled the policy of the west, maintained some authority and lent his imperial approval to a movement of Roman revival which swept Stilicho from power in 408. In the following years Honorius, although somewhat inept in his policies, managed to ward off barbarian conquests of Italy, which was the heartland of the Empire in the west, while conceding in fact the loss of large parts of Britain, Gaul and Spain. Many barbarian invaders were willing to recognize imperial authority and took the name of *foederati* but in practice they enjoyed a large measure of independence.

The Roman façade behind which barbarians such as Stilicho and Ricimer ruled became increasingly thin. Unlike their counterparts at Constantinople, the last Roman emperors in the west were unpromising material from which a *renovatio imperii* might have sprung. Many of them were boys or weaklings and the court, isolated behind the marshes and defences of Ravenna and influenced by lay pietism, was prepared to allow the imperial authority to pass to the barbarians and in Italy itself, especially after 440, to the Papacy and a revivified Senate. Honorius's nephew Valentinian who succeeded in 423 had a Roman Aetius to advise him but he and his minister maintained themselves in power by armed forces recruited largely from the Huns. After Valentinian III's death in 455, the *magistri militiae*, of whom Ricimer was the most outstanding, became 'kingmakers' rather than prime ministers and the following twenty years saw a succession of nine puppet emperors; with Odovacar's seizure of power in 476 all pretence was cast aside and the west was divided into Germanic kingdoms. The small kingdom of Soissons, still under a Roman, Syagrius, disappeared ten years later. In theory the Empire was indivisible and continued to be ruled from Constantinople but in practice the disappearance of a western emperor profoundly influenced the development of the barbarian states because the Byzantine emperors were too distant to exercise effective control; the disappearance no less affected the development of the Papacy. The old forms of government, Senate and consuls, might still remain in Rome but the western empire had gone only to be revived, and then in a very different form, in the time of Charles the Great.

At the beginning of the Christian era within the boundaries of the Roman empire in western Europe the population was predominantly Celtic, mixed with earlier races settled in the area. For many centuries before the establishment of the Empire, these Celtic peoples had mixed with traders from the eastern Mediterranean, with Greeks and with Italians. The name 'Romano-Celt' or 'Romano-provincial' is best used to describe the population of western Europe until the fifth century A.D. Outside the Empire and pressing against its frontiers were Teutonic Germans. By the later second century, if not before, the Germanic peoples were in a state of flux moving from place to place, usually westward, towards the wealthier settled lands of the Empire. This great movement of peoples, the *Völkerwanderung,* finally overthrew the Empire in the west and, although it is only its final stages from 406 onwards that are strictly relevant to our story, we cannot ignore this movement in the period between *c.* 180 and the end of the fourth century, for to do so would give the false impression of a sudden rush of barbarians into Roman territory. In fact Germanic influence had been increasing in the Roman world from the later second century. A survey of economic and social history does not call for a detailed consideration of the part played by Germanic tribes in the Roman army or by their leaders in Roman politics and administration but that influence, which started even before Stilicho's day, was considerable. Our interest is in the Germanic influence upon Roman society, upon the cultivation of land, the legal system and the Latin language; our concern is with ethnic changes which resulted from the fusion of Roman provincial and German settler. Also it must be noted that Roman influence on Germanic society was equally great.

Long before the Germanic tribes, in hostile attacks, poured across the *limites* of the Roman Empire, many Germans had infiltrated into Roman territory and had been given permission to settle on the land. As early as the second century, land-hungry Germans attempted to force their way into the province of Gaul and, although Marcus Aurelius and his son Commodus defeated the Marcomanni, from *c.* 180 continuing pressure existed. Nor was this pressure for admittance the result only of land hunger, for the west Germans were influenced by movements farther to the east; the Goths moved from the lower Vistula to the Black Sea in the later second century and fear of attack from the east impelled westward those Germans situated near the Rhine and the Danube. The Suevi and their allies moved from the middle Elbe and, known by the collective name of Alemanni, attacked the frontier repeatedly throughout the third century. At first the Romans, despite considerable losses, were entirely successful in maintaining intact the frontiers of the Rhine and the *limes* but under Gallienus, in about 258, they were compelled to give ground and the *Agri Decumates,* situated in the great wedge of land within the bend of the Rhine at Basle, were permanently occupied by the Alemanni. Farther north along the lower Rhine, bands of Franks established themselves on the left bank of the river and temporarily spread through the province of Gaul to the Iberian peninsula. To the east along the Dacian and Moesian boundaries, the Empire had to face attacks from the Goths. Though the Goths were defeated in battle, large numbers were admitted to the frontier areas to settle on the devastated lands and a similar policy was followed by Diocletian after 299 when Frankish prisoners of war were settled as *laeti* or *coloni* in the north-eastern part of Gaul. The more Germanic tribes settled within the Empire, however, the more difficult became the Roman position, for in times of stress when the frontier was breached Franks or Goths would tend to make common cause with their kinsmen from outside the Empire. Such attacks by the Franks, Alemans and Goths were frequent between 360 and the end of the fourth century.

Towards the end of that century, in 376, the Visigoths sought a home in the Empire. Leaving the province of Dacia which they had wrested from Roman rule to the Huns and the Vandals, Alans and Suevi poured across the Rhine in 406. These events marked the final stages of the *Völkerwanderung* and these movements were to bring the Germanic peoples control not only over all Britain, Gaul, Spain and Italy but also over north Africa; a control which was tempered by respect for Roman ways. If the most striking example of Romano-Teutonic cooperation to preserve civilization is to be seen in the combined action against Attila in 451, there were also many signs that the Teutons wished to enjoy rather than to destroy Roman institutions. Not all the barbarian leaders were immediately success-ful in establishing kingdoms; Alaric, though he sacked Rome in 410, failed to set up a Visigothic kingdom in Italy but his followers did so in Gaul and later in Spain. The Franks founded a kingdom in north-eastern Gaul, the Burgundians in the south-east of that province, the Suevi in the north-west of Spain, the Vandals in north Africa and first the Rugii and then the Ostrogoths in Italy. So by 476 the Empire in the west, apart from the land ruled by Syagrius in northern Gaul, had ceased to exist.

The rulers of these barbarian kingdoms had many difficult prob-lems to face, problems that could be successfully resolved only by enlisting the cooperation of the conquered Roman provincials. The first essential was the establishment and firm continuation of their rule. Between 476 and the mid eighth century when Islam had conquered much of the area held by the barbarian kings, most of the Teutonic rulers managed to maintain their authority but of all the barbarian rulers the Franks were by far the most successful. By the conversion after 493 of Clovis and his followers to Catholic Christianity rather than to the Christianity of the widespread Arian heresy, the Franks did not arouse so much antagonism between themselves and the defeated Romano-provincials as did other Germanic tribes. In fact the inhabitants of Gaul welcomed the firm rule of Clovis and assisted him in his conquest (at Vouglé in 507) of the Visigoths whom they hated not only as barbarians but also as Arian schismatics.

In Italy and Spain, however, an accommodation between Germanic conquerors and Romano-provincials was not so easily or so quickly achieved. The crucial factor, it would seem, was religious antagonism between the invaders converted to Arian beliefs and the Catholic natives, but in Italy the followers of Odovacar and also of Theodoric were far less numerous than the Franks and intermarriage with the provincials was much less common than in Gaul. Except in north Africa, disputes over land were not the cause of hostility between conqueror and conquered. Even as early as 415 the Visigoths under Wallia had received by arrangement with the Emperor Honorius a third of the produce of the Roman provincials in Aquitaine where they were settled, and in Italy later in the same century Odovacar's Rugians and the Ostrogoths took a third of the produce of the landed estates. Although no firm figures can be given, there are many reasons for believing that the population of the Empire had been declining for some centuries before the barbarian invasions. Italy, Gaul and the Iberian peninsula were underpopulated; these areas could therefore maintain a much higher population and it was generally unnecessary for the Germanic settlers to confiscate the lands of the Romano-provincial inhabitants. The newcomers took over the lands of the fisc (the imperial treasury) and practised 'thirding'. Some of the settlers were regarded as *hospitati* and received a third part of the land or a third of the produce of the estates of their 'hosts'.

The practice varied in different parts of western Europe according to the fertility of the soil and to the density of the immigrant population. In northern Gaul, where the proportion of Franks to Romano-provincials was higher than in southern Gaul, Clovis and his entourage took over the lands of the fisc and there was probably some degree of confiscation, whereas farther south little disturbance of landowners took place. In Spain the Visigothic kings had decreed that the Germanic *possessor* could claim two thirds of the produce from the former owner and the cultivators of the estates and the code of king Euric (466–84) confirms that this method of supporting Visigothic warriors had been devised in the second decade of the fifth century. The Burgundians also took two thirds of the great domains, leaving the remaining third in full ownership of the natives of the land. The Vandals in north Africa pursued a policy of outright expropriation, at least in the neighbourhood of Carthage, enslaving the Roman provincials who had owned the land and making them work their former estates for the benefit of their conquerors. It is not surprising that the Vandals aroused a greater hostility on the part of those they ruled than any other Germanic tribe. Perhaps it was their numerical weakness as much as their Arian ardour that made them such stern persecutors of the Catholic provincials. In the lands of the Rhine and the Danube the Alemanni and the Bavarians confiscated private lands as well as occupying the lands of the fisc. Expropriation however, was not general; the settlement of the Germanic invaders on the land presented few problems for there was land in plenty and to spare.

Not only did the political boundaries of western Europe change between the late fourth and the mid sixth centuries as Germanic kingdoms replaced the *imperium Romanum* but the entry and settlement of Visigoths, Ostrogoths and Lombards, Alans, Suevi and Vandals, Burgundians and Franks, Angles, Saxons and Jutes also involved ethnic and linguistic change. The outstanding feature of the invasions was the numerical weakness of the conquerors. We can assume that there was no general desertion of the invaders' homeland and that the majority of the warrior bands were young men who, in due course, would wish to marry and settle down. Some, no doubt, married women who came from the invaders' Germanic homelands but many wished to marry Romano-provincial women. Although over the centuries a blending of different racial stocks occurred, in the short run difficulties arose. Some Romano-provincials may have despised the Germanic tribesmen as barbarians but a loathing of the

Arian heresy reinforced by legal prohibition prevented marriage between the two races.

In Roman law, marriage had been regarded as the union of a man and a woman for the purpose of having children as members of a family in the Roman Commonwealth. From earliest times both had to be citizens of Rome or of a nation recognized for this status by the Romans. Certainly Roman citizenship had been extended very widely but not to barbarians and *c.* 373, by order of the Emperor Valentinian, provincials were forbidden, under threat of capital punishment, to marry barbarians. Forbidden marriages were not legally valid and dowry and marriage gift made were forfeited to the state. The *Breviarum Alarici*, published by the Visigothic king Alaric II *c.* 506, made no alteration in the Roman law which forbade the intermarriage between Romano-provincial and Goth. Such intermarriage was not finally allowed until 654 when a new legal code, the *Liber Judiciorum,* was promulgated by Receswinth, although there is reason to believe that it had been connived at since the reign of Leovigild (568–86). Even if that is so, the Visigoths had been established in the Iberian peninsula for well over 150 years before any considerable fusion of the races could have begun and even after 654 mixed marriages remained few in number.[1] Similarly in Italy, neither the followers of Odovacar nor Theodoric's Ostrogoths intermarried with the native inhabitants. The gulf between the barbarian and the Roman in Italy was very great and not until about 660 to 670, when another tribe of Germanic invaders, the Lombards, began to intermarry with the native population was any substantial fusion effected.

In Francia, however, fusion came much earlier. In northern Gaul, in Toxandria, the Franks who had settled there as early as 358 formed the majority of the population, but even in central and southern Gaul intermarriage between Frank and Celtic provincial took place from the end of the fifth century. Clovis's conversion to orthodox Christianity shortly after 493, by removing the religious animosity between conqueror and conquered, apparently made this inter-marriage possible. So the native stock remained an important and separate part of the population in most parts of western Europe, for only in the lands on the right bank of the Rhine and in the territories

[1] J. Vicens Vives, *Approaches to the History of Spain*, p. 159.

through which the rivers Main and Danube flowed did the Germanic tribes almost exterminate the Romano-provincials.

The numbers of the barbarian settlers and the date of their fusion with the native peoples influenced the linguistic changes of the period. In England spoken Latin died out at the time of the Anglo-Saxon invasions; in Toxandria (modern Belgium and parts of modern Holland and north-east France) the Franks settled in such large numbers that Latin was no longer, or rarely, spoken and this accounts for the Flemish and Dutch spoken today in most parts of this area. But in other parts of Gaul the Frankish settlement was so thinly spread that its influence upon the spoken language was limited to the introduction of new words into the debased Latin current in those regions. The two languages of the Roman Empire were Latin and Greek which latter tongue was still spoken in the Rhone delta at the beginning of the sixth century. In the main, however, Greek was confined to the eastern part of the Empire and underwent less change than had Latin in the west. Already in the later second century Latin was beginning to alter, case endings were tending to disappear, and it was spoken with a different accent and different idiom in Gaul and Spain from those current in Italy. St Jerome in the fourth century commented upon the poor Latin spoken in the west. The Frankish inability to impose a Germanic language upon the area in which they settled assured to the people of modern France a Romance language: *a fortiori*, in Spain and Italy Romance languages emerged which were even nearer to Latin. This was only to be expected where intermingling of the races was so long delayed, for in Italy, as we have seen, some two centuries passed between the end of the Empire and the beginnings of ethnic fusion. In the linguistic field the Latin of Cassiodorus and of Gregory of Tours is ample evidence of the changes that had taken place between the mid sixth and the late sixth century in Italy and Gaul.

Spain, north Africa and Italy suffered partly though not solely from this lack of unity between the races. Although the view that the native population was effete, despite some evidence that may be adduced to substantiate it, should be treated with caution, it appears that new Germanic blood did something to make Merovingian Francia a more active, successful and vigorous kingdom than either

Visigothic Spain or Lombardic Italy. In time the population decline of the third and fourth centuries was checked and increased numbers necessitated the clearing and cultivation of forest land.

The gradual mixing of Roman provincial and Germanic invader is reflected in the mixture of late Roman and barbarian art. Ostrogothic and Lombard jewellery in cloisonné with garnets and other semiprecious stones was made in a popular Gothic style which had many affinities with Germanic brooches, but the Latin crosses on it showed the influence of late Roman art. On the other hand mosaics and ivory diptychs, either from Constantinople or subject to heavy Byzantine influence, though somewhat barbarized, continue the imperial tradition. As far as can be seen from the small number of buildings that survive from the fifth, sixth and early seventh centuries, in architecture the Germanic kings copied the styles of east Rome. The most important examples of building in western Europe at this period are in Ravenna, a city in which Byzantine influence was unusually strong, but even elsewhere the style was followed. Large colonnaded churches of the basilica type with a terminal apse over which was a domed roof were built by Germanic kings: they were decorated with mosaics, which, like their architectural features, sprang from Roman or Byzantine models. From the later sixth century the architectural style of St Sophia was copied in places as far apart as Kiev and Périgueux, Aix-la-Chapelle and the oases of Upper Egypt.

The apartness and yet the gradual fusion of Romano-provincial and Teuton are reflected in the legal systems which governed the life and conduct of the two separate elements in the European population of these centuries. Under the eastern Emperor Theodosius II a codification of the Roman law was published in 438. It was this Theodosian Code that was the *lex Romana* known and accepted by the barbarians, for the great code of Justinian of a hundred years later, though it replaced the Theodosian Code in the east, was little known in western Europe until the eleventh or twelfth centuries. After 438, laws made at Constantinople did not apply to the west unless the western emperor adopted them. During the later fifth and sixth centuries the Romano-provincials throughout the west were living under a Roman law slightly different from that of the Romans directly ruled by the emperors of the east, but the law was for them a cherished tradition to which they were attached and from which the Germanic invaders did not wish to separate them. The Angles, Saxons, Franks, Burgundians, Lombards and others all had their laws and customs which had been handed down to them by oral tradition. These laws were, in due course, reduced to written codes and, while the Romano-provincials were governed by Roman law, the German settlers were subject to their own code. Provision had to be made for the settlement of disputes between two parties subject to different legal codes but this does not appear to have caused much difficulty. Some confusion was caused by the multiplicity of legal codes, for at one time in Gaul alone six codes were in force under which different Germanic tribes lived.

The Franks had the Salian, the Ripuarian and the Chamavian codes and there were the Burgundian and Visigothic codes. Even after the conquest of the Burgundians and Visigoths by the Franks, they continued to be judged by their own system of law and the Gallo-Romans from whatever part of Francia were judged by the *Breviarium Alarici*. The first redaction of the law of the Salian Franks was issued by Clovis between 508 and 511, and a little later appeared a shorter code for his Romano-provincial subjects alone. About the same date Theodoric in Italy issued a code usually known as the *Edictum Theodorici*. More important than these, however, was the *Lex Visigothorum* published by Alaric II in 506, for it contained a large number of the constitutions from the Theodosian Code. The parts applied to private legislation among the non-Visigothic population are referred to as the *Breviarum Alarici* which formed the basis of law study in the west until the early twelfth century. The Merovingian kings made laws applicable to both their Germanic and their Gallo-Roman subjects which tended to cause the rapid disappearance of differences between them from the later sixth century onwards, although it was not until some 200 years later that the subjects of Charles the Great acknowledged a reformed law which still contained the elements of the tribal codes. By this time, however, the law defined in the capitularies played such a prominent part that the different position of the Romano-provincials and the Germanic tribesmen had virtually disappeared. Some differences in law still remained between Franks (Salians and Ripuarians), Burgundians, Bavarians and other tribes, but there was little difference between them and Gallo-Romans. In fact the Roman provincial had ceased to exist in the western Europe of the late eighth century.

In the east no such drastic change occurred in the political, social or economic life. With plentiful supplies of manpower the emperors at Constantinople were able to preserve the integrity of their state and so assure a continuity in law and administration which slowed down the pace of change. Even there, barbarian races settled within the Empire but they never permanently or even for lengthy periods usurped the imperial power. Ethnic fusion took place between invaders and natives from the later sixth century onwards but the barbarian was contained and absorbed into the 'Roman way of life'. In fact this way of life was more Greek than Roman for, although the Roman tradition in law and government remained, Greek was the language of most of the inhabitants and it gradually ousted Latin. The east was not faced with a flood of foreign settlers with new languages, with the problems of several codes of law or with the problems of ethnic fusion such as troubled the west in the fifth century. The administrative system continued in the eastern part of the Empire, for few changes were made in offices, functions or titles until the reign of Heraclius (610–41).

Between 400 and 800 European society was more deeply affected in some ways by christianization than by political, linguistic, ethnic and economic changes. The adoption of Christian marriage from the fourth century onwards put an end to the voluntary restriction of births that had been common in earlier centuries and that together with a greater measure of care for 'underprivileged' citizens (hospitals) tended to increase the population; nor must the part played by the infusion of new Germanic blood in the west be overlooked. Gradually Christianity put down or transformed old pagan practices and certain forms of sport; gladiatorial shows were replaced by chariot races; the Olympic Games were suppressed in 394 and the Eleusinian Mysteries ceased after Alaric sacked the temple in 396. But it was not until the sixth century that Justinian closed the schools in Athens which had been the centre of pagan philosophical teaching for almost a millennium; at that time, too, pagans ceased to have any share in government. A hard struggle had been fought in Rome itself where the old gods were openly worshipped until, after 382, the

Emperor Gratian did much to suppress these practices and through-out western Europe in the fifth century pagan literature circulated and pagan rites were sporadically maintained. But that same century saw the incorporation of many of the old heathen festivals into Christian rites: harvest festivals and patron saints did duty for pagan feasts and the old gods. Christianity indeed was so strongly estab-lished throughout Europe before the main barbarian attacks that it was able to survive and in time to convert those settlers within the old Empire who were not already Christians. In this conversion the settlers received not only a new religion but something of the laws, institutions and culture of the classical world was handed on to them.

We should not deceive ourselves into thinking that no disastrous decline in cultural standards took place as a result of the shattering of the unity of western Europe. Such a decline was patently obvious not least to contemporaries. Western Europe had become german-ized but it had also become christianized, for all but the extreme north and north-west of the continent had been freed from pagan-ism by 800. Of recent years the trend among some scholars has been to underestimate the catastrophic nature of the break-up of the Roman Empire and it is true that standards had been slipping long before the end of the fourth century.[1] But European unity had been shattered and the continent was thrown into the melting pot with fewer changes in the east than in the west but with some change everywhere. Standards of government and administration fell less in the east than in the west but even there change occurred. Art and architecture were profoundly affected by the conquest of Christianity and by the introduction of designs from Asia. In this shifting world Byzantium played a leading role and the influence of the great imperial city was felt throughout Europe. Its commodities were available even in England, as the finds of the Sutton Hoo site have shown. The year 400 saw a Europe on the way to fragmentation, the year 800 saw unity restored in some measure to the western part of the continent; in this changing world the economy underwent much change; rural life in some ways was transformed and commercial links were broken and reformed.

[1] R. S. Lopez, *The Birth of Europe*, p. 49.

CHAPTER 2

Rural Change and Expansion to c. 1000

Although it is impossible to quantify, there may have been some population growth in part of Europe between *c.* 500 and 1000. The clearing of forest and the cultivation of heavy clay soils would not have been undertaken had there been no more mouths to feed and could not have been achieved without an increased labour force. This growth was probably unevenly distributed in area and in time, but evidence from the Île-de-France, the Ardennes and Burgundy argues a certain expansion in those regions, although the Hungarian and Norman ravages may even have brought about a decline in European population in the tenth and early eleventh centuries. This expansion in agricultural production caused some change in the countryside in the five centuries after the collapse of the western Empire and its replacement by the barbarian kingdoms. It is not easy to separate the changes in estate management from those in agricultural techniques, but an attempt will be made to leave to the next chapter the questions of the acquisition of labour and its status in society and of the way in which the manorial estate was worked.

The outstanding contribution of the Romans to agricultural techniques was the intensive working which their agronomists preached and which their landowners put into practice. The fallow was intensively worked and when corn was in the ground the soil was kept loose and free from weeds. Land sown with corn in the autumn was hoed in January or February, then again in early March and was given a thorough weeding in early May before the crop was cut in June or early July. In addition to grain, the Romans had also encouraged the growth of fodder crops, such as vetches, lucerne, chick peas and farrago (a blend of barley, vetches and other leguminous plants) which the cattle ate green. They recognized that soil fertility was limited by the absence of manure and their agricultural writers such as Cato (234–149 B.C.) and Varro (116–28 B.C.) recommended stall feeding: the straw was laid on the floor of the stalls, the animals fouled it (where straw was not available oak leaves and bean stalks were used) and this fouled straw was the most valuable manure. Wood ashes were also used and Isidore of Seville mentioned stubble burning. Green manuring, the digging in of lupins, bean stalks and vetches, was advised by Cato in an attempt to make some land produce crops every year and Columella suggested a rotation of crops of cereal, vetches, cereal, farrago.

This system of rotation in Mediterranean Europe only just managed to survive the political wreck of the Empire in the west. The methods of ploughing and the size and shape of fields continued, but nearly everywhere intensive cultivation ceased and fallow was almost universal. The reasons for this are that the Romans had never really managed to suppress fallow except on very fertile soils, e.g. those around Mount Vesuvius, and that fallow and the working of it was often as much necessary to maintain humidity as it was to maintain goodness in the soil. A three-course rotation was no use in the Mediterranean area because spring corn did not succeed there, as it tended to be dried out before it was ready to be harvested, and spring-sown oats were especially valuable in feeding cattle. Hence a shortage of cattle was a feature of Mediterranean husbandry and this shortage was intensified by the declining forests in that region since forest was essential as a supplement to cattle feed. This lack of cattle meant that little manure was available and thus any attempt to get rid of fallow generally in southern Europe was impossible, although in some districts of northern Italy progressive farmers managed to work a system without fallow.

The paucity of the evidence does not allow more than tentative suggestions to be made about the evolution of agricultural techniques in the centuries after the fall of the western Empire. What was specifically Mediterranean in Roman technique survived in southern Europe throughout the Middle Ages and, indeed, had some influence upon agricultural practice in north-western Europe. The long upheavals of the age of the barbarian invasions did not break the influence that classical agriculture had upon some areas far away from the Mediterranean for it was practised mainly upon light soils.

These soils were not over-moist in the Mediterranean regions but, allowing for the higher rainfall, the methods of cultivation employed, say, on the light chalky soils of the downlands of south-eastern England were not dissimilar to those used on the Italian limestone soils.

The two most important considerations are the type of plough, which had a direct bearing on the shape of the fields, and the amount of fallow, which set the pattern of the agrarian calendar. Although research in these areas advises caution, in general, a great difference existed between northern and southern Europe, a difference that may have existed to some extent in the times of the Roman Empire but one that was to become more acute, if, indeed, it did not really appear, after the downfall of the Empire in the west. In the post-imperial period these differences in agricultural technique became more marked and were to remain until the nineteenth century; in fact in some areas fallow is still the rule until the present day. Europe south of the Loire and the Alps had, in the main, a two-course rotation whereas northern Europe eventually – although not in some parts until the late twelfth century or even later – adopted a three-course rotation.

This contrast was attributable to various factors. The subsoil was of basic importance but it was perhaps of less significance than the moisture content of the topsoil which depended upon climate. The main objective of the Mediterranean system was the preservation of moisture. The contrast between the two systems, however, owed much to the different types of plough employed in the two regions.[1] In the Mediterranean region the light scratch plough was used; in Latin *aratrum*, in French *araire*. This type of plough had a symmetrically shaped share of iron, although sometimes it might be made of hard wood; it did not penetrate the ground to a great depth (15–20 centimetres) and usually had no coulter. Sometimes a coulter was mounted before the share and sometimes the coulter, which cut through the soil, was a separate instrument which the scratch plough followed. J. B. P. Karslake's view that the finding of coulters of the Roman period at Silchester indicated that heavy ploughs were in use in Britain[2] was countered in 1938 by R. Lennard who showed that

---

[1] A. G. Haudricourt and M. Jean-Brunhes Delamarre, *L'Homme et la Charrue.*
[2] *Antiquaries Journal*, XIII (1933), 455 ff.

coulters were sometimes attached to light wheel-less ploughs[1] and most scholars have accepted his judgement. The scratch plough was adequate for the light soils but it was no use on the heavy soils that existed even in southern Europe, notably in the valley of the river Po in northern Italy, but were to be found principally in the temperate zone. But while it was adequate, the best yields could only be obtained by expending much time and labour upon ploughing. The fallow was accordingly ploughed at least three times. The soil had to be pulverized and the weeds kept under in order to preserve moisture, and to that end the fallow was worked in January and February, secondly between March and May and again after the first autumn rains. Moreover, because the scratch plough does not turn the soil over and leaves a piece of undisturbed earth between each furrow, it was necessary to cross plough in order to secure the requisite pulverization. This cross ploughing tended to create squarish fields. The scratch plough was sometimes used, e.g. in Scandinavia, as it still is in Syria and Sardinia, to plough long strips so that the shape of a field does not incontrovertibly argue the use of any particular form of plough but, nevertheless, the scratch plough usually argues fairly small equal-sided fields. This lightweight plough was drawn by a pair of oxen and some of the light soils of southern Europe were even cultivated without ploughs by means of digging and hoeing with a toothed hoe.

The temperate zone of Europe contained much more heavy clay soil than did the Mediterranean zone and it was these heavy clays that demanded for their cultivation a heavy plough. A plough heavier than the *aratrum* was known in classical times. A passage in Pliny's *Natural History*, written in the first century A.D., has been much discussed by scholars. Having described this plough as being pulled by eight oxen, he continues 'non pridem inventum in Raetia Galliae duas adderent tali rotulas quod genus vocant plaumorati'. Since 1886, discussions have continued about 'plaumorati', a word that is meaningless and represents a corrupt text; if the correct reading should be, as was then suggested, 'ploum Raeti', we have the first use of a non-classical word to describe a plough different from the *aratrum* or scratch plough. How far this heavy plough was used

---

[1] 'From Roman Britain to Anglo-Saxon England', *Wirtschaft und Kultur: Festschrift zum 70 Geburstag von Alfons Dopsch* (Leipzig, Rohrer, 1938), pp. 69-70.

in the imperial period is a matter in dispute among scholars as yet undetermined. It would appear on philological grounds that *carruca,* the Latin equivalent of the French *charrue,* which means a wheeled plough, was not used in that sense as late as *c.* 507–11 when the *Lex Salica* was drawn up. At that time *carruca* still meant a two-wheeled cart, but by 724–30, the *Lex Alemannorum* may show that the word indicated a two-wheeled plough[1] and the latinized *plovum* appearing in 643 (*Edictus Rotharii*) probably indicated the heavy type of plough in contradistinction to the *aratrum.*

Doubt has been thrown upon the fact that it required eight oxen to pull this heavy plough and E. M. Jope declared that it did not seem that eight oxen were ever yoked to it at once and that no illustration shows more than four.[2] Uncritical acceptance of the Domesday eight-ox plough team has helped English agrarian historians to think that the heavy clays were brought under cultivation for the first time by the earliest Saxon farmers who brought the plough with them from their Germanic homelands. There is virtually no evidence that the heavy clay lands were first cultivated by the Angles and Saxons; but there is some to show that these heavy lands had been cultivated in Roman times and that this cultivation may have suffered a setback in the late imperial period and when the Germanic invaders wrested land from the Romano-British population. Such research as has been done in England tends to revive the view of continuity between the methods of cultivation in Roman and Anglo-Saxon times. H. P. R. Finberg in an essay entitled 'Roman and Saxon Withington' suggested such continuity of cultivation on a villa estate in Gloucestershire[3] and, although he agrees that some areas of the country, particularly Kent, may have been cultivated by free peasant proprietors, it is clear that some parts may have retained the servile tenures of the Roman villas, and from this he concludes that the methods of cultivation may have remained substantially unchanged from Roman to Anglo-Saxon times. Withington was an estate upon which mixed farming was undertaken, for the hill pastures (*dun* = a

[1] G. Duby, *Rural Economy and Country Life in the Medieval West,* p. 19, denies this view.

[2] C. Singer *et al.* (eds.), *A History of Technology* (London, Oxford University Press, 1956), vol. II, p. 91.

[3] University College of Leicester Dept of English Local History Occasional Paper No. 8 (1955).

ridge; specialized meaning, hill pasture) were obviously an important part of an estate that produced wool as well as cereals.

Whether the really significant step in bringing into cultivation the heavy clay lands is to be attributed to the use of a plough with wheels or a plough with a mouldboard has been another controversial point between agricultural historians. It seems clear that it was the heavy plough with a heavy mouldboard that created long strips,[1] because such a plough was difficult to turn and the strips were therefore lengthened. The affixing of wheels merely regulated the depth of the furrow. The wheeled plough spread very slowly from Lombardy, its place of origin according to Pliny, during the Roman period, principally into areas outside the Empire. Parts of Germany where land was cultivated sporadically may well have seen the use of the heavy wheeled plough to clear long neglected strong lands. Here a heavy ploughshare would have been necessary and to put it on wheels would make it more easily transportable from place to place, whereas the weight of the share had previously to be limited to what could be carried on an animal's back. The mouldboard, a device for guiding the furrow slice and turning it over, was not known before the eleventh century and it is hardly clearly recognizable in drawings earlier than the fourteenth century. It was, in all probability, invented in Flanders because it was in origin only a flat wooden plank serviceable in the strong stoneless lands such as Flanders clay.

This heavy plough with an asymmetric share obviously required greater tractive power which, certainly down to the eleventh century, was provided by an increased number of oxen. The *polyptyque* of Irminon, abbot of Saint-Germain-des-Prés, makes it clear that in the early ninth century oxen were regarded as being for the plough of whatever type and horses for carrying man and his baggage. Probably as early as the late eleventh century horses were used for ploughing in the Paris region and by the fifteenth century oxen were rarely used there, whereas in parts of Italy oxen were retained – certainly until twenty years ago. The relative merits of oxen and horses as draught animals will be discussed in a later chapter for it was much discussed by agrarian writers of the thirteenth century.

[1] View expressed by C. S. and C. S. Orwin, *The Open Fields* (Oxford, Clarendon Press, 3rd ed. 1967), p. 32.

One of the developments of technique in the temperate zone was the practice of marling, a practice which, according to Charles the Bald, had started in the reign of his grandfather Charlemagne. Marl is a clay that contains carbonate of lime and when mixed with topsoil it proves a valuable fertilizer. Its use was one of the great innovations of the temperate regions and an edict of 864 (Edict of Pitres) forced *coloni* to cart marl. Marling was not possible everywhere but it was widespread in parts of France and England. Paring and burning of the topsoil was used as another method of fertilizing the soil but it does not appear to have been a method that was widely employed. Another and more significant technical development was the introduction and use of water mills for the grinding of corn between 800 and 1000.

Gradually in the temperate zone a timetable of agricultural work emerged which was different from that of southern Europe. By the ninth century the first ploughing of the year was usually for the spring sowing and took place in March; indeed where barley was to be sown the ploughing might be done in February. Then, in May the fallow received its first working, a ploughing that might be delayed in eastern France and western Germany until June. A second working of the fallow was made just before the autumn sowing. This timetable was to alter in the later Middle Ages as more frequent ploughings were introduced.

Although the harrow was not a medieval invention, the Romans made little use of it and it does not appear to have been used in the western temperate zones until after the imperial period. Whereas the Romans used it primarily for tearing out weeds, in the medieval world it was employed for covering seed. A harrow clearly is depicted in the eleventh century Bayeux tapestry and at first it consisted of a square wooden frame with thorns, variations in the shape occurring later. Because it was essential to cover seeds quickly, the horse, which moved much faster than the ox, pulled the harrow. Another invention of the early Middle Ages, the flail, helped to speed up the process of threshing. The instrument may have been invented by late Roman times, for St Jerome in the fourth century seems to refer to a jointed flail, but threshing was certainly mostly done in classical times by oxen or horses treading out the corn or by beating with a single stick. The flail replaced the beating stick in the early Middle Ages.

These developments in agricultural technique and especially the growing use of the heavy plough led to the equation, to quote Marc Bloch, coulter + horizontal share + mould board + wheels = strips = open fields = communal agriculture. We can presume that this evolution was in some measure forced upon farmers to feed a growing population. The heavy plough, the use of which was probably not widespread before the fifth century, made possible greater productivity in agriculture by opening up the heavy clays and by cultivating soils to a greater depth than could the scratch plough. It could only be used in areas of some density of settlement, for the plough itself was costly and it was costly to operate in that eight – or at least four – oxen were required to pull it and an isolated family would not have enough animals to employ it. Hence the plough could only be used in village settlements and by communal arrangement. German scholars have postulated a large increase in population, probably at the end of the sixth century and certainly in the seventh, in central and south-western Germany, and in the Rhineland and in some districts a fourfold increase had taken place compared with the population of the later Roman Empire. This increase here seems to be connected with the growth of open fields, which indicates the more widespread use of the *carruca* or wheeled plough. The ridge and furrow that was created by the heavy plough on wet lands that needed drainage probably dates from this period in these parts of Germany; also to these centuries may date the strips curved in a slight S-shape because this curve was produced by the manoeuvring that was necessary to turn the large plough team. The increase in arable cultivation which is a feature of the period from 400 to 1000 led to a better balance between animal and cereal production. In the remaining centuries of the Middle Ages, or more precisely in those centuries between the eleventh and the early fourteenth, the process of reducing the forest and the waste and increasing the arable was to be taken much further, but the first attack on the forests and wastes of northern and western Europe came in the 600 years or so after the downfall of the Roman Empire in the west.

In general, the plants cultivated in this period were the same as those grown in classical times. Some of the corns were improved and spelt, rye, oats and buckwheat were fully developed only in the Middle Ages. Barley was widely grown in the temperate zone, for it was of all corns the most tolerant of climatic changes; it ripens, for example, in Scandinavia farther north than rye. Barley was used in the Middle Ages both for porridge and bread, fermented it was made into ale and in southern Europe horses ate barley rather than oats. It was sown both as a winter grain (*hordeum hexastichum*) and, more frequently, as a spring grain (*hordeum distichum*). At the time of Charlemagne it took the leading place among cereals, but its popularity declined as it was realized that rye drained less nourishment from the soil. Millet suited light soils and some varieties matured in three months; it was grown during the Middle Ages in the Pyrénées, south-western France and northern Italy. Sorghum was introduced by the Arabs, although it may have been known to Pliny. But the great growth of oats and rye gave medieval Europe an aspect different from the Europe of the Roman Empire. Oats were nearly always sown in the spring and rye nearly always in the autumn. So much was this the rule that in Germany the land under the winter crop was often known as the *Roggenfeld* and that under the spring crop as the *Haberfeld*. Oats were regarded by some classical authors as a weed, although Columella ranked it as a fodder crop, but the Germans made porridge of it and throughout the north, in Germany, northern France and in Scotland, it provided human nourishment in the form of porridge. But its great importance was as a feed for horses and horses were far more numerous in the Middle Ages and more significant in medieval society than they had been to classical society. Rye had also been regarded as a weed grown along with wheat but it was developed in the north because it resisted cold better. Pliny first mentioned it and it occurs in Diocletian's edict of prices as *centenum sive secale*. It spread to Gaul, probably in the fourth century, but it was only after the downfall of the western Roman Empire that it became the dominant corn in the centre and north of Germany and the chief corn crop on the poor soils of central France and northern Belgium. The Anglo-Saxons must have known it and brought it with them for it was much grown in England and the barbarian invaders of Italy took it and grew it even in southern Italy where it was known as *germanum*.

Some writers have thought that the balance of foodstuff consumed was improved in the Middle Ages but the consensus seems to be that such improvement occurred from the eleventh century onwards when, to quote Lynn White, 'Europe was full of beans'. However, in the centuries before the millennium, turnips, beans, peas and lentils were grown. If some expansion in the textile trade may be postulated, it may be argued that the output of dyers' weed, woad, madder, saffron and teasels increased and flax and hemp were important crops in some areas. In southern Europe cultivation of the vine and the olive continued as in Imperial times but the imbalance between agriculture and animal husbandry became more marked, for a law of the Emperor Valens (363–78) indicates a grave shortage of cattle which remained as a feature of the Mediterranean agrarian economy. At least from the fifth century those parts of the temperate zone that had been within the Roman Empire had many fruit trees: apple, pear, plum, peach, cherry, quince and fig as well as walnut, chestnut and hazel.

In stressing the expansion of European agriculture especially in the temperate zone where much virgin soil was brought into cultivation in the 500 years after the foundation of the barbarian kingdoms, we must not overlook the profound importance of the marshes, moors and forests to the rural economy of this period, and indeed to that of the entire Middle Ages. They were doubly important; firstly rural dwellers depended, to a much greater extent than they do today, upon the collection of wild fruits and berries, and secondly they were often the principal source of food supply for animals. Above all they provided the feed for the large herds of swine which ate acorns and beech mast and which supplied the most widely consumed meat, at least until the later fourteenth century. Rivers and marshes helped to supplement the diet, perhaps always deficient in protein in the medieval period, by providing fish. The forests and copses produced the timber which was required for building and for firewood, and the marshes the osiers for fencing and the rushes for matting, while the moors were often suitable pasture for sheep and the Alpine uplands provided summer pasture for cattle. Nor should the importance of the bee to the rural economy be forgotten. Honey was the sweetener used by the mass of the population of medieval Europe and beeswax had uses other than the making of church candles.

The picture that emerges then between *c*. 500 and 1000 is a picture of a modestly expanding rural economy. Expansion and change were greater in the north than in the south where the economy stood still or tended to decline. In the temperate zone the development of virgin lands or lands that had been little cultivated meant that the balance of production was tipped in the favour of the north which became the area of experiment and challenge in early medieval farming practice.

CHAPTER 3

The Growth of the Manor

The estate owned by a lord and having dependent tenants upon it,
known in England as a manor and in France as a *seigneurie*, formed
the farming unit most frequently found over large areas of western
and central Europe throughout the Middle Ages. This type of large
rural estate did not spread uniformly throughout Europe; in some
places it developed much earlier than in others, in some regions
nearly all the available land was cultivated in estates of this pattern,
while in others vast numbers of small peasant proprietors remained.
Parts of France and Italy underwent this seignorialization long before
Germany and England and in 1200 the great estate in Germany was
still at a stage of development as regards the exploitation of labour
services which had been reached by many estates in the district
between the Loire and the Meuse at the time of Charlemagne. By
the ninth century, the areas where the great estate was most firmly
established were north-eastern and south-eastern Gaul, most of
Italy, Catalonia, the Rhineland, and parts of central and southern
Germany. England and Denmark were not to become seignorialized
until well into the tenth century. In the south-western part of Gaul
and in the Saxon plain seignorialization was never complete, for here
the large estates of several thousand acres existed alongside much
smaller estates, the owners of which knew no control save that of
the state. These free holdings, called allods, remained especially
numerous in Aquitaine. Finally areas existed such as Friesland,
northern Holland, and Dithmarschen (the district between the river
Eider and the mouth of the Elbe at the western end of the Kiel canal),
Norway and perhaps Sweden, which never knew the manorial
estate.

The class of villein serfs, which formed the majority of the
population of Europe by the early twelfth century, was composed of

men whose forbears had risen from slavery and also of men whose ancestors had once enjoyed a much greater degree of freedom. This levelling process had been going on at least from the sixth century and with increased rapidity between the later ninth and the early twelfth centuries. In considering first those who had risen to the rank of serf from the lowlier rank of slave, we must look back almost to the beginning of the Christian era. Conditions made it no longer profitable or even in some instances possible to cultivate large estates (*latifundia*) by gangs of slave labour. Several ancient writers on agriculture pointed out that slaves were not interested in their work, and that estates were not well run by their labour unless they were very closely supervised. At a time when slaves were plentiful and therefore cheap, estates might be cultivated in this way without too great a capital expenditure, but the long Augustan peace reduced the supply of slaves, and from the second century A.D. at the latest other methods had to be found of working these large estates. Even before Christian influence became strong, it had been a virtuous act to free a slave; from the third century manumission was a work of Christian charity. Many of the freed men acquired small pieces of the vast *latifundium* but, though free, they still owed certain services to their masters. Also, small proprietors, *coloni*, took holdings, for the dwindling population during the later centuries of the Roman Empire made estate owners anxious to find anyone who would till their land. The scarcity of slave labour, and possibly the influence of Christianity then, brought about a change in the methods of cultivation of the *villa*. On such an estate, which would vary in acreage, some land was normally worked by the lord (*dominus fundi*) but the greater part of it comprised small holdings worked by the 'hutted' slaves, those who had been given a hut (*casa*), or by the *coloni*, free men who farmed land that they did not own.

The government's policy was to attach both the *coloni* and the *servi casati*, the 'hutted' slaves, to the soil and in furtherance of that policy already before 375 an edict had forbidden a lord to sell rural slaves whose names were on the tax rolls apart from the sale of the land they tilled. At a later date a lord was legally prohibited from diverting these 'hutted' slaves from the cultivation of the land to other – presumably domestic – tasks. Although his lord no longer gave him board and lodging, the 'hutted' slave was still subject to his lord's authority which meant that he had no access to the courts of law, that he was deemed unfit for Holy Orders and that, in theory at least, he was compelled to serve whenever he was bidden. As late as the ninth century the holdings of these men were called, in those extensive monastic surveys known as the polyptiques, and in royal documents, *mansi serviles* and, although freemen are found holding these tenements and the unfree holding the *mansi ingenuiles* of the freeman, the nomenclature of the holdings demonstrates clearly the double origin of the tenant class.

The more important element, however, in the tenant class of the ninth century or in the class of villein-serfs of the twelfth century is not the slave but the freeman. In assessing this element of freemen whose status had been depressed, we must deal separately with the *coloni*, the free farmers on the estates within the Roman Empire, and those freemen, mostly of Germanic stock, led into and settled within the Roman provinces by their warlike chiefs. From the third century, the economic difficulties of the Imperial government and the measures it took to overcome them attached the *colonus* more firmly to the soil, as those same measures bound the artisan to his trade and the decurion to his municipal office. It was an age of stagnation and bureaucratic control. Economic forces were even more compelling than government legislation, for as early as the mid third century great landlords were constraining their tenants, freemen though they might be, to stay on their holdings after the expiry of their leases. This action was illegal, but the poor were open to pressure from the great, for the landlord had become responsible for producing the *colonus* for military service and for collecting his tax payments. By the fourth century any *colonus* who had cultivated the land for thirty years or more was recognized by the state as being bound to the soil; he was described as a *colonus adscriptitius* and it is apparent that even in the previous century a *colonus* deserting his land received severe punishment. Justinian wrote of the *adscriptitius*, omitting the word *colonus*, yet even in so doing he still clearly distinguished him from the slave. The control of the great landlord over the *colonus* grew but at the same time some advantage accrued to the tenant himself, for he could not be evicted from the land although he might be moved from one part of the estate (*fundus*) to another.

We see then that both economic forces and governmental legislation even before the collapse of the Empire in the west had been tending to depress the status of the *coloni* although at the same time they were being given a fair measure of security. It is difficult to assess how far this legislation succeeded in fixing the *colonus* to the soil and where legislation and economic laws clashed, as they did to some extent, between the fourth and the sixth centuries, powerful reasons for leaving the soil sometimes nullified state enactments. The decline in population proved a strong factor which compelled many great landowners to be ever watchful in maintaining their labour force. Our evidence as to the degree of enforcement of legislation tying tenants to the soil is scanty but, in the absence of any effective imperial police force, it can hardly be doubted that many farmers escaped from the land. Some sixth-century writers, indeed, complained of those who, seeking to better their social status, escaped from their holdings. If the forces of law and order were weak in the later years of imperial rule, they were in some respects even weaker in Merovingian Gaul and in Italy under the Lombard kings: moreover, neither Lombard nor Merovingian law forbade tenants to leave their holdings. The state stood aside. Thus, in a number of ways the great landowner acquired control over his tenants. If the state would not or could not prevent a tenant leaving his tenement then the lord himself took over the task. As early as 388, private prisons for freemen had had to be prohibited but it is significant that the *dominus fundi* had been seeking to extend to his free tenants the jurisdictional powers which he undoubtedly held over his slaves. Whatever might be the legal position, lords were extending their authority and we hear of a good bishop of Arles at the end of the fifth century who only inflicted a few strokes upon his free dependants and his slaves. Justinian's code in the next century allowed the moderate chastisement of the *colonus* and in this way his status was reduced. While in law the *colonus* remained a free man he was already suffering some legal deprivations.

The view that the Germanic tribesmen who followed their warrior chieftains into the Roman lands were all free men may have to be modified. The name *Frank*, which scholars have now decided does not mean free, cannot be employed to advance the theory that the tribesmen were free and equal. The writings of Tacitus make it clear that the Germans had farmers who were slaves, and doubtless many 'clients' attached to the chiefs of invading German tribes, although they were freemen, were so dependent upon their lords that their free status might be in jeopardy. Moreover, half-free cultivators of the soil existed on the estates of great German lords; the Saxon *Laten*, the Frankish *Liten*, the laets. This gradation of social class which the Germanic tribes brought with them into *Romania* and similarities in social status led to the establishment of an equivalence of status between the Germanic conquerors and the conquered Romano-provincials. That the majority of settlers was formed of free men has not yet been seriously challenged by scholars and we have, therefore, to consider how it was that their free status, like that of the *coloni*, gradually deteriorated into one of semi-servitude.

The answer to this question is twofold. The thirst for power and prestige on the part of the great men and the demand for protection and security by the small freeholder are together responsible for the depression of the status of the free peasant proprietor or ceorl as he was called in Anglo-Saxon England. The seven centuries from 400 to 1100 were uncertain times and within that long span only some 150 years from *c.* 700 to *c.* 850 saw the re-emergence, and that only in some areas of Europe, of a limited state authority. The absence of strong central government especially between *c.* 400 and *c.* 600 and again between *c.* 850 and *c.* 1050 gave free rein to the local anarchy of petty tyrants. This lack of governance compelled the weak to seek protection.

Already in the last century of Roman rule in the west, men were seeking patrons and offering up their small holdings to a lord to receive them back as benefices on condition that they paid dues and services to their protector. But the idea of a lord or chief with tenants dependent upon him is, in all probability, much older even than the fourth century for, both in the Celtic Gaulish society of Caesar's day and in the Germanic society of the time of Tacitus, chiefs are to be found who owe their position to their 'clients'. The tribesmen gave presents to the lord, and many of these gifts became fixed by custom and ended up as obligations. The tendency for the weak small landholder to secure the protection of the great was natural and it was intensified by the lack of strong central administration. Some loosening of the power and authority of the kin-group at the time of the *Völkerwanderung* may also have contributed to the practice of seeking protection.

Although the French scholar Marc Bloch warned that the practice of commendation, especially of handing land over to a lord and receiving it back again as a dependent tenure, did not arise from an economic crisis,[1] economic conditions in the early Middle Ages were in general unfavourable to the small holder. The full effects of the reduction in the circulation of money are, indeed, incalculable but presumably he was deprived of the ability to amass a reserve from which he could pay his taxes and other dues. In an age when new lands were being opened up to cultivation – and this was probably more true of England than of the continent in general – the pioneer with inadequate capital would always be in a precarious position. The German freeman, the cultivator of a small holding, say of 12 hectares, found himself particularly vulnerable to one bad season or to an attack of disease which might kill all his animals. It was in such circumstances that he might have to look to a large local landholder, either lay or ecclesiastical, with his more substantial reserves, to protect him and his family from death by starvation. Such life-giving help could not be obtained without some concessions and the starving peasant might bind himself and his heirs to a lord and become his man.

Finally religious piety was the mainspring behind many grants of land. The local monastery or the local bishop proved a powerful protector. In a period when the authority of the church became more prominent than it had previously been, in an age when the supernatural powers of a local saint might be highly venerated, the local monks who kept his relics might be regarded as highly efficacious protectors. A small holder could, of course, merely seek the *mund* or protection of a lord, promising to pay him an annual gift or to assist him in various ways, or, on the other hand, he might commend himself to a lord offering him his land and receiving it back again as a dependent tenement. Services and dues would follow, as appears from a survey of the lands of Santa Giulia of Brescia *c.* 900, which records 'there are here fourteen freemen who have handed over their property to the hall, the condition being that each shall do one day's work a week'. One has only to recall the

[1] M. Bloch, *La Société féodale, Liens de dépendance*, p. 376.

uncertainty of the times, the invasions of Vikings and Magyars, the force of religious piety, to appreciate the small man's need of security.

How did the great seek to extend their power and prestige? Partly they enlarged their control by their own ruthless actions, but they were in part helped to wider authority by the state itself. Frankish kings granted many estates to churches and to great men with wide immunities, so allowing the lords to exercise jurisdictional authority over the men on their estates even though these tenants were free-men. As the royal officials were excluded from these vast estates, and the tenants excluded from the royal courts, the status of the tenants on such estates gradually deteriorated. But the lords themselves were not inactive. Relying upon the power of the old Germanic chief to compel his followers, the power known as the *ban*, lords, especially in the troubled period after *c.* 850, placed many new impositions upon their tenants. These obligations, called in French *banalités*, compelled tenants to grind their corn at the lord's mill, to bake their bread at his oven and to press their grapes at his wine-press. For these services a fee would be charged and on some manors the lord claimed the exclusive right to supply, for a fee, the bull or boar necessary to maintain the tenants' herds. It was precisely where the royal authority was weakest, as in France in the later ninth and tenth centuries, that these impositions became most widespread and most onerous. In Germany on the other hand these *banalités* hardly existed until a much later date. Other impositions such as *chevage* (head money) and the *taille* appeared during the anarchy of the later Carolingian era. *Chevage*, an annual payment, was originally paid by freed slaves, and, along with reliefs, the two payments became sym-bols of a man's subjection to his lord, although in the first place the latter contributions were certainly regarded as donations made to the lord in payment for his protection. The *taille* was probably more ancient in origin, based upon the obligation of a subject to support his chief. As with the *banalités*, so the *taille* became widespread in France while in Germany only a small number of lords levied it, namely those who had the powers of *haute justice*. In fact the imposi-tion of these additional burdens was closely connected with the jurisdictional powers, either delegated or assumed, enjoyed by lords. In conclusion, it is quite clear that the burden of services and charges fell more heavily upon the twelfth-century tenant than upon his eighth-century predecessor. However, the amount of labour service performed on the lord's land diminished during these four centuries as population grew and the lord's demands were more widely spread among his tenants.

What were the distinguishing features of the vast estates upon which the lord's dependants worked? Generalization is most difficult here: there were many differing types of estate. Differences sprang from geographical and political factors as much as from climatic and soil conditions. In the regions of Europe that were seignorialized three principal features of these large estates are to be found; the lord's demesne (*terra indominicata*), the holdings of the tenants and the common land and forest. The management of the agricultural operations upon the demesne, and indeed in a sense upon the whole estate, was directed from the lord's dwelling house, or more correctly, from a group of buildings which included also the lord's barns, cattle sheds and workshops. These buildings, sometimes fortified, were called in Latin *curtis*, the court or enclosure; in Italy the word used was *corte*, in Germany *Hof*. The Normans employed the term *manoir* to describe the lord's dwelling house, and the predominant part played by it is demonstrated by the transference of the word manor to include the whole estate.

The lord's demesne was, in the main, cultivated by the labour of the tenants although even at the earliest period some regular labour, either slave or hired, was also a necessity. In theory the tenants did service on the lord's holding (*mansus indominicatus*) when required, but custom, as early as the ninth century and probably earlier, played an important part. We find that the obligation to serve was, by this time, being firmly placed upon the tenant's holding (*mansus*) and that the amount of service required might vary from one *mansus* to another, but land, of course, could not perform the duties – these had to be done by men and women. Perhaps the most usual period of service on the lord's demesne was three days a week but in some places it was even more. But it must be borne in mind that this service was incumbent upon a full holding and that each manse had one family, and probably more than one, living upon it. This being so, the tenant of a manse might work three days a week on his lord's land but other members of the family would be able to cultivate his holding. Indeed at harvest time the custom sometimes compelled the holder of a tenement to bring one or two workers along with him to work on the lord's holding but on such occasions the lord, under this same customary obligation, fed his tenants. In some regions these tenants formed the main source of labour available to the lord for the cultivation of his demesne while elsewhere hired labour, or even slave labour, played a more significant part. Many large estates in pre-Conquest England were cultivated by *famuli*, who were slaves or near-slaves, but on the continent at this period such labour was perhaps less frequently employed. At any rate, on a Farfa estate in the ninth century only ninety-three slaves out of 1400 tenants were enumerated and a century later on the estates of Santa Giulia of Brescia there were 741 slaves as against 4000 tenants. These figures include those who were purely domestic slaves. In some regions, however, it would appear that hired labour played a significant part in demesne cultivation from an early period and a predominant part at least from the eleventh century.

The tenants' labour therefore cultivated the demesne to some degree but it also supplied other requirements of the lord. Other duties such as carting, and supplying the lord with wooden implements or with wax from their hives, emphasized the dependent status of the tenants. Freed slaves and their dependants were often compelled to work in the lord's house in the workshops, known, despite the fact that both sexes were employed there, as *gynaecea*: here they spun wool and wove cloth. In some places the tenant even had to provide the lord with metal tools but in such instances the lord supplied the necessary raw materials. Subordination to the lord of the manor was also driven home still more by many services of a frivolous nature which tenants had to perform. Duties such as flogging the moat round the lord's castle so that the frogs in it would not disturb his rest, or performing ritual dances before the lord were thought by Marc Bloch to have been derived from duties owed by men to their tribal chieftains long before the Roman occupation of Gaul. Payments for permission to marry a daughter or for a son to enter Holy Orders or for the misconduct of his womenfolk reinforced the dependent status of a tenant on these estates.

These manors, at any rate, in the region between the Loire and the Meuse were often vast. Many comprised about 300 holdings (*mansi*) and were probably about 4000 hectares in extent. The percentage of land held in demesne also varied widely. On estates of the French kings and on those of great nobles and of principal churches the demesne often reached between a quarter and a half. Near Paris at Villeneuve-Saint-Georges and at Palaiseau the *mansus indomincatus* totalled 32 per cent and 35 per cent respectively of the cultivated area of the estates. In woodland country, however, it was frequently less. Where a religious house had been given an estate in an area not of nucleated villages but of scattered settlements the demesne remained small.

It cannot be too strongly stressed that these serfs were not slaves, possessing as they did a patrimony, an estate, however burdened it might be, which could be passed from father to son according to fixed laws of inheritance common to the district with which the lord did not interfere; the serfs were far removed from the slaves of antiquity. Within the ranks of those who could be termed villein-serfs, from the early twelfth century we find gradations of freedom. At the top of the scale were those who had originally commended themselves to a lord without surrendering their land. The *muntmen* in Germany in the twelfth century had a higher status than other tenants although tenants in France known as *commendés* had, by that same date, nothing but the name to distinguish them from other dependent tenants. In England the Domesday socmen were often free in so far as their tie with their lord appears personal rather than tenurial. Like the English socman the German *Landsasse* and the French *libre vilain* could choose his own lord. By the later tenth and early eleventh centuries the idea of the free man had changed: the free man was regarded as one who could choose his own lord as a vassal did. But these *Landsassen* and *libres vilains* still had duties to perform to their lord; they were not the holders of allods who were completely free from control by great men and subject only to the state. On some monastic estates groups of tenants called *cerocensuales* appeared who enjoyed the revenues from their lands in return for the payment of wax to the monasteries at major church festivals. In Bavaria and adjacent parts of Austria there appeared the *Barschalken* about whose precise status so much dispute has arisen.

Most of the dependent tenants were bound by custom to perform certain duties on the lords' lands, but south of the Alps many more

tenants held land by contractual agreement. In Italy the written contract had to some degree survived the troubled years after the dis-
integration of the Roman empire in the west. The *livello*, usually
granted for twenty-nine years, was frequently renewable, but this
temporary lease differed from the hereditary tenure that existed in
Germany, France and England. Nevertheless, the idea of serfdom in
Italy was the same as it was north of the Alps. In Catalonia similar
ideas existed but in Asturias, Leon and Castile the link between lord
and cultivator appeared less close. Other dependent tenants were
distinguished by the size of their holdings. The bordiers and cottars
held by servile tenure but their duties were less onerous on account
of the small size of their holdings. Probably their origin is to be
found among people who had squatted on the manor and whose
forbears had never possessed a full tenement, *mansus* in Latin, *Hufe*
in German, in English hide. These *mansi*, at any rate by the ninth
century, had been divided and taxes therefore had to be levied on
each hearth. The status of their forbears was the sign which classified
other dependent tenants: thus descendants of freed slaves were
known as coliberts and held *mansi lidiles*.

We see then a considerable variety in the status of dependent
tenants. The growth of the pattern of cultivation of the soil by such
tenants took a long time to form and was closely connected with the
subordination of the small to the great landowner in matters other
than economic. Jurisdictional subservience cannot easily be dis-
entangled from economic dependence which was being formed in
the upper ranks of society between the great lord and his vassal.
Both movements reflected the weakness of the state and of central
administration in western Europe in the early Middle Ages. However, it must not be assumed that the whole of western Europe was
formed into large estates with subordinate tenants upon them, for in
some regions considerable numbers of free tenants remained and
there were even whole villages that were entirely free from any
control by a great local lord.

But where the manor was established it allowed a relatively small
proportion of the population, the lords of the manor, to live in
idleness and abundance and to devote their time to fighting and to
exercising power over their fellow men. This exercise of power was
probably more important, at least down to the twelfth century, than

the maximization of profit, for the medieval lord was generous in the sense that display of wealth by supporting the largest possible number of dependants was regarded as right and proper.

The peasant standard of living varied immensely even at the earliest period of manorial development, for the manses varied greatly in size, for example from 17 to 30 hectares at Poperinghe to 4.35 to 9.65 hectares in four villages belonging to the abbey of Saint-Germain-des-Prés, although it must be borne in mind that size may have been related to the quality of the soil. Also the number of people living on a manse would vary. A manse given to Saint-Germain-des-Prés had twenty people living on it: two married brothers, one with three children and the other with five, a sister with six children and an unmarried sister. The larger holdings provided an animal for the plough team but tenants both with and without animals had to do compulsory labour on the demesne, the *corvée* in French, which word meant a 'demand' or 'requisition'. The free manses usually provided animals for ploughing and carting while other obligations, such as cultivating with the spade or hoe and dipping and shearing sheep were attached to the servile tenements. The services which the tenants performed varied according to technical developments. The invention of the water mill released much labour from the wearisome work of grinding corn by hand just as additional working of the land called for more labour. By this exploitation the lord in effect appropriated the surplus productive effort of the peasant families. But it must not be forgotten that the peasant, however integrated into the manor he might be, had links with other groups with different interests, for the manor rarely coincided with the village settlement and the community of the vill was older than the manor; the map of rural Europe became a palimpsest upon which the manor had been traced without completely obliterating the traces of earlier rural settlement.

CHAPTER 4

Trade and Commerce in the Early Middle Ages

In medieval Europe an overwhelmingly large proportion of its inhabitants lived in the countryside and obtained its livelihood from agriculture or from animal husbandry but, even in the early Middle Ages, trade and commerce employed some, both inside towns and without. The fall of the Roman Empire in the west in the fifth century did not bring about any vital change in the rural economy of western Europe; still less did it affect the industrial and commercial life of that area. Both in estate management and in trade, changes which went on for many centuries after the fall of the western Empire began well before that event and it is essential to look back to the third century of the Christian era to understand those developments in industry and commerce. Just as in the agricultural sphere, the Roman state tended to intervene increasingly in commercial affairs and this policy of restriction was continued, in some measure, by the Germanic kingdoms, heirs to the Empire in the west.

The world of free private enterprise, which was the world of the Emperor Augustus, had given place to an era of rigid state control under the Emperor Diocletian (284–305). The first and second centuries of the Christian era, down to *c.* 235, formed a period of economic prosperity and the middle years of the third century to 284 marked an intermediate epoch between the *laissez-faire* period of the early Empire and the rigid caste system, brought about by state intervention, of the later Empire. The political upheavals of the mid third century coupled with the economic measures taken by the imperial government profoundly affected urban life; Autun, which had had an area of 200 hectares, provides a striking example of this decline for it was rebuilt in 305–6 on a 10 hectare site. Cities throughout the Empire, with the possible exception of Britain, were shrinking both in area and population from about 275 onwards. The stagnation and decline of cities was the result not only of barbarian raids but also of population trends. Conditions of urban life seem to imply either a low fertility rate or a high death rate or indeed both factors may have been operative. But towns were centres of trade and the political uncertainty of the third century and the increasing burden of risktaking reduced distant trade. This diminution in what Pirenne described as 'le grand commerce', to distinguish it from local exchanges between a town and its surrounding district, probably stimulated the production of goods locally. The *villae* manufactured many goods which had previously been produced either in towns or bought from towns for use on the estate, and this further undermined the position of the towns. High interest rates made it prudent for the manufacturer or the trader to limit his risk which, in the absence of joint-stock enterprises and the principle of limited liability, had to be borne by the entrepreneur alone. The countryside revenged itself on the town which for centuries had been parasitic upon it. This reduction in urban activity is indicative of the fact that the economy was in decline.

This stagnation in the economy was not unconnected with the political disorders of the late third century. The Germanic invasions together with the attacks from a revived Persian Empire greatly increased governmental expenditure on arms, and during the period when parts of Gaul were overrun, taxation was not coming in from that province in full. The government's finances were in a desperate condition and the emperors had two ideas for remedying the situation: the one was to require citizens to perform public functions without pay, the other was to debase the coinage. By the latter device the government hoped to increase its profits from the issue of money and to have more coins available to meet its growing expenses. Debasement is always a dubious method because traders are always going to appreciate that coins no longer have the same value; especially is it dubious in a currency where the value of the coin depends upon its metal content. The touchstone, and more sophisticated methods of assaying, soon informed merchants that the silver content of coins was being diminished, and even without these refinements the reduction in the size of coins made the debasement obvious. Gold coins were little affected. Constantine renamed the *aureus* the *solidus*: it contained 4·55 grammes in weight and remained unaltered until the eleventh century. But the silver *denarius* slipped disastrously: in 301, 50,000 to the gold pound; in 305, 120,000; in 324, 168,000; in the later years of Constantine, 172,000; in the late fourth century, 473,000; and in the mid fifth century, 504,000. In Egypt a gold *solidus* in the early fourth century was worth 4000 Egyptian *drachmae*; in the fifth it was the equivalent of 180 million *drachmae*. The silver coins became bronze coins washed with silver and by the fifth century even that pretence had been abandoned so that the *denarii* became bronze coins of smaller and smaller size until the *minissimi*, as they were called, were about the size of the head of a nail. This runaway inflation – almost on the scale of the German inflation of the 1920s – led to heavy price rises and it is against this background that Diocletian issued his edict of prices in 301.

In this edict, Diocletian laid down the maximum prices for goods and services. It was extremely detailed, listing, for example, eighty-four different articles of wool and over 2000 of linen. It is an important source for commodities available and for services performed. Diocletian's maxima were high and should not seriously have interfered with trade but, as so often happens, the price edict forced goods off the market into a black market; Lactantius tells us of this effect. Whether, in economic theory, such a policy could have succeeded inside a virtually closed economy of substantial size is an interesting discussion for the theoreticians, but for the historian the exercise is known to have been a failure. In order to prevent the further rise of prices by black market operations, Diocletian withdrew the edict. The first quarter of the fourth century saw some improvement in the economic well-being of the people but it was only temporary and there was no return to the great commercial exchanges of the period before the mid third century.

The other remedy which the government thought would solve its difficulties was to fix people in their jobs, so that they could not avoid the payment of taxes and so that they might perform public functions with the minimum of gainful reward. The government aimed to do this by drawing into the state apparatus the *collegia* or gilds of craftsmen. These gilds in the first and second centuries had been loose organizations and a *laissez-faire* system of economic enterprise was common. By Diocletian's time, however, the gilds were no longer voluntary, they were bodies controlled by the government whose members were forced to carry on their trade and even compelled to pass on their obligations to their heirs. Just as a *colonus* could not legally leave the soil, so the *collegiatus* was forbidden to quit his trade and, among the bakers, control was taken to such lengths that they were forbidden to marry any but the daughters of gild members. The shipowners (*navicularii*) were compelled to put vessels of a prescribed tonnage (10,000 *modii*) at the disposal of the state although tax remission was given in return. The shippers in 326, 334, 337 and 380 were specifically released from fiscal burdens but they became tied to their trade and, in effect, their heirs were bound by the laws of inheritance to follow them in it. They were under obligation to assemble a crew and organize a voyage in the state service at a fixed rate of 4 per cent of the value of the cargo in kind plus one thousandth of its value in gold so that the shippers might scarcely suffer any loss. But in 412 and 414 the percentage paid to shippers bringing grain to Rome from north Africa fell to 1 per cent and the death penalty was decreed for any shipper who delayed in port, speculated with the cargo or traded illicitly. It may be argued that the importance of supplying the capital with grain justified these draconic measures but the degree of state control and the inflation may betoken a stagnant economy.

After the widespread adoption of water mills at Rome a separate gild of millers was set up of which we have knowledge from the end of the third century. The millers and bakers, the oil merchants and the pork butchers (*suarii*) were all responsible for the distribution of free allocations to the Roman populace. By the beginning of our period most traders, for example, fishmongers, potters, innkeepers, silversmiths, were organized in gilds and were compelled so to be in order to carry on their trade. The system was one not of nationalization but of government-controlled private enterprise. Disputes have arisen among scholars as to why this semi-planned economy arose but it was due, principally, to the fact that private enterprise proved unequal to the task of feeding the population and of producing and distributing goods. This inability may well have been because profit margins were too low but government control undoubtedly still further sapped private enterprise. Burdens of administration were also thrown upon a hereditary caste of *curiales*.

This system of state control, although it might compensate him for loss of income (*solacium*), left him little initiative and so the economy stagnated still more. Although the needs of the army were supplied by the provinces in kind, an imposition known as *annona*, it is untrue to infer that money was driven out and that a return to a barter economy occurred. The payment of taxes *in natura* led to the building of public storehouses (*mansiones*) and this type of payment along with transport difficulties caused a decentralization of the economy. State employees were paid in vouchers which were in effect drafts on the public storehouses, and muleteers were requisitioned to transport *annona* and for the working of the public post. Municipal councils were compelled to supervise the rest houses along the roads.

Despite the payment of taxes in kind, money levies continued. In the towns, taxes were still paid in gold and silver and, down to 450, senators paid a super-tax called the *follis* and a levy in gold (*aurum oblaticum*) upon the emperor's succession and on every fifth anniversary of it. In 364 a tax on the profits of the trading classes (*collatio lustralis* or *chrysargyrum*) was paid every five years in gold and silver. The tax was extended later to innkeepers and brothel keepers. Zosimus and Libanius wrote of fathers enslaving or prostituting their children in order to raise the money required to pay the *chrysargyrum*. Moreover, the *annona* was converted to payments in gold (*adaeratio*) from the later fourth century onwards and disputes arose over the rate of conversion of these gold taxes into payments in kind. The collection of taxes in kind, especially in the fourth century, removed quantities of commodities from the workings of the market and thus reduced in some measure the scope of the money economy. The incidence of the *chrysargyrum* on the trading classes was a concealed benefit to the villa owners who produced goods for their estates and perhaps sold some goods on the market for they were not, as the Theodosian Code shows, subject to the tax; but villas producing goods for the market may well have been exceptional.

The taxative policy, the semi-planned economy and villa production were all inimical to private enterprise but even more hostile were state factories. Mention is made of these in the codes of Theodosius and Justinian and also in a list of dignitaries of the imperial bureaucracy (*Notitia Dignitatum*) which dates from the early fifth century. State arsenals, weaving mills (*gynaecia*), dyeworks (*bafia*), linen mills (*linyfia*) and embroidery workshops were under the control of a supreme official (*vir illustris comes sacrarum largitionum*) and these factories were designed to cater primarily for the army and, as supervision was needed, were in all probability large-scale enterprises. The dyeworks certainly fell into this category: they were manned largely by convicts and slaves and were unpopular places of employment as human urine and shellfish that might have been dead for six months were some of the raw materials employed in the dyeing processes. Attempts were made to restrict the workers in imperial factories to their occupations in the same way as gildsmen were being confined. These workers, although freemen, were lower in status than gildsmen and were paid in kind; thus another section of the community was withdrawn from the money economy.

But the writers of the fifth century still assume a world in which money payments are made. Landowners lend money, craftsmen work for themselves or for others for wages and pious women sell property for gold and give the money to the poor. Such things could not have happened in a barter economy. It appears that a currency shortage existed in some provinces but what seems to have happened from *c.* 300 to *c.* 430 is that two economies existed. The general public was satisfied with distributions in kind while a sufficiency of gold and silver coin circulated among the rich. By the 430s gold and silver were more plentiful than they had been, for the state had by several means expanded the gold supply. An edict of 365 had allowed anyone to leave his job to go prospecting for gold upon payment of eight scruples a year, later reduced to seven, to the treasury.

We must now turn to the main issue, to the vexed question as to how far 'le grand commerce' continued at the period of the great Germanic movements of the late fourth and fifth centuries. Was the thriving commerce within the Empire and from lands outside it to the east broken by the Germanic invasions as scholars once thought? Was the unity of the Mediterranean ruptured? That interprovincial trade continued in the fourth and fifth centuries is undeniable but it was checked in many ways. Gilds of shippers and river transporters seem to disappear in the fourth century and perhaps the army transporters (*bastagarii*) may have carried goods. The export of the metals iron and bronze to the barbarians was forbidden and, from 374, the export of gold was prohibited. Arms, wine, corn, oil and fish sauce were not to be exported beyond the frontiers. On the other hand, Ausonius in Gaul reports the receipt of oil and fish sauce from Spain, and Sicily was sending corn and horses to Rome. What can be generally agreed is that the period from 300 to 450 was one of decline in economic exchanges and that the west suffered more than the east.

The difficulty for some centuries had been a growing imbalance of trade between the eastern and western provinces of the Empire. In the period after 300 this imbalance become more marked for the east was more economically advanced than the west and had the commodities, silks, spices, jewellery and grain which the west wanted and, in return, the west had little to offer to the east except slaves and hunting hounds, so the goods imported from the east had to be paid for in gold. The consequence was that stockpiling of gold occurred in the eastern provinces while the western provinces were unable to pay for imports. This imbalance, together with the fact that after 476 the united political control over the area around the Mediterranean was ruptured by the establishment of barbarian kingdoms, led an earlier generation of economic historians to the conclusion that 'le grand commerce' from one end of the Mediterranean to the other ceased in the fifth century.

This view was assailed by two European scholars, Alfons Dopsch and Henri Pirenne. Dopsch countered the view that the Germanic settlers were barbarians and established that they were much more civilized than had at one time been thought. Just as they did not wish to destroy the administrative framework of imperial government, so they did not wish to destroy the trade routes of the Empire. The Merovingians, he asserted, inherited the commercial life of the Romans and passed it on to the Carolingians.

Pirenne did not agree to continuity between Merovingians and Carolingians but he did assent to the view that the Merovingian Franks and other Germanic peoples continued the commercial life of the late Roman Empire. He demonstrated that commercial links with the east remained throughout the Merovingian period. References to Syrian and Jewish merchants in Francia are fairly common and reference was made to them by Gregory of Tours who wrote his *Histories* between *c.* 573 and *c.* 594. Marseilles still remained at the end of the sixth century a great trading centre for supplying western Europe with Levantine goods. One of the key points in Pirenne's argument was the use made of papyrus which had to be imported into western Europe from Egypt. The Vandals, it had to be admitted, interrupted trade in the middle years of the fifth century by their piratical raids but the Mediterranean became freer after the death of Gaiseric in 477. Sidonius Apollinaris feared in 468 that the corn supply for Rome might not get through but Pirenne denied that the Vandalic piracy of this era caused the break-up of Mediterranean commerce and asserted that it was only a temporary difficulty and that some commercial exchanges took place even during the 460s and 470s. Pirenne also based his argument for the continuity of trade between the eastern and western Mediterranean on a demonstration that the monetary system of the Frankish kings was Roman or Romano-Byzantine. Gold was used for the *solidus* and silver for the *triens* and the *denarius*. Because the coins were similar to those minted at Constantinople, he argued that this showed the continuity of trade and he believed that down to *c.* 700 trade continued through Marseilles and that Mediterranean goods and influences were dominant in Merovingian Francia. Merchants brought Levantine goods and took back slaves who were plentiful as a result of warfare between Germanic tribes and between Germans and Slavs.

From the sixth century Byzantine merchants, having difficulties in trading to the east because of the Persian wars, turned their attention even more to the west. The Persian wars had blocked the trade with China and, although in the sixth century some Nestorian monks had smuggled silkworm eggs into the eastern Empire, the silk supply was inadequate. It was in these conditions of frustration for eastern merchants that they turned more easily to the Mediterranean. Moreover, under the Emperor Justinian (527-65) the Mediterranean became safe again for travel as he reconquered north Africa, large parts of Italy and parts of Spain for the Empire. Because the Lombards, in Italy after 568, were on bad terms with the Franks, the Alpine trade with Italy was replaced by trade links between Francia and Byzantium via southern Italy which the emperors at Constantinople still held. Pirenne's thesis was that after *c.* 570 trade across the Mediterranean even began to expand until the early eighth century.

In his famous book *Mahomet et Charlemagne*, he expressed the view that Mediterranean trade, 'le grand commerce', was disrupted not by the Germanic invasions of the fifth century but by the Islamic advance of the later seventh century. This was what caused the economy of Europe to decline during the Carolingian period, and Pirenne believed that from *c.* 700 an era of stagnation developed. As a direct result of this economic stagnation, he thought the Carolingian rulers were forced to adopt a domanial economy where production was concentrated on the great *villae*, an economy which was scarcely removed from a barter economy – 'a gloomy period of stagnation and retrogression in economic life'. This break in trade was the result of the discontinuity of what had kept it going, namely the plentiful supplies of gold from Constantinople which were obtained from the mines of Nubia. After the Islamic conquest of Egypt in 641 the eastern Empire was deprived of this source of supply of the precious metal. Some papyrus still managed to get through, as is shown by a grant to Corbie in 718, but, generally speaking, after the mid seventh century Byzantine gold was no longer coming to the west and Byzantine merchants began to make good their loss of western trade by turning to the Ukraine. By *c.* 700, then, the focus of Byzantine trade had turned to the east as it had done in the later fourth and fifth centuries. The drying up of cross-Mediterranean trade caused the Carolingians to turn to the north and such trade as there was centred round the mouth of the Rhine at Duurstede and at Quentovic, near Etaples in the Pas-de-Calais. Silver took the place of gold and it spread into southern Francia as the currency for such trade as prospered there. Pirenne thought that the abandonment of gold was a sure sign of the decline of 'le grand commerce'. The Carolingian Empire was harried by raids from the Saracens and from the Norsemen which it could not prevent. Dopsch did not agree with Pirenne's thesis of a stagnating economy and insisted that no sharp break existed between Merovingian and Carolingian trade.

Pirenne's views in some respects, are no longer accepted by scholars. Baynes thought that his references to Syrian merchants in Gregory of Tours did not prove continuity of trade,[1] and Lopez,

---

[1] N. H. Baynes, 'Pirenne and the unity of the Mediterranean world', *J. Rom. Studies*, XIX (1929), 230–5.

although he agrees that culturally the Islamic advance was more disruptive of the Roman world than had been the Germanic settlements, disagrees on many points of economic detail.[1] He argues especially that many of the 'disappearances' from western Europe which Pirenne said coincided with the Moslem control of the western Mediterranean were not contemporary either with the Arab advance or with each other. To take first papyrus which was manufactured in Egypt: although Egypt was overrun between 639 and 641, the Merovingian chancery continued to use papyrus until 692. Gold currency was struck in Francia until the second half of the eighth century and there are traces of the continuation of trans-Mediterranean trade in oriental luxury textiles during the ninth and tenth centuries. In fact, the production of some textiles out of which royal garments were made, purple cloth and gold thread, had been closely controlled from about the third century, and also the producers of papyrus in Egypt were compelled to sell the best qualities (*basiliké charté*, i.e. royal papyrus) to the ruler and public notaries were expected to write their deeds on this type of papyrus and to pay a tax on every legal document. This was what authenticated the deed and strict rules were made about them by fifth- and sixth-century emperors. From Justinian's time royal charters were sealed with gold seals and the emperor signed his name in purple ink while imperial officials used silver ink. As Lopez has shown, the supply of papyrus did not cease with the conquest of Egypt; on the contrary, the works, largely staffed by Christians, went on producing it and the Moslems continued to export it to Constantinople where the Code of Justinian, still in force, demanded that certain documents be written on papyrus. The papyrus had been marked with the name of the *basileus*; this was replaced by an invocation to the Trinity but 'Abd al-Malik (Caliph, 685-705) ordered that this invocation and the sign of the cross, which was placed on supplies sent to Constantinople, should be replaced by an Islamic inscription. Even this was tolerated for a time by Justinian II, but about 690 he could stand it no longer and, after a diplomatic break with the Caliphate, the export of papyrus from Egypt was terminated.

Thus it is incorrect to say that the Moslem advance caused the cessation of Mediterranean trade, but rather that the break came

[1] R. S. Lopez, 'Mohammed and Charlemagne: a revision'.

some fifty years later and was the result of hostilities between the Empire and Islam. These hostilities brought about the cessation of the circulation of Byzantine gold coinage in Islamic territories and in the Mediterranean area generally. Only in the tenth century, when the Egyptians ceased the manufacture of papyrus, because paper had taken its place in the Islamic dominions, did papyrus disappear completely and the emperor at Constantinople and gradually the whole of western Europe went over to the use of parchment: the Papacy resisted the change until nearly the end of that century. So Pirenne's arguments on papyrus are unsound and his thesis that there was a sudden abandonment by the Carolingians of the Merovingian gold coinage cannot be maintained, for both Charlemagne and Louis the Pious struck gold coins. As Renouard said, he has failed to substantiate the thesis that economic life persisted in western Europe with the same intensity through to the eighth century.[1]

Yet, as Vercauteren has written, not all Pirenne's theories can be overthrown.[2] What emerges from the most modern and informed scholarship is that trade over the years from the beginning of the fourth century to the end of the ninth fluctuated. In the Mediterranean basin it declined in the fourth and early fifth centuries, revived in the sixth and early seventh, was reduced again at the end of the seventh and in the early eighth centuries and probably continued at a low level throughout the ninth century.

Neither Germanic invasions nor Moslem advance completely killed it and compensating trade links existed elsewhere. In the north, trade flourished in the sixth century and in the later eighth and ninth centuries and was connected with a great trade revival effected by the Vikings, who established trade links from Scandinavia to Constantinople through Russia. Any idea of a more severe trade depression in Carolingian than in Merovingian times is not now accepted. But that overall trade exchanges between western Europe and eastern Europe and places farther east declined over the whole period is undoubtedly a fact because of the diminution of purchasing

---

[1] Y. Renouard, *Hommes d'Affaires Italiens* (Paris, Colin, 1949), p. 8.

[2] F. Vercauteren, 'Monnaie et circulation monétaire en Belgique et dans le Nord de la France du Ve au XIe siècle', *Settimane di studio ... di studi sull'alto medioevo, Spoleto*, VIII (1961), 279–311.

power (gold) in the west,[1] but whether the decline was catastrophic is open to question. It would appear that potential effective demand for eastern goods in the west was satisfied, for in the late tenth century the great lay and ecclesiastical lords had much unspent wealth in gold bars and jewellery which were melted down and used when trade began to revive towards the end of that century and in the following one. Lopez thinks that the gold supply may well have been inadequate, and this may have checked the economic growth of the eleventh century, but that the trade of the fifth to the ninth centuries was not seriously restricted by lack of the precious metal. However this may be, it would seem reasonable to postulate a decline from the flourishing trade of imperial Rome that existed in the first 250 years of the Christian era. One fact must constantly be borne in mind: throughout these six or seven centuries we have little more than occasional chronicle references and some archaeological data, in the form of coin finds, upon which to write the history of European trade.

[1] For the monetary reasons which led to the replacement of gold by silver in the west, see P. Grierson, 'The monetary reforms of 'Abd al-Malik', *J. of the Economic and Social History of the Orient*, III, 3 (1960), 241 ff.

CHAPTER 5

The Revival of Trade
and the Growth of Towns

As we have seen, we must avoid theories of catastrophe in European trade in the period between c. 400 and c. 1000 but the overall picture that clearly emerges is that western Europe was, in comparison with the Byzantine Empire and the Islamic Caliphate, an underdeveloped area. An area, hampered by political struggles and lack of security, which, although it had not entirely reverted to a 'natural' economy, certainly saw less money in circulation; an area where payments were made from debtor to creditor either in coins or in commodities at the option of the debtor. These payments under the optional system were usually payments from peasants to their landlords but they were also known in other types of transaction. In international trade, coins were at all periods preferred for it was more difficult for a merchant from a great distance to arrange business on the basis of a barter exchange. However, even large transactions were sometimes expressed for settlement in *solidi* when it is obvious that a certain weight of precious metal is indicated.[1] Coins were in short supply in this period, partly because the velocity of circulation was slow, also because of the tendency to hoard, and the fact of a very unbalanced distribution of income proved a handicap to the smooth working of a monetary system. The great revival of trade in the later tenth century was a triumph for a 'money' economy over a 'natural' economy. That money had survived at all in the west was due to the high standard of the Byzantine *solidus* and its use as an international currency from c. 400 to c. 700. This gold *solidus* of the Byzantine Empire was known as the *nomisma* to the Greeks and as the bezant in western Europe where in the thirteenth century it was also called the

---

[1] C. M. Cipolla, *Money, Prices and Civilization in the Mediterranean World*, p. 617.

hyperperon; to the Moslems it had the name of the dinar and was used by them until *c.* 690.

Because trade between Francia and the eastern Mediterranean declined (perhaps more severely after 700), the Carolingian kingdom turned away from Mediterranean trade and so when the revival came it was led by the Italian cities. After the mid ninth century parts of Europe collapsed into worse anarchy than had probably been experienced even in the fifth and early sixth centuries. The vast regions over which Charlemagne had ruled lost their political unity after 843 and the northern coastline of modern France, Belgium and Holland suffered severe Viking raids for a period of seventy years between 840 and 911. The Vikings, sailing up the river valleys and sometimes leaving their ships and going even farther on horseback, sacked Paris, Bourges and Orleans and in 924 and 926 the Magyars swept across southern Germany and northern Italy reaching as far as the city of Strasbourg which they devastated. Further trouble occurred in the Mediterranean where the *status quo* that had existed in the central part of the sea for 300 years was shattered when, in 878, the Byzantine Empire lost the island of Sicily to the Moslems. Ten years later the infidels had established a base at the foot of the Ligurian Alps at Garde Frainet and thus hindered traffic through the western Alpine passes. This entailed the passage of any Mediterranean goods which northern Europe might require through the more easterly Alpine passes and through Germany. The Ottonian emperors founded a strong state there in the tenth century, especially after the defeat of the Magyars on the river Lech in 955. Trade in the Mediterranean probably reached its nadir in the last quarter of the ninth century; but it was the darkest hour before the dawn.

In the early tenth century, although Byzantine and Moslem fleets continued to dominate the western Mediterranean sea, 'a commercial and also a military counter-offensive of "western Europe"', as Lopez has called it, was just beginning. In old seaports such as Naples, Ravenna and Pisa and in new centres such as Venice and Amalfi and in the towns of Pavia and Milan, a revolution was beginning which gradually displaced the Byzantines and Syrians as middlemen in the trade between east and west and which eventually, by the late twelfth and early thirteenth centuries, made Italians dominant in the eastern Mediterranean itself. The Italian ports that pioneered this

revival in western Mediterranean trade were small cities such as
Amalfi, Gaeta, Salerno and Bari which had been forced into trade
two centuries earlier. The ravages of the Lombards had compelled
those districts still under Byzantine control to trade in order to make
a livelihood and these Italo-Byzantine towns became prominent
from the early tenth century onwards. Above all, Venice which had
been but a fishing centre was trading actively with Constantinople
in the later ninth century, and on the profits of this trade the Venetians were able to supply themselves from Lombardy with grain and
wine which they did not produce at home. These Italo-Byzantine
cities acted as outposts collecting goods for transmission to Constantinople, and their inhabitants, as Byzantine citizens, had access to the
local depots which the imperial authorities set up in the principal
harbours and at road termini and also to the controlled lodging
houses in the capital at which merchants had to stay.

The Venetians were especially favoured in return for lending
ships to the eastern Empire for military transportation and for the
Imperial post. Under this concession Venetian vessels paid only two
gold *nomismata* when they came in through the Dardanelles while
the ships paid fifteen *nomismata* when they went out. In addition to
legitimate trade with Byzantium, there was smuggling both into and
out of Constantinople. Despite imperial decrees forbidding the
trade, the merchants of these Italo-Byzantine ports smuggled in
slaves and smuggled out precious textiles, which, if they were worth
more than ten *nomismata* a piece, could not (along with gold, war
materials and basic foodstuffs) be legally exported. The legitimate
trade, however, was sufficient to induce many merchants from
Venice, Amalfi, Gaeta and Salerno to trade in Constantinople
although they could not establish permanent colonies there, since
residence in the *xenodochia* or lodging houses was restricted to three
months at a time.

Not only did these ports trade with Constantinople but they also
had links with Moslem countries. The comparative abundance of
Arab coins found in western Europe shows that the balance of trade
with Moslem lands was more favourable than with the Byzantine
Empire. Imports consisted of spices, perfumes, ivory, textiles and oil
and the exports were slaves, timber, iron and wooden and iron
implements. Trading with the enemy or with the potential enemy

little stirred the conscience of these Italian merchants for when, in time of war between the Empire and the Caliphate, the emperor placed a ban on the export of timber and iron (there was a standing prohibition on the export of slaves) only the Venetian doges attempted to enforce it.

Unless we accept the view recently expressed that no European trade revival took place until, in the eleventh century, Norman incursions had declined and feudal anarchy had been tamed,[1] we can assign the key role to Venice in the tenth century. The commercial monopoly of the Italo-Byzantine seaports might have been threatened if Charlemagne's direct negotiations with Constantinople or with Hārūn al-Rashīd in Baghdad had come to a successful conclusion but they did not, and rights that he would have granted to the entire Byzantine Empire were given to Venice. The Franco-Venetian *pactum* of 840 laid the foundation for the supremacy of Venice over the other Italo-Byzantine seaports in western trade. The foolish policy of Amalfi, Naples and Gaeta in collaborating with the Moslems undermined their privileged position in the Byzantine Empire. By the beginning of the eleventh century the predominance of Venice was established beyond doubt as small Istrian ports such as Comacchio and even Ravenna itself declined. Venice was virtually independent of Constantinople yet its merchants still enjoyed the advantage of Byzantine citizenship and it maintained diplomatic relations with all the Moslem powers. It spoke as an equal to the Lombard and later kings of Italy and to the western (Holy Roman) emperors. Foreign merchants were treated in Venice as they were in Constantinople and compelled to lodge in state-controlled *xeno-dochia*. Moreover, before the eleventh century Venice had no serious rival among other Italian ports for it was not until after 1000 that Genoa began to recover from the decline which Lombard invasion had brought upon it and Pisa, although it was the only city to continue active trading, was no serious challenge.

But we must turn from a consideration of the revival of southern European trade to look at the north. It has become customary to discuss the commerce of northern and that of southern Europe as if they were almost completely isolated. This was not so. Although at some periods the exchanges between the two systems were minimal,

[1] R. de Roover, in *Cambridge Economic History of Europe*, III, p. 43.

the two trading areas were never completely cut off, for southern Europe, despite more northerly viticulture in the Middle Ages than now, supplied wine to the north and northern Europe provided slaves to the south. The northern trade was not in luxuries but in indispensable commodities. The only luxury item was the rich furs but the staples were foodstuffs, such as grain, butter, cheese and fish, and timber, metals and salt. Following upon the introduction of the three-field system and the horse harness, many parts of Francia, north of the Loire, were able in Carolingian times to produce an exportable surplus of agricultural products which were sent to regions where the population could not maintain itself in foodstuffs, particularly to Scandinavia and Frisia and later to Flanders and Brabant.

Whatever view may be taken about the stagnation or otherwise of the economy of Charlemagne's empire, we know that his lands traded actively with England for the king himself mentioned trade matters when he wrote to Offa of Mercia in 798. The letter made provisions for the proper treatment of the merchants of the two countries when they were in each other's territories and established that pilgrims were to be free of toll. Moreover, Charlemagne asked that the Mercian cloaks sent to his domains should be of the same breadth as previously. The emperor set up customs posts to regulate trade between his empire and the Slavs to the east and with the Avars who lived in the middle Danube valley. Evidence also exists which demonstrates that the Frisians were great traders in the north in the seventh and eighth centuries. But all this does not prove anything more than a low level of commercial exchanges.

The anarchic period after *c.* 850 in the north was not all loss. Few aspects of history have been more thoroughly revised in recent years than our assessment of the part played by the Vikings and, although it is undeniable that they were great plunderers and destroyers, they are now seen as explorers of hitherto unknown lands and pioneers of new trade links. Although they plundered Duurstede, there is evidence that some Norsemen traded to the same port. Scandinavian commerce reached its highest point between the late ninth and the eleventh centuries. In their voyages the Norsemen penetrated westwards to Greenland and the coast of North America and to the Bosporus in the east; their contribution to such skills as ship construction was outstanding and they undertook voyages that had never been undertaken previously in man's history. The source of much information, the sagas written in Icelandic (i.e. Old Norse), have to be treated with caution both because the earliest ones date only from the twelfth century and also because heroic poetry is not always a reliable source for the economic historian. However, several examples of Norse boats have been excavated. The Oseberg boat, on view in the maritime museum in Oslo is 21 metres long by 5 metres wide and had fifteen pairs of oars, while another vessel, the Gokstad boat, had a mast 12·6 metres high with a single sail which demonstrates that the ships were propelled both by oar and by sail. Ships such as these could make 10 knots and carry forty to a hundred men. Whether the Northmen left their homelands because of an increase in population which made the food supply insufficient, whether to live in a more suitable climate, or whether from a passion for adventure, we shall probably never certainly know but the Norwegians, Swedes and Danes, for they were already distinct peoples in the late eighth century, poured out of their homelands from the 790s on.

From the point of view of the development of trade links, the Swedes made the most important contribution to the opening up of a new trade. Under the name of Varangians they opened up a route which, at first, went from the bay of Riga up the river Dvina to Polotsk or Vitebsk and from there to the upper waters of the Dnieper near Old Smolensk and down the river to the Black Sea where Byzantine traders took their wares. In 839 some of them appeared in the train of the ambassadors from the eastern emperor who came to the court of Louis the Pious. They called themselves Rus or Rhos – Russians – which was the primitive name given by the Finns to the Swedes. The route down the river Dnieper was, however, unsatisfactory for two reasons. Firstly, the river had rapids and, secondly, it flowed through territory where there was no strong governmental authority; both these drawbacks could be obviated by using the Volga, for astride that river the Khazars, a Turkish people, had established themselves in the early eighth century and Itil on the lower Volga was an entrepôt for goods destined for Constantinople coming from central Asia and the Far East. The Varangian route, as revised, therefore ran from the Gulf of Finland up the river Neva to the southern shores of Lake Ladoga, down the Volkhov river to the site of Old Novgorod; then the goods were taken overland to the Volga at Tver and so down to Sarai or Itil. The goods the Swedes carried, furs, timber, wax and slaves, were sold either to the eastern Empire or to the Moslem world, for Arabic silver coins, found at many places along this route, are proof of such a market. In addition we have a ninth-century Arabic account by Ibn Khordadhbeh of the routes taken by the Rus. They paid a tenth on their goods either to the Byzantine emperors or to the Khazars and sometimes the Rus crossed the Caspian Sea and took their merchandise to Baghdad.

Taken collectively, the Norsemen made a spectacular transformation in the European economy. Commerce which had been centred on the Mediterranean almost exclusively until the end of the seventh century, and still centred there in the eighth, was given in the ninth and tenth centuries a northern shift. Although Carolingian and English ports had a little significance, the expansion of commerce in northern Europe was mostly the work of the Norsemen, for in addition to the work of the Swedes, the Norwegians discovered Iceland in the ninth century, Greenland in the tenth and, in all probability, the eastern seaboard of the United States. The difficulties of interpretation of the Vinland map are many but few scholars now doubt that America was discovered by the Norwegians *c.* 1000. Where they struck land is a more controversial issue: perhaps it was Labrador, Newfoundland or Nova Scotia. The west coast of Greenland was settled in 981–2 and one authority states that Eric the Red, named Leif, discovered Vinland in 1003 and that another expedition went in 1005 led by his brother Thorvald who with thirty men stayed there for three years. About 1010, Thorfin Karlsefni took 180 men and women intending to settle but three years later, discouraged by the hostility of the natives, they gave up. Nearer home, the Norwegians settled in the Faroes, Orkney and Shetland and, by 900, there had been established what has been termed 'the empire of the North Sea'. This commercial expansion cannot be compared in overall significance with the tenth-century trade revival of the Italo-Byzantine cities for perhaps the volume of trade, apart from the route through Russia, was small and its value in no way comparable to that with Byzantium and Moslem lands. But it helped to increase the importance of northern Europe as against the south and to establish the two systems of medieval commerce, which 300 years later were to be dominated respectively by the Hanse and certain Italian city states.

But the revival of trade cannot be separated from the growth of towns. R. de Roover's view that the trade revival came after the tenth century, although based upon different premises from those expressed by Pirenne, agrees, more or less, chronologically with the latter's thesis. Pirenne argued that towns did not really exist until the tenth century, although in a few instances he might have been prepared to agree to date some to the end of the ninth, and that they could not exist until the trade revival of that era, a view which H. van Wervecke has endorsed.[1] The latter's opinion is that the criticisms levelled in the last twenty-five years against Pirenne's thesis do not invalidate it because the arguments that have been advanced to counter it relate to towns of secondary importance. The Pirenne thesis of a closed domanial economy (*geschlossene Hauswirtschaft*) down to the later tenth century, which implied an absence of towns, can no longer be accepted even though some of the work of rehabilitation of early towns may have gone too far. In fact the trend of modern scholarship has been to spotlight the urban survivals from the Roman era while the 'Belgian school' asserts that these towns, admittedly more in northern than in southern Europe, had declined and that they were no longer active trading centres engaged in 'le grand commerce'. Archaeological work has shown that the town plans of Tongres and Trier in the Middle Ages did not retain the chequerboard layout of the Roman period as did Turin and it would appear that the ecclesiastical element grew at the expense of the commercial section of the population in the years before 1000. At Lyons in the first half of the ninth century between 300 and 350 persons lived in religious establishments and by the following century it would appear that ecclesiastical, capitular and abbatial property predominated in some towns.

However much controversy may have arisen as to the dating of the rise of towns and however much stress may be given to continuity or the lack of it from the Roman period, undoubtedly, from the eleventh century, urban life played a more important part in the

[1] H. van Wervecke, in *Cambridge Economic History of Europe*, III, p. 4.

C

European economy than it had done for 600 or 700 years previously. It was not until agriculture reached a sufficient extension and efficiency that urbanization could gain momentum, and even from the eleventh century it moved only slowly and irregularly. Towns at first still contained open spaces that could be used for food production and these did not disappear even in Paris before the end of the twelfth century. But by the early or mid thirteenth century many towns had expanded considerably. Continental scholars,[1] aided by the devastation caused by World War II, have done much research on the area of medieval towns, and new methods of evaluating ground plans have offered new explanations for town growth and size. German towns of medium size covered on average about 50 hectares while some of the smaller ones were contained within an area of between 4 and 10 hectares. Growth is well illustrated by the city of Cologne which covered 118 hectares in 1106; in 1180 new walls were started which eventually enclosed 396 hectares, an area which sufficed the inhabitants until the nineteenth century.

Without entering the controversy over urban origins and about the tenure by which burgesses held, a controversy well summarized by J. Tait for Europe as well as for England,[2] it is apparent that the town was a fortified place. The town wall was the most tangible and striking demarcation between town and country and the walls could provide shelter not only for urban dwellers but for those living in the surrounding countryside in time of emergency; the Anglo-Saxon *burhs* were specifically built for such a purpose. At the gates of this *burg* or fortified area a trading quarter, known in Latin as *portus*, arose and this district, also called *suburbia,* although it might have had some rough defences, was not usually walled until the late twelfth century.

There seems little doubt that the inhabitants of the towns held their tenements by a free tenure from the start and not by servile tenures. Certainly the towns were centres of new thought and action; however oligarchy-dominated they might at times have become, the cities were on the whole centres of progressive and even radical

[1] Especially and most recently, E. Keyser, *Städtegründungen und Städtebau in Nordwestdeutschland im Mittelalter*, Forschungen zur deutschen Landeskunde, vol. CXI (Remagen, 1958).

[2] In *The Medieval English Borough: Studies on its Origins and Constitutional History*, (Manchester U.P., 1936).

ideas. The degrees of autonomy achieved by towns differed greatly from one part of Europe to another. The great Italian cities of Venice, Florence and Genoa were, in effect, sovereign states which controlled their own affairs and ruled considerable areas outside the city. The Flemish towns, although never achieving complete independence from the count, had substantial control over their own government, whereas cities in countries where central government was strong, above all in England, were limited to running their own administration and finances.

The late twelfth and thirteenth centuries saw much town planning and the establishment of new towns. The kings of England both in England itself and in Gascony played an active role. By 1297, when Edward I held a meeting of town planners at Harwich,[1] more than 120 planted towns had been established in England, from the Norman plantations of New Windsor, Ludlow, Richmond (Yorkshire) and Bury St Edmunds to Richard I's creation of Portsmouth and John's foundation of Liverpool. In the thirteenth century, Harwich, Stoney Stratford, Dunstable, Royston, Baldock, Wokingham, Maidenhead and Reigate could be matched by the *bastides* planted in Gascony and particularly around Bordeaux. These planned towns were frequently built on a chequerboard pattern although the slope of the land or the course of a river might sometimes modify the ground plan.

Pedestrians set the scale of medieval towns. Wide streets were unnecessary as there was little wheeled traffic, and none that required fast passage, and the result was that, in the main, streets were lanes giving access to houses. Houses were more important than streets. The smallest type of house in Germany was about 4·5 metres wide with one or two rooms on the ground floor and a similar number above, with no rooms in the attic; good examples of such dwellings are still to be seen in the *Fuggerei* in Augsburg. Craftsmen's houses invariably had two storeys with a workroom on the ground floor. As craftsmen began to supply the surrounding countryside, more craftsmen came in and a permanent site was often provided for their transactions. This was the *forum*, as distinct from the *mercatus* or weekly market. The original market, a provision market for the

[1] M. W. Beresford, *New Towns of the Middle Ages* (London, Lutterworth, 1967), pp. 1ff.

inhabitants, was frequently known as the Fishmarket, but as towns expanded in the later twelfth and thirteenth centuries a principal street was often widened for a new market. This is the origin of the *Neumarkt* of so many German towns.

In the great trade revival the towns played a crucial role, for they had as their main concerns two aims: to defend the trading interests of the town and to defend the interests of the consumers. It is now generally agreed that before the late thirteenth century the practice of merchant gilds, which were granted to towns as a whole and not to individuals, was less restrictive than in the fourteenth and fifteenth centuries. The defence of the town's trading interest, by restriction of foreigners, by their exclusion from retail trade, by the practice of hosting and so on, was not common before about 1280 to 1300. Also the policy of securing a plentiful supply of victuals led municipalities to introduce statutory maxima for food prices. They introduced in many places the 'standard loaf' which varied in size and quality with the price of grain. Consumer protection was more effective in some towns than in others; where the crafts were strong, and particularly the victuallers' crafts, attempts to keep down prices were less effective than in those towns where merchant gilds wished to minimize food prices in order to hold down wages and so retain a competitive position in the goods which they sold or exported. Even so, in a town such as Brussels, where in the fifteenth century the crafts were powerful, the food-producing gilds were not allowed to enforce 100 per cent membership of victuallers, and individuals were allowed to kill sheep for their own family use. Nevertheless, we read of more complaints against regulation and price fixing in the last two medieval centuries than at an earlier period. In looking forward, as we have done, to the role of towns in medieval trade, the purpose has been to stress their importance to the revival of trade which started in some parts of Europe in the tenth century and continued to flourish and expand until the first half of the 1400s.

CHAPTER 6

The Organization of Trade in Italy: Credit and Banking

The trade revival in southern Europe, and above all in the Italian peninsula, was by the millennial year truly launched and in the three succeeding centuries a great era of commercial and industrial expansion ensued. Growth in these two areas was essentially urban in character, hence the increased size of towns, which can be demonstrated by the fact that many cities had an early wall built about the end of the eleventh century which was replaced by a second wall dating between 1250 and 1350. This rebuilding is a clear indication of urban population growth although it is almost impossible to quantify it as virtually no complete censuses exist for any town before 1350, but we know that before the middle of the fourteenth century Milan, Venice, Naples and Florence had over 50,000 inhabitants with Florence sheltering probably double that number and Venice nearly 200,000. Genoa, Bologna and Rome had about 50,000. North of the Alps fewer large towns existed; although Paris was a giant with 80,000, Ghent had 56,000, Bruges about 35,000 and London 35,000–40,000. Venice dominated Mediterranean trade at the opening of this 300-year period but Genoa, after three centuries of decadence resulting from the Lombard conquest of Liguria and the deterioration of Roman roads across the Apennines and along the coast, began to rival the queen of the Adriatic. The rise of Genoa was assisted by the decline of Pisa in the tenth century. But although the Italian cities might rise and fall in the 'league tables' of Italian commercial prosperity, it is almost certain that all of them carried on a greater volume of trade than any other single town north of the Alps during this period, and by the twelfth century Venice, Genoa and even smaller Italian mercantile cities had surpassed in wealth the greatest business centres of the ancient world, and they went on a century later to reach the pinnacle of medieval trade. Businessmen of the western Mediterranean were to be found in England, southern Russia, the oases of the Sahara, India and China.

There can be little doubt that this great commercial expansion in Italy between the late tenth and the mid fourteenth centuries was given its main thrust by population growth and in turn this growth expanded the market. Increase took place, though at differing rates, all over Europe both north and south of the Alps and thus the market in goods that Italian merchants alone could supply developed favourably, despite setbacks, over three centuries. But economic growth took place first in the Italian peninsula: Piacenza, for example, in 819 had only one fair lasting one day; in 896 it had five fairs one of which lasted seventeen days. The direction of Italian expansion was set, to some extent, by political as well as by economic factors. The rise of the Papacy as an international power which dominated the peninsula from the mid eleventh century onwards led to a counter-offensive against infidels and schismatics, and the Crusading movement between 1095 and 1204 had a considerable influence in setting the direction of Italian commercial expansion towards the Middle East. Of course, its main trade links with Constantinople, and to a lesser extent with the Moslem states, had already been forged before 1000 but the demands of the Crusades especially in shipping reinforced the interests which the Italian ports had in the eastern Mediterranean and led to their growing involvement in overland trade with China.

This commercial revolution had important effects upon the class structure of the society of many Italian city states, for the lesser nobility entered trade even though the ranks of the non-noble filled the ranks of the business class in Italy as elsewhere. An increasing percentage of the urban population engaged in trade so that in time wealth rather than birth became the basis of distinction between one class and another. The Pitti palace in Florence only exceeded in size and grandeur many mansions in Florence and Venice built with money acquired in trade – a situation common in Italy but unheard of north of the Alps. Moreover, social mobility was a marked feature of these centuries of commercial expansion; apprentices rose to become masters and successful craftsmen became entrepreneurs while new men made fortunes in commerce and money lending.

The books kept by Genoese notaries show how members of all sections of the community engaged in trade; it was for some the medieval equivalent of a flutter on the stock exchange. Several of the great towns of northern Italy, Languedoc and Catalonia became metropolitan; that is they engaged in long distance as well as local trade, they drew their foodstuffs from distant areas and they had a profound influence on the terms of trade.

It is easier to establish the reasons for and the direction of this movement which R. S. Lopez has called a 'commercial revolution'[1] than to ascertain the origins of the class of merchants and of the sources of the capital that they employed. What the origins of the capital were has been greatly disputed among economic historians and no certain answer has yet been reached in the debate. Werner Sombart took the view that in so far as early merchant capitalists were former landed proprietors or domanial officials their capital was formed by accumulated ground rents, but this view has been clearly proved to be untenable in some instances by Jakob Strieder.[2] The latter was, however, researching into the capitalists of the city of Augsburg, and in particular into the Fuggers, at the close of the Middle Ages and what he wrote about the circumstances of the fifteenth century may well not be applicable to an earlier period. It has been shown for the twelfth century that the profits of trade were so enormous that it would appear that accumulation of capital originated in such profits rather than in incomes derived from landed property,[3] but again we cannot be certain that what was valid in the twelfth century was equally applicable to the late tenth and eleventh centuries. If merchants had all been parvenus then their capital must have been limited and certainly the Italian nobility did not live solely in the country but in addition had town residences and entered trade. In whatever way capital may have been formed, and in all probability more than one method was used, considerable quantities of it were employed in financing numerous ventures or voyages.

Sometimes the merchants of the Italian city states would send out goods which they would sell and with the proceeds buy imports;

---

[1] *Cambridge Economic History of Europe*, II, pp. 289 ff.

[2] *Zur Genesis des modernen Kapitalismus*.

[3] F. Edler de Roover, 'Partnership accounts in twelfth century Genoa', in A. C. Littleton and B. S. Yamey (eds.), *Studies in the History of Accounting*, p. 90.

sometimes trade was in the nature of barter of one cargo of goods for another and sometimes they would send out gold or specie with which to purchase imports. The return on capital, as befitted the greater risk, was considerably higher than that which could be earned from investment in land. From the early eleventh century the Italian towns were providing northern and western Europe with essential spices, such as pepper, cinnamon, saffron and ginger, with sulphur, alum, camphor, myrrh, incense, sandalwood, logwood, velvet, cloth of gold, taffeta, dyes, perfumes and jewels from the Moslem world, and they were supplying timber, pig iron, wrought iron, grain, woollen cloth, salt meat, salt and (albeit illicitly) slaves in return. Their trade with the Byzantine Empire was also on a large scale. All these enterprises needed considerable outlays of capital to keep them afloat.

The techniques the Italians used to finance this large-scale business enterprise were highly sophisticated and the lack of them in northern Europe was to some extent the reason for the smaller scale of commercial undertakings among the merchants of the Hanseatic League and for the failure of the north German and Scandinavian economy to reach the heights of that of the Mediterranean. But it has been argued that Hanseatic commerce, being based on a single axis from Lübeck to London and Bruges in the west and to Danzig, Riga, Revel and Novgorod in the east, was simpler than the multifarious ventures of Italian merchants. At an early period in Italy merchants devised techniques to regulate shared undertakings. These partnerships are first known to us from the cartulary of a Genoese notary Giovanni Scriba who began to keep his record in 1156, although it has been argued on the strength of phrases used in some Venetian documents that one type of contract, the *commenda*, may go back to the ninth century. The *commenda* was the type of contract used for a venture financed entirely by a merchant who stayed at home, the investing partner (*stans*), and in which the travelling partner (*tractator*) invested nothing but was rewarded for the considerable risk which he ran in undertaking a sea voyage. The division of the profits under this type of contract was three quarters to the investing partner and one quarter to the travelling partner. In another form of partnership agreement, the *societas maris*, the profits of the voyage were shared equally between the partners but the *stans* provided only two thirds of the capital while the remaining third was supplied by the travelling partner who had to be remunerated both for his capital outlay and for the risk of the journey. The investing partner must not be thought of as a sleeping partner in the business for it was he who decided where the travelling partner should go, whether he should take goods or specie with him with which to acquire foreign wares and what type of goods he should purchase for import. Moreover, he would take charge of the sale of the goods brought back by the travelling partner and so be able to allocate the profit.

Medieval international trade was unlike that of the present day in so far as goods were not already sold to customers when they left the shores of the producing country: they were taken to foreign countries and sold often at fairs though sometimes by private arrangement, and on occasion not all the goods were disposed of when the travelling partner had to return. In such an eventuality he might either bring goods back with him or leave them to be sold by state officials. Three sheets of paper inserted into Giovanni Scriba's cartulary demonstrate the profitability of overseas commerce in twelfth-century Genoa. The two partners Ingo da Volta, the investing partner, and Ansaldo Baialardo, the travelling partner, undertook three ventures between autumn 1156 and August 1158, two of which were in all probability to Provence or Catalonia and one was to Syria, Palestine and Egypt; in two years, Ingo trebled his capital and Ansaldo had secured from nothing a capital stock of £142. The final venture was a sophisticated arrangement whereby the partnership was in part a *commenda* and in part a *societas maris*. The records of these contracts tell us much about the type of people who invested in maritime trading ventures. Nobles, clerics, widows, artisans and shopkeepers all appear as investing partners some of whom can hardly have had much commercial experience or expertise and it can only be assumed that such investors had advice from knowledgeable individuals. These agreements, in addition to defining the rules for the sharing of profits, restricted the partners' liability in the event of loss, whereas in a *compagnia* the partners' liability was unlimited.

Various ways of reducing risk were tried. The sea loan, which was different from a straight loan in that repayment was contingent upon the safe arrival of the ship, was condemned by Pope Gregory IX in 1236 and, soon after the middle of the thirteenth century, it was replaced in Genoa by the *cambium maritimum* in which the lender's gain was concealed in the rate of exchange. In the thirteenth century continuous searches were being made to find a solution to the problem of risk which commercial ventures inevitably entailed but it was not until after 1300 that insurance loans became at all common. The shipowner in the late Middle Ages made an advance to the shipper on the understanding that the repayment of the loan plus the freight charges would only be due upon the safe arrival of the ship at its destination. But this was not complete coverage, for the shipowner was rarely willing to advance more than 25 per cent to 30 per cent of the cargo's value. Another device for risk-sharing was for ships to be owned not by one man but by several shipowners who each held so many shares – *partes* or *loca navis* – in the vessel. In these many ways did merchants and shipowners seek to safeguard themselves during the great commercial expansion of the years between 1000 and 1350.

The expansion was to some extent held back even in Italy by shortage of credit and shortage of credit was attributable in part to the teaching of the medieval church on usury. Canon law became increasingly specific in its condemnation of taking any interest upon money that was lent. The view held by Aristotle that money was barren was accepted by the early church in so far as money was regarded, in a distinction made by Roman law, as a consumptible, and therefore to demand usury was like selling a thing and then asking a charge for using it. This meant that the church from Patristic times condemned the taking of any interest upon a *mutuum* and both St Ambrose (340–97) and St Jerome (*c.* 340–420) among others wrote against it and many church councils (Arles 314, Nicaea 325) forbade the taking of interest by clerics. The prohibition was extended to the laity in the ninth century. But it is significant that the twelfth century was the time when an onslaught was made on the pernicious practice of usury, for intensified commercial activity was making the problem a serious one from the church's point of view. The Second Lateran Council of 1139 (canon 13) excluded usurers from the consolation of the church; by the Third Lateran of 1179 they were to be excluded from communion. Canon 25 of the Council of 1179 states that the practice of usury had spread almost everywhere (*in omnibus fere locis tantum usurarium ita inolevit*) to such an extent that many people had left other forms of commerce to engage in it (*ut multi aliis negotiis praetermissis quasi licite usuras exerceant*).[1] In 1215 canon 67 of the Fourth Lateran Council implies that Jews were taking over the business of usury from Christians and orders the latter to break off contacts with Jews who were harrying Christians in matters of debt. To some degree the church was successful in the second half of the twelfth century in getting the problem under control, but the teaching against usury throughout the thirteenth century indicates considerable opposition to ecclesiastical doctrine. St Thomas Aquinas (*c*. 1225–74) summarized the whole position in his *Summa Theologica* and dealt particularly with the difficult problem as to whether the lender should receive any payment for the time that elapsed before he was repaid the principal. St Thomas recognized that the lender suffered through late payment of the loan and that a loss arose for him, the so-called *damnum emergens*, but he was not prepared to accept the view that a recompense should be given to the creditor for the cessation of gain. The argument ran that the lender might have made a gain by using his money if he had not loaned it; that by so doing he had been prevented from making a gain, the so-called *lucrum cessans*; this Aquinas would not approve because, he argued, the man had not already made the gain and recompense should not be made for a hypothetical gain, for something he did not have.

The teachings of the church, admirably suited though they might have been to the primitive agricultural societies of which Europe so largely consisted at least until the end of the twelfth century, were out of place in the developing exchange economy which was affecting all but the most isolated parts of the continent from about 1150 onwards. Some, of course, were not responsible to the teachings of Holy Church, although similar doctrines against the taking of interest obtained in the Moslem world. The Koran (suras 2, 3, 4, 30) prohibited the taking of usury to all true believers. But Christians in the eastern part of the Empire continued to live under Roman law, which had never forbidden the taking of interest upon loans; for them the basic law was the *Codex Justinianus* (IV, 32, 26) which had limited the interest rate that could be taken within a range of from 4 per cent to 8 per cent per annum. Subsequent adjustment of the

---

[1] C. – J. Hefele, *Histoire des Conciles* (Paris, Letouzey & Ané, 1907–38), vol. V, pt II, p. 1105.

rate to the current value of the coinage had, by the eleventh century raised the rate to between 5·55 per cent and 11·71 per cent.[1] Both Byzantine and Syrian Christian merchants were not therefore restricted by any anti-usury laws. Naturally the Jews were not bound by any provisions of Canon law and they remained, in some respects, suppliers of capital until the late thirteenth century, but in the later part of this period their operations were mostly in pawnbroking and small money-lending and their share of international trade began to decline as Italian participation grew. The Lateran Council of 1215 enacted that Jews were only to charge moderate rates of interest[2] and laid down sanctions which included boycott; it also urged princes to prevent Jews lending money at interest presumably by state legislation. Louis IX of France followed the spirit of these decrees and passed such legislation and the Council of Vienne (1311) declared that all secular legislation in favour of usury was null and void. The expansion of commerce demanded the invention of some method of avoiding the strict letter of the Canon law so that capital might be tapped for commercial enterprise. This remained throughout the Middle Ages a difficult operation, for most people regarded land as the true basis of wealth and land gave prestige as well as income so that more favourable terms had to be offered to attract capital to industry and commerce. Methods of banking and accounting were developed in Italy from the twelfth century onwards which helped to minimize the risk to invested capital and to secure for it an attractive return.

Undoubtedly Italian banking owed much to Byzantine and probably even to Roman and Greek precedents; the tenth-century *Book of the Prefect* records that bankers at Constantinople were engaged in money changing. Genoese documents of the twelfth century mention the *bancherius*, who was in all probability merely a money changer, but by about 1200 he had invaded the field of banking proper. Neither must we forget the growth of banking in other Mediterranean countries. There is some evidence from the sworn statements of Guglielmo Cassinense that by that date it was common practice for merchants to have bank accounts and to make payments

---

[1] G. Ostrogorsky, *History of the Byzantine State* (Oxford, Blackwell, 2nd ed. 1969), p. 190, note 1.

[2] C. – J. Hefele, op. cit. pp. 1365–6.

by book transfer rather than in specie. Also traces exist of the so-called dry exchange, that is of the use of foreign currency which the borrower did not need for bona fide trading purposes and on which interest concealed in the rate of exchange was charged. The earliest developments in Italian banking occurred at Siena and by the last quarter of the thirteenth century the city had become the principal banking centre of western Europe with Piacenza as its rival; both were represented at the Champagne fairs (see pp. 80–2). Much has been written of the technical achievements of medieval bankers in accounting and about the precise date at which double-entry book-keeping was introduced.[1] The matter is still in dispute and the traditional view of the date and place, *c.* 1340 in Genoa, has by no means been completely overthrown, although Florence has become a serious contender for the honour. The growth of more sophisticated techniques and the expansion of banking went together but we may look first at the expansion.

Late in the thirteenth century the Sienese firms, of which the Salimbeni and the Buonsignori were two of the largest companies, began to give ground to the Florentines. At this time also Lucca became a prominent banking centre. The Florentines copied the Sienese and formed large mercantile companies of which the Bardi, Peruzzi and Acciaiuoli were the most famous but a list of which included the Alberti, Frescobaldi, Scala, Cerchi, Rocci and Scotti among many others. The Bardi had a book capital of 90,000 florins but that did not exhaust their assets and the 'big two', Bardi and Peruzzi, were regarded by the Florentine historian Villani as the pillars of Christendom. Many of the great Florentine banking houses failed through granting excessive credits to monarchs, in particular to Edward III of England and to the Angevin rulers of Naples. But this did not bring about the end of Florence as a banking centre, for in the fifteenth century a bank perhaps more famous in name though smaller in size than the Bardi or the Peruzzi – the Medici – emerged. The records of the Bardi are scanty, those of the Peruzzi fuller. The multifarious activity of these banking companies is illustrated by the large number of their branches: the Peruzzi company was in Avignon, Barletta, Bruges, Castello di Castro (Sardinia), Cyprus, London,

[1] R. de Roover, in A. C. Littleton and B. S. Yamey (eds.), *Studies in the History of Accounting*, pp. 115–74.

Majorca, Naples, Paris, Pisa, Rhodes, Sicily, Tunis and Venice; and the Medici was in Naples, Milan, Pisa, Rome and Venice, Avignon, Geneva (transferred to Lyons in 1466), Bruges and London. Also banks participated in trade as well as in the banking business of making loans to traders and trading was more important than banking in the earlier period and still very significant to the Medici.

It was the relationship between Florence and the Holy See, increasingly close in the second half of the thirteenth century, which helped to develop Florentine banking, for the firms of that city obtained most of the business of collecting papal taxes and it was the danger of transporting bullion and specie which caused bankers to devise safer methods of credit transfer. Non-negotiable bills of exchange had certainly arrived in the fourteenth century and at the close of the Middle Ages these bills were perhaps discounted in the modern manner. Italian bankers were collecting papal taxes, for example in England, using the English money collected to purchase wool there which was shipped to Florentine clothiers who paid the bankers in florins which could be paid to the papal treasury, or the amount of the taxes could be credited to it as a ledger entry. Moreover, Italian banking houses were enabled to obtain the repayment of money owing to them by means of papal pressure, for sentence of excommunication was not infrequently pronounced against recalcitrant debtors.

Banks were performing many but not all of the functions which were theirs in the nineteenth century and are theirs today; above all they were offering credit and to do this they had to secure deposits. Many people in an age not noted for the strength of its law and order were pleased to have some place of safe deposit for their valuables and for their money but, despite the strict injunctions of Holy Church, they were often unwilling to deposit cash unless some return was given upon it. The bankers, therefore, were in the habit (this indeed was the Medici practice) of giving bonuses to depositors, which were designated gifts in order to circumvent the Canon law but which were really the equivalent of interest payments and without which bank deposits probably would have been inadequate. After 1311 when bankers could be convicted on the strength of their own account books they had to be extremely careful and what was in fact an interest payment was called a *dono* or a *discrezione*.

But the medieval banks were not central banks. They did not issue currency, which was the function of the sovereign, though he might delegate his rights; they did not control the overall quantity of currency and credit in circulation; they had not developed the cheque. The Bank of St George established in Genoa in 1408 was the first public bank and its dissolution in 1444, prematurely as R. de Roover thinks,[1] may have held back the growth of central banking. In the fifteenth century Milan became a prominent centre of banking with its most famous house, the Borromei, having branches in London and Barcelona; but Venetian techniques remained behind those of the Medici and Borromei. North of the Alps the expansion of banking was almost entirely the work of the Italians who dominated the money market throughout the Middle Ages. Only the Hanseatic League succeeded in warding them off and even it was successful in keeping them completely out of only one area – the Baltic. Collard de Marke and Guillaume Ruyelle at Bruges were money changers and deposit bankers in the 1360s and 1370s who used fairly sophisticated techniques but in fact they were copying the Italians. Only in southern Germany did some firms emerge with systems independent of Italian influence. These Italian banks were great partnerships and partners' investments had to be rewarded. One of the partners of the Peruzzi was Messer Domeneddio – the Lord God – the profits on whose shares were given to the poor. To keep track of these divisible profits accurate book-keeping was essential.

It used to be thought that the first indisputable example of double-entry book-keeping occurred in the accounts of the municipal stewards (*massari*) of Genoa *c.* 1340. By the beginning of the fourteenth century the time for a change-over from the paragraph form in which records had been kept to the placing of debits beside credits was propitious. The earliest example of the paragraph form of records yet found dates from 1211 in Florence, for prior to that tallies had been used. The more durable partnerships of the later thirteenth century evoked a demand for more precise knowledge as to where the partners stood, and another factor that influenced the development of accounting was the fact that agents had to keep lists of the goods which merchants sent them and they started a system

[1] In A. C. Littleton and B. S. Yamey (eds.), *Studies in the History of Accounting*, p. 135.

whereby receivables were counterbalanced by sales. It was perfectly possible to keep accounts in paragraphs leaving spaces for the infilling of later details but it was much more convenient to put debits beside credits, either on two opposite pages or on the same page vertically divided into two columns.

The dispute among experts in accounting studies is over the time and place at which this double-entry system first appeared. It has been claimed that the account book of Rinieri Fini, the agent of a Florentine banking house at the Champagne fairs between 1296 and 1305, satisfies the requirements of double-entry[1] but others have denied this.[2] Similar dispute rages over the Farolfi ledger of 1299–1300, also from Florence, and it has been claimed that a Sienese accountant for a few days between 8 and 11 December 1281 placed receipts next to expenditure in the modern manner. But not only was double-entry important in the development of accounting, the keeping of subsidiary books was of great significance.

The secret book which showed how the profits were divided demonstrates that in the Alberti firm intervals of one to five years elapsed between share-outs and during the period of the current partnership no new partner could be admitted nor could any withdraw. All had to wait for the pay-out at the termination of the partnership and, even if a partner died, his heirs had also to wait.

The tabular form of entry, described in Genoa in 1327 as accounts *ad usum banchi*, was probably developed by the money changers whose tables (*tavole*) supplied the word 'tabular', but use of such form does not necessarily imply acquaintance with double-entry. A bilateral arrangement plus the double recording of each entry, once on each side of the ledger, is still clearly seen for the first time in the stewards' accounts of the Genoese commune for the year 1340, though it is possible that the system may go back to the year 1327 when, because of frauds, the Genoese financial system was over-hauled. It would appear that northern Italy was more advanced than Tuscany in its acceptance of double-entry book-keeping; Genoa and Milan pioneered while Florence did not use the bilateral system until

---

[1] A. Castellani, *Nuovi Testi Fiorentini*, 2 vols (Florence, Accademia della Crusca, 1952), vol. I, p. 7.

[2] R. de Roover, in A. C. Littleton and B. S. Yamey (eds.), *Studies in the History of Accounting*, p. 117.

the late fourteenth century. On the other hand Tuscany kept accounts in Italian while the north continued to use Latin well into the fifteenth century. The use of day-books and waste-books and the system of posting items to the ledger all begin in the fourteenth century. Perhaps the soundest assumption that can be made about double-entry is that it originated in Italy between 1250 and 1350 and that it probably emerged simultaneously in several Italian cities. In Florence the phrase used by Paliano in 1382 that he was keeping his accounts *alla Veneziana* suggests that in the Tuscan capital the system came from Venice, although in fact Venice was not so far advanced in the practice of taking trial balances as were Genoa and Milan.

The accounts of that famous merchant of Prato, Francesco di Marco Datini (*c.* 1335–1410), illustrate the transition from single- to double-entry, for his first ledgers of 1367 to 1372 do not employ double-entry while from 1390 they clearly do. Among the Datini archives are to be found bills of exchange, insurance policies, bills of lading and rudimentary forms of the cheque which demonstrate the sophistication of business administration in later medieval Italy. Wherever traces of double-entry book-keeping appeared north of the Alps, these can be attributed to Italian influence and a detailed study of the book-keeping of northern and western Europe shows how far behind Italian practice these areas were, for it was not until the sixteenth century that Italian accounting methods were adopted in Europe generally. Luca Pacioli's treatise on accounting (*c.* 1494) described a system that was well known in Italy and was even more complex than his readers might believe but it was a system virtually unknown outside the peninsula.

CHAPTER 7

Medieval European Trade: South and North

Although Italian towns undoubtedly led the way in the commercial revival of Europe in the tenth and eleventh centuries, by the twelfth century some towns in the Low Countries had begun to rival Italian ones, and in industry even to outstrip them. In fact the growth of industry in a small area of north-western Europe made some towns industrialized in a sense that was not applicable to any Italian city before the late thirteenth or early fourteenth centuries and then only to Florence and Milan and possibly to Venice. By about 1150 the county of Flanders had become a compact predominantly industrial area as textiles were being made in considerable quantities for the market at St Omer, Douai, Lille, Bruges, Cambrai, Valenciennes, Ypres and Ghent and in adjacent territories at Louvain, St Trond-Huy and Maastricht. Of course, cloth was made all over Europe in the Middle Ages and an accurate assessment of the proportion of the population that dressed in homespuns can never be made but once men and women reached a degree of affluence they sought to dress in cloth of a better quality, and from the second quarter of the eleventh century some of these Flemish towns together with Arras, then in the county, began to satisfy those needs. Without attempting here to judge what factors caused such industrial growth in this particular corner of north-western Europe, it must be affirmed that the area witnessed a phenomenal expansion both in industry and commerce between the mid-eleventh and the mid-twelfth century. It was part of the significant changes which Europe experienced from the eleventh to the fourteenth centuries – changes that should not, however, be overestimated. The introduction of the horseshoe and the horse collar, the designing of speedier galleys, the invention of the compass and the astrolabe, the improvement of road surfaces by the use of the French *pavé du roi* or of Lombard circular stones, opened the way for this commercial expansion but none of these inventions added much power and speed to desperately slow and inadequate methods of conveyance. There was nothing like the railroad, the screw propeller, the internal combustion engine or the aeroplane to push forward the commercial revolution of the eleventh to the fourteenth centuries to the same extent as the industrial revolution of the late eighteenth, nineteenth and twentieth centuries has been pushed forward.

The expansion of population, which was taking place all over Europe from about the millennial year with a consequent rise in production, especially in north-western Europe, expanded the market demand for Levantine and Oriental goods which Italian merchants were in a unique position to supply. Moreover, in addition to the traditional raw materials, certain regions of the north-west could supply fine woollen cloth which found a ready sale in some of the areas from which the imported goods came; to some extent, therefore, the terms of trade probably moved slightly in favour of northern Europe and this favourable movement became more pronounced in the thirteenth century. Secondly, Italian trade was stimulated by economic growth in Italy itself which stemmed from the rise to preeminence of the Papacy; as a result, pilgrims flowed in larger numbers to Rome, and increased papal revenues also stimulated the growth of the Italian banking industry. Thirdly, expansion and direction came to Italian commerce as a consequence of the counteroffensive against Islam which showed itself in the *Reconquista* in Spain and between 1096 and 1291 in the Crusades. The western Mediterranean was cleared of Saracen pirates, so making sea travel much safer than it had been before the mid eleventh century with a resulting diminution in the loss of goods in transit. The Crusades, moreover, stimulated the demand for Oriental goods, as so many western-European knights had been exposed to new tastes and new products; many of them became acquainted for the first time with cane sugar, citrus fruits, dates, figs, cotton textiles and fine leather work. All these factors brought about a vast expansion in Italian trade both in the Mediterranean and beyond. The trade of southern Europe was basically the acquisition of goods from the Byzantine Empire, from the Moslem lands and from India and China and the selling of those goods to northern and western Europe, and with the proceeds the importing of raw materials or semi-manufactured goods for the industrial processes of certain Italian towns. Some of these raw materials and northern products were re-exported to the Byzantine Empire and the Moslem countries of the Near East. What towns were active in this trade, what routes they employed and how the exchanges were made with the north must be considered.

Pisa and Genoa were the first Italian towns to profit from the part they played in the Crusades. As a result of providing transport for the first and subsequent Crusades these two towns on the Tyrrhenian Sea acquired concessions in the captured Syrian towns. Pisa had a local trade in bulky products such as iron, salt and grain and its venture into the Levantine trade made its merchants among the chief suppliers of spices, silks and fine cloths until it was defeated and eclipsed by Genoa in 1284. Pisa's privileged position was based upon the help it provided during the siege of Jerusalem in 1099, for which, despite the fact that the Holy City had fallen before the arrival of its contingent, it was granted a quarter in the port of Jaffa. Genoa secured its reward in Antioch where the new ruler Bohemund granted its merchants thirty houses, a bazaar and a well. Venice, which had hung back from participation in the First Crusade because it did not wish to offend the Byzantine emperor who viewed with suspicion the establishment of Latin kingdoms and principalities in territory which had belonged to the Empire, decided in 1100 to aid Godfrey of Bouillon and in return secured rights in all cities to be taken subsequently by the Crusaders. Venice had since the later tenth century been the principal city trading to Byzantium and Alexius I in 1082 had crowned the many concessions made to it by a grant of unlimited freedom of trade throughout the Empire, of immunity from customs duties and the right to have their quarter in Constantinople.

G. Luzzatto pointed out the nature of these Venetian, Pisan and Genoese colonies in the ports and other Syrian towns.[1] The concessions might vary in spatial dimensions but the grantees would

[1] G. Luzzatto, *An Economic History of Italy from the Fall of the Roman Empire to the Beginning of the Sixteenth Century*, trans. P. Jones (London, Routledge, 1961), pp. 73 ff.

always have a *fondaco* or warehouse and these *fondachi* were established throughout the Near East. Along with territory went jurisdictional rights; resident Italians lived under their own law and were judged, at least in civil and commercial matters, by magistrates of their own cities, often called consuls. These Italians soon moved into Moslem lands and established *fondachi* in Egypt at Alexandria where goods from India and China and the Nile valley could be more easily obtained at a lower price. These commodities from the Far East (Pegolotti's treatise written probably in the 1340s tells how many items were in the trade) were brought by ship from China and India along roughly the same routes as in classical times to the Persian Gulf, Arabia and the Red Sea into Moslem countries, so that Europeans had no direct contact with the producers and suppliers; Islam had raised a barrier against European contacts with the Far East. In these ports of the Levant or inland at Aleppo, Antioch or Damascus exchanges were effected between the representatives of the southern European trading area and the Islamic importers of foreign goods, and also the merchants selling goods produced in the Moslem lands themselves. Political events had a profound effect upon trade routes. Throughout the twelfth century, in addition to the routes through the Syrian ports, Oriental goods were obtained through the Black Sea and Constantinople, a trade in which Venice enjoyed a near monopoly. On this latter route the Crimean peninsula played a key role, for the Venetians traded in Cherson and later had a colony at Sudak.

Two events, the attack in 1204 on the Byzantine Empire, traditionally but erroneously called the Fourth Crusade, and the establishment by 1241 of the Mongol Empire, which by that date controlled a vast area from Peking to Poland, deeply influenced trade routes. The former event was undoubtedly the result of Venetian machinations although a successful outcome was not unwelcome to other powers including the Papacy, and the Latin victory was to place Venice in an overwhelmingly strong position in the Aegean, the eastern Mediterranean and the Black Sea. For over half a century until 1261 the eastern Empire was reduced almost to impotence and during this period Venice established itself in many of the islands of the Cyclades, principally Andros, Tinos, Mykonos, Paros, Naxos and Milos from which occupation springs the adherence today to the Roman rather than to the Greek Orthodox church of many of the inhabitants. Venice also secured a foothold at Chalcis (Negroponte) in Euboea, the ports of Modon and Coron in the Peleponnesus, Durazzo and Corfu. Although the two latter were lost, they were recovered in the fourteenth century. But above all Crete was and remained the most important Venetian possession from which they dominated the trade of the eastern Mediterranean. Venice, indeed, had not taken up the three eighths of all Imperial territory conquered, as had been agreed upon in the pact made between the doge Enrico Dandolo and Baldwin of Flanders, but it had secured strong points most of which were to remain in its hands until the sixteenth century.

Genoa and Pisa at this period were placed in a less favourable position but nevertheless managed to expand their trade in imperial territory and when Genoa, by concluding the treaty of Ninfeo, backed Michael Palaeologus who succeeded in driving the Latins out of Constantinople in 1261, the Ligurian city's position was greatly enhanced. Venice, although it maintained those bases secured during the previous half century, lost its privileged position as regards exemption from customs duties but it still drove a flourishing trade despite the greater popularity of the Genoese at the Byzantine court. Pera, the Genoese quarter of Constantinople on the other side of the Golden Horn, and Caffa in the Crimea became the two dominant centres of trading influence possessed by Genoa but it had trading bases elsewhere in the Black Sea and also on the Caspian. In fact Genoa had established *fondachi* at Antioch, Jerusalem and Acre between 1097 and 1109. Genoa, moreover, dominated the western Mediterranean for it was in control of the trade with the north African coast to the west of Tripoli in Libya, where it had established itself at Bougie, Ceuta and Tunis by the mid twelfth century. Also it did much business with the ports of Languedoc and Catalonia, principally with Aigues Mortes and Barcelona. After the defeat of Pisa at the naval battle of Meloria in 1284, Genoa had no rival but Venice. Genoese hostility to Pisa had been furthered by an alliance with Lucca and, to counter this, Pisa had made an alliance with Florence in 1271 by which the inland town had been enabled to use the port, but this treaty proved no lasting security for some thirteen years later Genoa defeated its rival. These two Italian towns, Venice and Genoa, were importing goods from the Near East and from China and India which had been brought by the traditional routes.

A great shift in routes was effected by the establishment of political power by one authority over a vast area from Korea to Poland. The conquests of the Mongols under Ghengis Khan and his successors meant that by the 1240s the whole of eastern Europe and Asia from Wroclaw to Peking was pacified to such an extent that travel was both possible and safe for western European merchants. No longer were Italian merchants compelled to rely for Oriental goods upon middlemen, either Persian, Byzantine or Arab, but they were able to trade directly. Some time in the 1260s Marco Polo's father and uncle were able because of the security of the roads to travel from a Venetian colony on the south-eastern coast of the Crimea to Sarai on the Volga and thence via the Caspian Sea and Bukhara to Shang-tu (Coleridge's Xanadu) or Peking. In 1269 they were back in Acre with requests from Kublai Khan to the Pope that Christian missionaries should be sent to China. When they left again in 1271 with young Marco, aged seventeen, they took a different route. Starting from Ayas, not far from Alexandretta, they journeyed via Yazd and Kerman to Hormuz on the Persian Gulf, then north through Persia to Balkh, along the upper Oxus to Wakhan; they then crossed the Pamir plateau and continued through Kashgar, Yarkand and Khotan to somewhere near Lop Nor. From there they crossed the Gobi desert to Su-chow (Kinchüan) and Ch'ang-an (Sian) and in 1275 arrived at Shang-tu. There they were greeted by Kublai Khan who had assumed control over large parts of the Mongol Empire in 1252 and who was undisputed ruler of China and of the area from Korea to the Arabian desert and Poland from 1279 until his death in 1294. He made Peking the capital of all China, residing there in the winter and at Shang-tu in southern Mongolia near Dolon-nor in the summer. For many years the three members of the Polo family remained in attendance at the court of the Mongol emperor who asked their advice and who was unwilling to let them return. During their seventeen-year stay many personal and trade links were forged connecting Europe with the Far East. The Polos' return journey, following the traditional sea route, began from a place called Zaitun, probably Chin-Chiang in Fukien and brought them home through Singapore, Malacca, the Nicobar Islands, Ceylon and the Malabar coast to Hormuz which they reached in 1294. Thence proceeding north to Tabriz where they spent nine months, they eventually reached Venice by way of Trebizond. Direct contacts had been made with China and Europeans were able to penetrate the barrier that Islam had raised against such contacts between the seventh and the thirteenth centuries. During this period of Mongol dominance Venice gained a lead over Genoa by its greater exploitation of the overland route which terminated at Venetian posts on the Black Sea.

From the time of the Polo journeys until the fall of the Yüan dynasty in 1368 and the conquests of Timur (Tamerlane) from the 1370s to the 1390s when Persia, Russia and India were subjugated, these overland routes were kept open but the upheavals of the late fourteenth century together with the blockage of communications caused by the advance of the Ottoman Turks brought about increasing supply problems if not an actual diminution in the quantity of Oriental goods available in the fifteenth century. The opening of more direct routes to the east in the thirteenth century brought about a saturation of the European market for some eastern commodities and many Italian merchants had to accept lower profit margins during that century and the subsequent one. But from the third quarter of the fourteenth century the three factors previously mentioned blocked the overland routes to the east and within forty years attempts were being made to obtain eastern spices by new routes. It was perhaps partly this insistent demand for pepper and other spices from the Far East which led Prince Henry the Navigator of Portugal to explore the west African coast, and the settlement of such island groups as the Azores and Madeira enabled sugar, the supplies of which had been interfered with by the Ottoman advance, to be grown for the markets of northern and western Europe. This blocking of the overland route also led to increased rivalry between Venice and Genoa and the war of Chioggia (1378–81) hastened the decline of the Ligurian port. Relatively, the period of direct contact between Europe and the Far East within the Middle Ages was a short one but it was one of great significance and importance.

Yet it is easy to exaggerate the importance of the trade that Italian cities had with Byzantium, the Moslem countries and the Far East. Certainly Pegolotti in his treatise known since the eighteenth century as *La Pratica della Mercatura* lists well over 300 articles which entered into commercial exchanges in the early fourteenth century, although in reaching that number it must be pointed out that he listed twenty different types of cloth, twenty-three different sorts of silk and some twenty-five wines. Pepper and other spices and plants or seeds used for medicinal purposes bulk largely in his recital of commodities and many of these articles, especially jewels, had a high value for their weight; but the volume of trade was, nevertheless, small. G. Luzzatto has pointed out that all the eastern commodities brought into Venice in the fourteenth century were usually carried in three state convoys which went each year, one to Constantinople and the Black Sea, another to Beirut and a third to Alexandria.[1] Each convoy had only two to four galleys, the size of the largest vessel being not more than 500 tons, and a great deal of the space was taken up by a crew of sixty oarsmen, to which must be added at least twenty cross-bowmen and often also further reductions in available space resulted from the carriage of pilgrims. The food and water that these people consumed *en route* made additional calls upon space. Approximately only 2000 tons of merchandise arrived in Venice annually from the Byzantine Empire and the Near East; at Genoa the volume of trade was probably similar. It appears that cotton imports increased about the middle of the fourteenth century, for cogs rather than galleys were sent to the ports of Cyprus, Armenia and Syria to fetch it but even so it is doubtful whether the total annual weight of cargo exceeded or even reached 5000 tons. But the value of the cargo was considerable, for early fifteenth-century chroniclers estimate the value of goods on board each galley at around 200,000 ducats. Venice also had a much more bulky trade in salt and corn, supplying the Po valley with the former commodity and receiving the latter from Romagna, the Marches and Abruzzi and also from Crete, Sicily and Rumania and even occasionally from Egypt. But this trade had no significance in the south-north commercial links of medieval Europe.

Journeys undertaken by Italian importers of Oriental goods to the consumers of their wares in England and Flanders came rather late, for it was not until 1277 that Genoese galleys sailed via Cadiz and Seville to France, England and Flanders. Venice soon followed along this sea route although until the early fourteenth century it had

[1] G. Luzzatto, op. cit. p. 87.

always attracted northern European merchants, especially Germans, to come to the Adriatic port to obtain what they wanted rather than encouraged Venetians to travel to the fairs north of the Alps. Flemish cloths had been sold in Italy and other Mediterranean lands in the first half of the twelfth century. But direct contacts were made between Italians and the merchants of northern Europe at the great fairs, for as northern commerce began to expand in response to a growing demand for luxury goods, use was made of a complex of towns in the province of Champagne as an exchange point. Fairs remained throughout the Middle Ages and beyond the principal centres at which international exchanges took place. Even before the twelfth century the great fair of St Denis north of Paris had been visited by Italians probably as early as the 1070s. From 1114 we have continuous information about the Champagne fairs. Six fairs were held annually in four towns, two at Troyes on the Seine, two at Provins, one at Lagny on the Marne and one at Bar-sur-Aube. At Lagny the fair for the winter commenced on 2 January and the one at Bar-sur-Aube on Shrove Tuesday. At Provins the first fair started on the Tuesday before Ascension day. The 'hot fair' at Troyes was on 24 June, while the second Provins fair was on 14 September and the 'cold fair' at Troyes on 2 November. These fairs became international for not only did all regions of France send their merchants but by the early thirteenth century merchants came from northern and central Italy, especially from Milan, Cremona, Piacenza and Asti, and from Flanders, Hainault, Brabant, Spain, England, Germany and Savoy. All types of merchandise were on sale, woollen cloth from Flanders and northern France, silks from Lucca, leather goods from Spain, Africa and Provence, furs from Germany, linens from Champagne and Germany. The Italians brought goods from outside Europe, spices, sugar, alum, lacquer and dye woods. Cotton goods were also on sale and trade was brisk in grain, wine and horses, but the most important sector was the trade in woollen cloth.

The Champagne fairs had at first been of local importance only and the earliest document, of 1114, relating to Bar-sur-Aube mentions only horses and other animals. At this time northern cloth merchants were still taking their cloths south to Italy, where they had travelled perhaps as early as 1100, but from about 1190 the

Italians came north and the Champagne fairs assumed their inter-national character. They had been controlled in the early period by the counts of Champagne but from the last decade of the twelfth century control passed to the kings of France. Taxes were levied on the stalls and on the residences of the merchants, entry and exit tolls had to be paid by them; there were levies on sales and purchases and dues upon weights and measures, and payments had to be made by Jews and Italians for safe conducts. The wardens of the fairs were responsible for order and controlled the fair seal, and a large admin-istrative and judicial personnel evolved which drew up documents relating to sales and adjudicated in disputes. Unfortunately none of the records of this commercial and judicial business has survived with the exception of a single leaf from a register of the Troyes summer fair of 1296: it contains fifteen deeds mentioning merchants from Piacenza, Genoa, Milan, Asti, Como, Savona, Florence, Montpellier, Narbonne, Avignon, Carpentras and St Flour. These deeds deal with the sale of cloth and horses. The importance of the fairs was guaran-teed by the safe conducts which the kings of France gave to those merchants who came to the Champagne fairs. As early as 1209 Philip II Augustus promised such documents to all merchants, especially to the Italians, and allowed them three months in which to leave the country if at any time his safe conduct was withdrawn. In 1245 the Roman, Tuscan, Lombard and Provençal merchants gained exemption from the jurisdiction of the fair wardens and were granted the right to use their own legal systems, a privilege which was confirmed by Philip the Fair in 1294–5.

The series of wardens' letters, continuous from 1274, tells us how the fairs were conducted, for the wardens assured the execution of agreements arrived at between merchants. Eight days were allowed for entry to the fair, ten days then followed for the sale of cloth, eleven for the sale of leather, hides and skins and nineteen for the sale of goods by weight and the settlement of accounts. At the conclusion of this period four days were allowed for the drawing up of the 'letters of the fair': so in all the fair lasted about six weeks. The arrangement of business was to the advantage of the northern mer-chants who could sell their cloth and leather and assess their earnings before they purchased the Mediterranean and Oriental goods which were sold mainly by weight. By the mid thirteenth century the

Italians had established permanent consulates. Siena did so first in 1246 and others soon followed. The consuls exercised authority over their fellow citizens but also represented their city in negotiations with foreign rulers and with the justices of the fair. They represented their citizens' interests both before a fair court and, if a dispute went to a higher level, before the *Parlement* in Paris. During the second half of the thirteenth century fifteen Italian towns had consuls at the Champagne fairs. The Italians also organized themselves in a *universitas* (gild) from 1278 onwards under the direction of a *capitaneus* or rector and the merchants of several Italian towns met together to agree upon routes of travel. The Provençaux had a similar organization but, unlike the Italians whose rector was chosen by the consuls, the *capitaneus* of the Provençaux was chosen by the council of Montpellier. A so-called 'hanse' of seventeen cloth-selling towns of Flanders, Champagne, Picardy, Hainault and Ponthieu was formed by 1230 and its origin goes back to the previous century; it had no head but the merchants of these towns held meetings to discuss problems common to the sellers of cloth.[1]

By *c.* 1320 the international importance of the Champagne fairs had ceased although even before that date their significance had become financial rather than commercial as they offered currency and bill quotations. A commercial recession, the origin of which has not been defined, began for the Champagne fairs about 1260. It has been attributed to heavy taxation by the French kings and to the rise in importance of Lyons, although it is now generally agreed that its rise followed the decline of the Champagne fairs and was not a cause of it. Others would attribute the decline to the wars of Philip the Fair (1285–1314), the competition of the sea routes at the end of the thirteenth century or to the industrialization of the north Italian towns so that they no longer imported Flemish cloth. Some have seen the substitution of gold for silver in international trade which took place in the second half of the thirteenth century as one of the causes of the decline of these fairs.

But fairs played a significant role in the trading system of northern Europe throughout the Middle Ages and into more recent times. Flanders, like Champagne had six important fairs, two at Ypres, and one each at Bruges, Thourout, Lille and Messines. Italian bankers

[1] *Cambridge Economic History of Europe*, II, p. 374.

known as Lombards came to the fairs, as did money changers who were local men, and documentation in the form of registered obligations remained, 7000 of which were destroyed at Ypres in 1914. These obligations were letters constituting promises of payment falling due at the next fair. In a sense the importance of the Italy-Bruges axis caused a decline in the importance of these fairs, for from the early fourteenth century commerce was so highly developed that it took place all the year round. Chalon-sur-Saône, Lyons and Geneva had famous fairs in the later Middle Ages. Chalon rose to real importance after 1280, Geneva got under way in the fourteenth and reached its zenith in the fifteenth century with four fairs a year, and Lyons, though it had been prominent earlier, was built up by the kings of France in the fifteenth century as a rival to Geneva. The spring fair was held on the right bank of the Saône, i.e. the French side, and the autumn fair on the left bank, the Imperial side. If fairs declined a little in importance in the highly developed areas of western Europe, they still remained of great significance in the trade of the eastern parts of the continent as a new east–west trade axis developed. Frankfurt in many ways replaced the Champagne fairs, for merchants there sold local and Flemish cloth, arms from Nuremberg, herring from Lübeck, dye products from Breslau, Italian glass and silk wares, Rhenish and Alsatian wines, Hungarian horses and goods from greater distances such as English cloth, Russian furs and Scandinavian herring. Fairs at Nördlingen and Leipzig played a prominent role in trade but in Scandinavia only the Scania fairs were of international importance. The Scania fairs had this significance because the English and Dutch fished in the Sound and sold their catch at these fairs held at Skanör in southern Sweden but elsewhere the trade, for example at Wisby, Stockholm and Bergen, was completely dominated by the Hanseatic merchants. In the fifteenth century, fairs sprang up at Malines, Antwerp and Bergen op Zoom and the importance of such fairs for south–north and north–south trade was perhaps as great as the development of the sea routes.

We have seen how the Italians dominated the trade between southern and northern Europe but there was an area of trade into which they did not penetrate, for Sluis and Newcastle formed the limits of their advance in a northerly and easterly direction. By the late thirteenth century the Germans were dominating the international trade of northern Europe. The origin of the prosperity and predominance of the Hanseatic League is to be found in the prosperity and predominance of a few German cities. Of these Cologne is outstanding. Even in the twelfth century, the wealth of the city was a by-word, as Caesarius of Heisterbach and Otto of Freising inform us, and although its wealth depended to some degree upon industry, it was mainly due to commerce. It managed almost to monopolize the trade of the Rhine valley, ousting the merchants of Utrecht, and in the thirteenth century the merchants of Cologne became the chief intermediaries in the trade between Flanders and central and southern Germany. It also played a prominent part in the trade in metal goods made in Namur, Dinant and Liège. Westphalian merchants in the early twelfth century had expanded eastwards and before the middle of that century they had gone beyond the Elbe into Slavonic lands where, in Lübeck, by permission of the Wendish prince they had formed a permanent settlement. After the city had been burnt a purely German town was founded in 1143 which in the late twelfth century established colonies at Schwerin, Wismar and Rostock. Farther to the east, Riga, founded as a German city in the early thirteenth century, helped to establish Dorpat and Reval. These German merchants followed or sometimes even preceded the settlement of the lands east of the Elbe by the Teutonic knights and by peasants. They opened up the Baltic trade in which Russia was the chief supplier and the principal market: a trade in furs, honey, pitch, tar, timber and rye. Later the Prussian towns of Marienburg, Elbing, Thorn and Königsberg, and still later Danzig, were established to become outlets for corn and timber which were the main products of Prussia, Lithuania and western Poland.

This eastward expansion had a profound effect upon the economy of northern Europe as a whole. The industrialized regions of the north-west, especially Flanders, had a new market for their cloth and an abundant source of supply of cheap timber and grain. England began to buy Baltic timber instead of Scandinavian and also Baltic grain, either for its own use or for re-export, while Flanders, which had relied upon grain supplies from northern France or from southern Germany, switched over to Baltic sources of supply at least between 1250 and 1350.

The rise of the east German towns greatly strengthened the economic position of Germany in Europe, for German merchants became dominant in Scandinavia and Russia, acquired great economic influence in the Low Countries and enjoyed exceptional privileges in England. In the fourteenth century the German towns combined into a powerful naval, military and political union of the Hanse. The establishment of the Hanse in the 1360s did not mark an advance in German expansion but was rather a union to preserve the dominant position of the great trading towns, for at that time German commerce had all but reached the final limits of its territorial expansion. It was in self-defence then that the merchants of the German towns came together and the Hanseatic League started with the formation of unions of Germans abroad, of which those at Wisby and London were the first. The term *Hansa* was used at first to designate the right of merchants to form trading associations and its first use is to be found in England, although by the beginning of the thirteenth century it was no longer applied to the burgesses of English towns but had become restricted to the organizations of foreign merchants in London. The traders of Cologne there formed a *Hansa* which eventually grew into the Hanse of the Steelyard comprising all or nearly all the German merchants trading in London. The Great Charter (*Carta Mercatoria*) of 1303 substantially increased the privileges of the German merchants in England, and the exemptions from toll that they received placed them in a more favourable position than other foreign merchants. Their corporate organization of the Steelyard received extensive powers of self-government and the merchants were judged by their own law. Similar corporate organizations with similar privileges were set up in other places. The most important were the two German 'factories' at the termini of the greatest trade route they exploited, namely at Bruges and Novgorod. The *Kontor* in Bruges was formed by German merchants who had been attracted to that city primarily by the Anglo-Flemish trade in wool but remained there because Bruges became, in the late thirteenth and fourteenth centuries, a leading centre for commercial exchanges to which traders came from all over Europe. The Hanse merchants had much to do with its continuing prosperity. They likewise dominated the town of Novgorod. The *Hof* or yard with warehouses and residential hostels was the centre of their communal organization and it received protection under agreements made with Russian princes. But there were similar, albeit smaller, communities of German merchants in outports such as Lynn, Boston, Hull and Bristol, and in Venice was to be found the *Fondaco dei Tedeschi*. In the Scandinavian ports they often held a quarter of the city and took part in municipal government; Bergen in Norway is the outstanding example of the high degree of control which the Hanse exercised in some places.

This commercial system formed by the German merchants was as close and as tightly knit as any that had appeared in Europe and it was already in existence at the beginning of the fourteenth century, although at that time the system owed its unity and cohesion to economic facts rather than to political ties. The rise of the Hanseatic League was a formalization of the system of consultation which had gone on among merchants from different German cities in various centres. Sporadic meetings of the 'home' towns were called to discuss matters raised by their merchants abroad, and by the middle of the fourteenth century such meetings were being held several times a year. The difficulties that were arising with Flanders and the growing tensions with Denmark, which culminated in the first Hanseatic war (1360–9), provided the political challenge that brought the towns together more or less permanently. In 1367 representatives of the towns met in Cologne to form a confederation and the League continued after the peace of Stralsund (1370). During the war predominance had been won for the city of Lübeck and from 1370 on German towns and outsiders both regarded it as the guardian of Hanseatic unity. In fact the economic interests of the German towns forming the League were, in the second half of the fourteenth century, disparate. Lübeck was suffering a decline as the Dutch pioneered the direct route round the Jutland peninsula, and Danzig, which rose to a powerful position in the 1340s and 1350s, also preferred this route. Baltic goods were less frequently unloaded and taken overland through Lübeck to the North Sea. The Teutonic Order which the League had to accept as a partner traded in such a way as to be almost a competitor of the League. Moreover, the western wing of the League, the Rhenish towns with Cologne at their head, had strong separate interests. The central group of Wendish towns led by Lübeck were the towns that maintained the

League's unity, but Lübeck's interests were really selfish ones designed to maintain its own importance by cutting to a minimum the direct trade between the North Sea and the Baltic through the Sound. It was for that reason that Lübeck was so hostile to England and Holland, the two countries that used the Sound route most extensively.

The German towns of the Hanseatic League were in a dominant position in the trade of northern Europe as were Venice and Genoa in the southern trade. To some extent they dominated English trade even into the fifteenth century, they had a large share in the prosperity of Bruges and they completely controlled the Scandinavian trade. In Sweden they controlled the mines and appointed half the municipal governments. In the thirteenth century the Norwegians had still been active traders but in the following century Norway also had fallen to the Germans. They, like the Venetians, were not to be seriously challenged until new world trading patterns arose in the sixteenth century.

D

CHAPTER 8

Economic Growth in the Twelfth and Thirteenth Centuries

Many dangerous pitfalls exist for the historian who attempts to analyse the economy of medieval Europe down to the thirteenth century in terms of modern economic theories of growth. The greatest difficulty, the one from which others spring, is the inadequacy of easily quantifiable data and it is virtually impossible to assess economic development, as the twentieth-century economist understands it, for the medieval period. To the economist, economic growth means an increase in the *per capita* gross national product[1] or, stated another way, a sustained and reasonably fast increase in *per capita* income.[2] The data available certainly do not permit us to posit growth according to such a definition, since no accurate calculation of the total population can be made for most medieval cities or states, and before 1350 the price data at present available lack the regularity, continuity, homogeneity and diversity necessary for the satisfactory measurement of the price level.

In such a primitive economy GNP is a notional concept. But the term 'economic growth' has been used to describe other distinct phenomena such as an expansion of activity in a pre-industrial economy which was not accompanied by any far-reaching technological or structural changes, or, secondly, a sharp acceleration in production accompanied by dramatic technological and structural changes which transform a relatively underdeveloped economy at least to a developing status.[3] In the former sense, we can talk of growth in the economy of medieval Europe, although the second

---

[1] 'Economic growth', *International Encyclopedia of the Social Sciences* (ed. D. Sills), 17 vols (New York, Macmillan, Free Press, 1968).

[2] B. E. Supple (ed.), *The Experience of Economic Growth*, p. 11.

[3] ibid.

definition is almost entirely irrelevant to that era. If we are to take growth as meaning a sustained rise in total population and in total product but not in *per capita* product, then it is certainly discernible in the period up to the early fourteenth century.[1] The lack of quanti-fiable evidence makes it impossible to make an informed guess at the growth rate. On the other hand impressionistic evidence can be pieced together to form a fairly coherent picture, which can be described in terms of modern theory, and this in turn allows us to make deductions about the general character of the economy.

Much recent sociological writing, moreover, has been directed to showing that the economy should not be regarded in isolation but that it is only one aspect of society. When in economic growth, the quantitative changes are of sufficient magnitude that they involve changes in organization in the system, it has been declared that the problem of structural change in the economy must be treated as a sociological problem.[2] If this is so, then it can be argued that changes that occurred in societal organization in medieval Europe were connected with the changes in the economy and we may agree with J. J. Spengler that 'considerable and sustained economic growth took place in Europe before the fourteenth century'.[3] A loosening of the social structure is both a cause and a consequence of economic growth which can only be seen as a special aspect of general social evolution.[4] Many of the primitive societies, for example Indian villages, have parallels with medieval village communities and some of the problems, both economic and sociological, which beset the backward countries of the twentieth century hindered the expansion of economies in the Middle Ages. Growth, it may be argued, means more than a rapid and sustained rise in real output per head, for on the social and demographic sides it produces alterations in fertility and mortality rates, in migration patterns, in family size and struc-ture, in the educational system and in the provision made for public health.[5] Moreover, the influence of economic development spreads into the areas of income distribution, class structure, the organization

[1] S. S. Kuznets in B. E. Supple, *The Experience of Economic Growth*, p. 53.

[2] Talcott Parsons and N. J. Smelser, *Economy and Society*, p. 246.

[3] In B. F. Hoselitz (ed.), *Theories of Economic Growth*, p. 3.

[4] 'Contemporary theorizing on economic growth', in B. F. Hoselitz (ed.), *Theories of Economic Growth*, p. 297.

[5] 'Economic growth', *International Encyclopedia of the Social Sciences*.

of government and the political structure. In so far as economic growth may be postulated between the later tenth and the early fourteenth centuries, it may be possible to say something about its influence upon some of these areas but frequently the statistics are lacking which would permit a very full commentary upon its influence over some sectors of society. To the extent that medieval man theorized about his society he regarded it not as a *Gesellschaft* or association like a firm but as a *Gemeinschaft* or community like a family: as an organism with the Pope as the head, the warriors as the arms and the peasants as the feet.[1] It was a society to which ideas of change tended to be alien. Even when technical advances were made, considerable opposition to them arose, as when weavers refused to accept thread from the new spinning wheels at Abbeville in 1288[2] or when the fulling of cloth by fulling mills was forbidden.

The economy of medieval Europe in general, leaving aside a few highly unusual areas, was an agrarian peasant economy which was characterized by a high degree of self-sufficiency within each community and even within each family. Moreover, it was marked by a relatively slow change in technique and by the relatively unimportant role of market exchange. Modern economists regard such economies as having high average death rates, which fluctuate as a result of variations in crops and in the incidence of epidemics.[3] Birth rates are stable at a high level to replace the death rates which are high because of poor diets, primitive sanitation and ineffective medical practice. This economy apparently did not grow until at least the late tenth or early eleventh centuries and not greatly until the twelfth century. What were the constraints, cultural, economic and political, that prevented growth in the economy?

Any attempt to answer these questions will involve glancing briefly at the cultural value systems of medieval Europe. Without in any way lapsing into the old-fashioned view which saw the Middle Ages through rose-tinted spectacles as the 'Ages of Faith', it is certain that the importance of religious motives formed the *Weltanschauung* of medieval Europe. To some degree, although it is

[1] W. Stark, 'The contained economy' in *Aquinas Paper 26* (The Aquinas Society of London, 1956), p. 4.

[2] C. Singer *et al.* (eds.), *A History of Technology*, vol. II, p. 649.

[3] A. J. Coale and E. M. Hoover, *Population Growth in Low-Income Countries*, pp. 9, 10.

difficult to say with precision how far, the people of medieval Europe were other-world oriented and to that extent they were not interested in the increase of material wealth. Such values were inculcated by the church which preached the dangers of increased worldly wealth and affirmed that, in some instances, to seek it was a downright sin.

Where accumulated wealth existed, it was the duty of those who enjoyed it to redistribute their capital assets either in the form of charitable outlays or by conspicuous consumption; it was not in keeping with the teachings of the church that they should be used to make more money. In an age that judged a man's status by his 'port', which depended largely on the size of his retinue, conspicuous consumption helped to provide employment and to redistribute capital.

The central importance of religion lies in relation to action not to thought, and organized religion, *ecclesia Romana*, influenced action greatly. Thus the value systems over most parts of Europe were not congenial to commercial or industrial expansion. Cultural value systems can be judged by the punishments and rewards they offer and by the differential expenditure of resources, time, energy and natural environment they employ. The value systems of medieval Christendom rewarded the saint and spent resources upon buildings to glorify God. Of course, some wealthy sinners diverted resources to other ends, for, by definition, values are distinct from conduct, but in general the climate of opinion of the regnant system of values did not favour economic growth.[1]

With such value systems, much stress was laid upon tradition and in traditional societies people tend to accept their positions as God-given and do not attempt to change them.[2] In medieval society some channels of vertical mobility (for example the church) existed, but as a rule society was stratified with social, cultural, economic and even legal barriers to movement. A serf was born to live his life and die as a serf who worked in accordance with customs and procedures known to all and this dispensation he accepted at least until the thirteenth century and in many parts of Europe into the fourteenth century. This traditional attitude led to a relatively static view of

[1] B. F. Hoselitz (ed.), *Theories of Economic Growth*, p. 4.
[2] A. and E. Etzioni (eds.), *Social Change: Sources, Patterns and Consequences*, p. 182.

society, for where people were born into pre-ordained social positions and occupations there were no working-force problems to solve. The government might be concerned with whether it had enough serfs and whether serfs had enough to eat but it was not concerned with whether he was employed or unemployed.[1] Also such traditional societies assumed that the world's stock of accessible resources was essentially fixed and, as a consequence, that economies accordingly were relatively static.

It is almost impossible to draw a clear distinction between cultural and economic constraints upon growth because they intermesh at many points. To take but one example, the cultural restraint upon amassing wealth meant that there was no precedence for saving and so capital creation was difficult. However, we can assess some constraints of an economic nature within the general framework of a traditional, if not indeed a traditionalistic society. Economic development was retarded by the difficulty of mobilizing the forces of production. These forces are, classically, land, labour and capital, to which must be added organization or entrepreneurial skill. Land of itself presented little difficulty, for vast tracts of empty land were available for cultivation and occupation all over Europe before *c.* 1150 to *c.* 1200 and it was only in the thirteenth and in the first decades of the fourteenth century, and then only in a few areas (notably in England), that land was in short supply. But land without the application to it of labour and capital could not produce economic growth and it is in the mobilization of these two factors that great difficulties were experienced. As we have seen, the value judgements of the Middle Ages offered little incentive to save and the teaching of the church on the taking of interest (see chapter 6) positively discouraged it, with the result that those individuals or families who had a surplus, and some had to borrow to acquire one, spent it upon conspicuous consumption. Money was spent on ill-considered charitable outlays and thrift appears to be a virtue not extolled by the church before the Reformation. Yet until there was some surplus, capital creation was, of course, impossible, but even when a surplus existed it was not easy to tap it for the expansion of the agrarian economy and still more difficult to attract it to industrial development. As will be seen, however (see pp. 93–4, 96–7), growth

[1] 'Investment', *International Encyclopedia of the Social Sciences*.

in the Middle Ages resulted rather from the mobilization of labour than of capital.

Serious hindrances to the modernization of the labour force were to be found in medieval Europe. As a result of the stratification of society, social mobility was low; social, economic and even legal barriers hindered movement from one societal group to another. Poor transport facilities were another hindrance to the easy mobilization of the labour force and social stratification inhibited men from undertaking new enterprises. One view taken by sociologists is that for men to undertake deviant behaviour the rewards must be attractive and that deviant behaviour is undertaken by those who wish to rise in the social scale; another theory is that those who undertake it are at the margin of a given culture or are in a social or cultural position in which they straddle more than one culture.[1] The latter are often known as marginal men because of their ambiguous position from a cultural, ethnic, linguistic or sociostructural standpoint and they are strongly motivated to make adjustments in situations of change. Such were the Genoese, Pisans, Sienese and Florentines north of the Alps. But in general there were relatively few of these marginal men about who, in the course of making adjustments to their environment, might develop innovations in social behaviour, for hermits, missionaries and monks who fell into this category usually developed other-worldly orientations. This lack of marginal men was doubtless a severe social constraint upon change. Social mobility in some ways was easier in the ninth and tenth centuries when, provided a wealthy patron would pay for the special training of a youth from the age of twelve years, for the equipment of a specially bred horse and for armour, the avenue to knighthood remained open. But from *c.* 1150 the knight was no longer an 'entrepreneur' but an entrenched land-based lord, for during the twelfth century the right to be dubbed knight became a hereditary privilege.[2]

In all probability at least until the twelfth century the aspiration levels of the 'working classes' were low and only in the fourteenth century does clear evidence emerge of any rise in those aspiration levels. The poor educational provision for the labour force also stood

---

[1] 'Economic growth', *International Encyclopedia of the Social Sciences.*

[2] A. and E. Etzioni (eds.) *Social Change: Sources, Patterns and Consequences*, p. 204.

in the way of economic growth. The mobilization of capital and labour was made more difficult, and growth thereby hindered, by the endemic wars of the Middle Ages which frequently pauperized whole areas. The Latin victors of the Fourth Crusade (1204) and Ghengis Khan, alike, pauperized the communities they conquered and some of those regions have remained impoverished to the present day.[1] The lack of law and order was also a constraint on growth in many areas of Europe before the late eleventh century, for central government had broken down in extensive parts of western Europe from the mid ninth century and was scarcely restored in some places until the twelfth century. During this era, feudal magnates had ruled uncertainly with periods of near anarchy and of tyrannical governance alternating. Indeed growth had to some extent been hindered by the breakdown in organized government which occurred at the fall of the Roman Empire in the west. There is little sign of any inventions or of the acceptance of them in the years between 400 and 1000. Such, in outline, were the difficulties facing the development of medieval society which restricted the growth of its economy; so formidable were they that the *essor* of the twelfth and thirteenth centuries appears miraculous.

Despite the gloomy prospect that has been so far outlined, growth did take place in the economy, as we have seen (Chapter 5), from the late tenth century in Italy and in Europe generally from the twelfth and thirteenth centuries. This growth was extensive rather than intensive. The rise in output was due in the Middle Ages to a rise in labour input: it was not, like modern growth, the result of greater capital input and of an improved quality of the labour force. In relation to agriculture the development was largely the result of more people working on a greater acreage of land and so increasing the total product.[2] Productivity increased but slightly in the absence of any major technological breakthrough in agriculture. It seems unlikely that the principal inventions were basically responsible for the increased agricultural product, although it is impossible to assess with precision the contribution made by the improvements, admittedly few by modern standards, which were effected.

The more efficient use of horse power, which was obtained by

---

[1] J. K. Galbraith, *Economic Development in Pr spective*, p. 18.
[2] See G. Duby, *Rural Economy and Country Life in the Medieval West*, pp. 106 ff.

better methods of harnessing the animal in the eleventh and twelfth centuries,[1] might have done something to increase the efficiency of the ploughing operation in some areas, notably the Île-de-France, but since most parts of Europe used the ox as the plough animal it is by no means correct to attribute great gains in productivity to the introduction of the horse collar. Undoubtedly an improvement took place in the design of ploughs whose efficiency was increased by the greater amount of metal in their construction from the eleventh century onwards. Although metal ploughshares were known from the tenth century B.C. the increased availability of metal from *c.* 1000 meant that more of it could be used, so strengthening and making the plough more effective, and there is also evidence of greater experiment with the use of wheels on ploughs and, in the eleventh century, of the invention of mouldboards. These heavier ploughs requiring at least a four-ox plough team undoubtedly improved the tilth of heavy clay soils, so tending to increase the yield from them. But sometimes inventions were held back by legal constraints: for example, the use of the scythe was possibly delayed because of the common rights to the stubble enjoyed by tenants of the medieval open fields.[2] The process of grinding corn was speeded up to some extent by the introduction of windmills into Europe but there were few before the thirteenth century.[3] Water mills were more and more widely used for grinding corn. These inventions in some measure would free labour for employment in other spheres: the grinding of corn is a good example, for it was hardly anywhere done at home by the housewife.[4] But the main increase in the product from the land came as a result of bringing more land into cultivation. This was achieved both by clearing scrubland, cutting down forest and draining marshland, all of which activities went on apace between the eleventh and early fourteenth centuries.

The most plausible model, it would appear, is that some population growth occurred in some parts of Europe probably in the tenth and early eleventh centuries and, as a superfluity of land existed, an

[1] C. Singer *et al.* (eds.), *A History of Technology*, vol. II, p. 553. Lynn White Jr, *Medieval Technology and Social Change*, pp. 60 ff., dates the introduction of the horse collar to the ninth century.

[2] ibid. p. 96.

[3] ibid. pp. 623 ff.

[4] ibid. pp. 601 ff.

increased population could be fed. This increased population grew rather more food than it needed to consume and this surplus could be used to feed a growing urban population, which, freed from agricultural labour, was able to produce consumer goods, chiefly textiles, and to exchange them for food. More people in towns were able to abandon agriculture and to devote themselves entirely to the manufacture of consumer goods. Some surplus must have been present to form the capital accumulation necessary for economic growth and from the late eleventh century some 'modernization' occurred in the labour force. Specialization in the labour force clearly emerged in the Flemish towns in the later years of the century, a specialization that permitted the production of a better quality cloth than had previously been known. Carders, spinners, weavers, fullers and shearmen all emerged as specialized craftsmen.

'Modernization' is also seen in the regulation of hours and conditions of labour. In earlier societies, and probably in medieval Europe before the later eleventh century, those who were self-employed worked until they had finished their task, but when they came to work for employers – as they did in many sections of the textile industry – gilds, municipalities or statutes frequently specified hours and sometimes conditions of labour.[1] It has been estimated that with dawn-to-dusk working, six days a week, and with ninety to a hundred days a year in all not worked, that the total hours per year were in the region of 2750 to 3000 hours, or an average of fifty-four hours a week. This figure was increased in the sixteenth century when the rise in numbers competing for jobs enabled employers to lengthen hours.

Three variables in growth are population growth, technological change and the emergence of entrepreneurial skills, and in the Flemish cities from the later eleventh century population grew and entrepreneurial skills developed while technological change was minimal or perhaps even non-existent. Entrepreneurial skills flourished despite opposition, for entrepreneurial behaviour did not belong to the category of social actions that were considered as constituting the 'good life'. Indeed as late as the fifteenth century this was true of certain kinds of financial entrepreneurship which was tainted by the official opposition of the church to usury.

[1] 'Investment', *International Encyclopedia of the Social Sciences.*

Urbanization was, of course, a stimulus to growth and especially to agricultural growth in the twelfth and thirteenth centuries. We have dealt elsewhere (see Chapters 5 and 6) with urban development but its importance was that it secured division of labour, which in turn meant that an increasing percentage of the European population was becoming freed from agricultural production. The labour force was being more profitably employed. It would appear that economic growth came between about 1150 and 1325 because European society was large enough to be able to make use of division of labour and also because the population had unfilled wants for goods and services, wants that had doubtless been stimulated to some degree by contact with the Near East. The cessation of major invasions after the tenth century and the improved political order within the framework of Christendom facilitated the growth of a European market. While medieval society was a typical non-industrialized society in its very low level of technological development and its dispersed control of the means of production, it had some division of labour, to some extent an exchange economy and some notion of a free contractual relationship of the labourer with the employer. Perhaps it would be truer to say that such a notion was not widespread until after the middle of the fourteenth century. So, despite all the constraints, growth came between *c.* 1150 and *c.* 1325, in response to the factors mentioned, but it was limited by the low level of technological innovation and the limited energy input which still derived largely from human, animal, wood, wind and water sources.

Several of the usual accompaniments of economic growth are clearly discernible. Despite the paucity of data, it can be seen that English prices were on average about one third higher in the period 1250–99 than they had been between 1200 and 1249 and showed a rise of 15 per cent in the years 1300–49 over the second half of the thirteenth century and some French figures demonstrate that prices were one third higher between 1301 and 1350 than they had been in the first quarter of the thirteenth century.[1] The rises in prices, which were more probably of the demand–pull rather than the cost–push type, kept economic growth going for a couple of centuries. As the economy became more specialized and market-dominated it may be

[1] 'Prices', *International Encyclopedia of the Social Sciences*.

that in the early years of economic development *per capita* real income rose, but by the thirteenth century population had increased to such an extent that it began to press upon resources and, in particular, upon supplies of foodstuffs and upon the amount of cultivable land available. This could not be sufficiently expanded to feed the ever-increasing number of mouths.

The movement was a classical one. At first increased supplies of food and other commodities allowed the population to expand. The increased food supplies did something to improve nutritional standards which, in turn, led to improved health, greater longevity and larger families. In accordance with Malthusian principles, the population expanded in due course up to and beyond the limits of subsistence. Beliefs and customs reinforced the economic advantages to a peasant family of a large number of births, for children contributed at an early age to agricultural production and gave security to parents in old age. A low income society has a mortality and fertility pattern that fits pretty closely the conditions which Malthus envisaged.[1] The population pressure upon resources has been well demonstrated by M. M. Postan and J. Z. Titow in their work on entry fines and the size of peasant holdings in thirteenth-century England.[2] Entry fines rose and the size of holdings upon many manors decreased remarkably between the beginning and the end of the 1200s. Perhaps an aspect of rapid population growth noted by A. J. Coale and E. M. Hoover as affecting modern developing countries[3] has validity for thirteenth-century Europe, namely that such rapid growth tends to diminish the amount of capital available. As prices rose and as the amount of land per family fell, the surplus available for investment diminished. In the absence of any technological advance in farming and given the chronic shortage of manure in medieval Europe, it was perhaps impossible for the economy to undergo the kind of reorganization which economists call economic development. If the rural population of England was as large at the end of the thirteenth century as it was at the end of the seventeenth,

[1] A. J. Coale and E. M. Hoover, *Population Growth and Economic Development in Low-Income Countries*, p. 10.

[2] 'Heriots and prices on Winchester manors', *Econ. Hist. Review*, 2nd ser. XI (1959), 392–411; and J. Z. Titow, 'Some evidence of thirteenth-century population increase', *Econ. Hist. Review*, XIV (1961), 218–24.

[3] A. J. Coale and E. M. Hoover, op. cit. p. 22.

as M. M. Postan has asserted[1] – and there seems little reason to doubt his views – then, given the more primitive methods of farming at the earlier period, large numbers of people must have been living on the starvation line. The large-scale mortality that resulted from famine in years of bad harvest indicates that a large section of the population was highly susceptible to diseases of malnutrition. The poverty of many peasants was, moreover, intensified by the fact that the land-lords in general took too large a share of their profits (see pp. 174–5). As J. K. Galbraith has said,[2] poverty may be the consequence of class exploitation and the division of the gross national product in the thirteenth century was notably less equitable probably than in earlier medieval centuries and certainly than it was between *c.* 1375 and *c.* 1500. The period of economic boom was a period of increasing poverty and hardship for many, probably for the majority of the population.

Some attempts were made, of course, to reorganize the agrarian economy and to expand in areas where expansion was possible at a lower cost in resources. Land which was unsuitable for arable frequently fed sheep and some increase in sheep flocks may have occurred in England and possibly in other parts of Europe during the thirteenth-century boom.

Some capital was diverted into industry and particularly into the textile industry where the fulling mills required expenditure on the building of dams and mill races to supply a constant flow of water to the new machinery. Similarly capital must have been spent on dams and races to power water-driven saws and, in addition, water mills were used in paper making and tanning.[3] Water power was, moreover, employed in irrigation, for crushing olives to obtain oil, for grinding pigment, for turning lathes and to power grinding mills for cutlery. Water-driven hammer forges were used in iron metallurgy from the twelfth century and water-powered bellows appeared about the same period. In fact, such technological improvements as existed in industry depended almost entirely upon the application of hydraulic power, and the water wheel, either overshot or undershot, became the most important prime mover of medieval

[1] M. M. Postan and J. Z. Titow, op. cit.
[2] *Economic Development in Perspective*, p. 5.
[3] C. Singer *et al.* (eds.), *A History of Technology*, vol. II, pp. 609 ff.

industry and encouraged the improvement of gearing and other mechanical devices. This advance paralleled and must have played a part in the economic growth from the tenth century and there is some reason for thinking that the advance slowed down when capital was in less plentiful supply towards the close of the thirteenth century.[1]

We have postulated that there may have been an increase in the *per capita* GNP until such time as too rapid population growth reduced the living standards of a large proportion of the people in the thirteenth century. And yet growth need not necessarily be measured in increased real income *per capita*. Economic growth may enable a society, or certain members of it, to enjoy more leisure or improved services. The increased total product may provide what we might term non-economic aspects of growth, for it is fully in line with modern thinking to see growth as a special aspect of general social development. The increase in total product permitted a larger number of non-productive people to stay alive and, indeed, to flourish in this period. Again lack of statistics does not permit accurate quantification but the numbers of scholars and teachers in the newly founded and growing universities, the numbers of monks and nuns in the more numerous monastic houses, the numbers of those entering the new mendicant orders and the numbers of seculars serving the parishes were expanding steadily throughout the twelfth and thirteenth centuries.

The intellectual awakening known as the Twelfth-Century Renaissance, although some would deny it that appellation, was both made possible by the creation of greater wealth which resulted from the rise in population and also had an indirect effect upon the economy by training more lively, thrusting minds. The students and teachers formed a body of clerks who were granted additional privileges such as protection from unjust arrest and trial before their peers and the right to strike, discontinue lectures or even to secede in protest against grievances or when their established rights were attacked. They governed their institutions of learning in a more democratic and less hierarchical fashion than did the church and the state. By the early fourteenth century there had been established in Europe about twenty major institutions, *studia generalia,* all of which

[1] ibid. pp. 640 ff, 651.

had come into being in the two preceding centuries. Their upkeep had only been made possible by the expanding of the economy. The monks also were 'a costly institution'[1] and their maintenance required great resources, as did the building of the thousands of abbeys constructed in Europe in the years between *c*. 1000 and *c*. 1250. In the thirteenth century, considerable although not such vast resources as had been devoted to the monks were lavished upon the friars and hundreds of friaries were established throughout Europe. By the 1200s most of the parishes of medieval Europe had come into being and their numbers did not increase before the nineteenth century. All these institutions provided services to their founders and to society at large. The founders of monasteries expected vigorous busy communities which would sing the daily round of prayers that would ensure spiritual benefits for them and for their ancestors and successors, while the people in the neighbourhood looked to these houses to supply alms in time of need, medical advice when they were afflicted by ill health and for some a permanent refuge in old age. They also undertook the education of boys, not all of whom were destined to enter the religious life. The friars provided welfare and even hospital services of a sort. These mendicant orders, like the monks, furnished opportunities for scholars to pursue their studies although, as Roger Bacon's career demonstrates, they did not encourage original thought. The universities provided education for a growing number of doctors, lawyers and clerks, although very few of the parish clergy achieved a university education. The parishes probably gave a living to more non-productive men than at any other period; it has been estimated that there were, on average, five men in orders in every English parish in the thirteenth century.[2]

But it was not only clerics who were non-productive in an economic sense. The economic development of the twelfth and thirteenth centuries permitted an increase in the number of non-productive laymen. Knights were accompanied by squires and other retainers. The expanding economy meant that a larger proportion of the labour force was engaged in ancillary services, and as markets rose so

[1] R. W. Southern, *The Making of the Middle Ages*, p. 155.
[2] J. R. H. Moorman, *The English Church in the Thirteenth Century* (Cambridge U.P., 1946), p. 53.

did the figures of those engaged in moving, storing and distributing products and in control functions generally. Moreover, greater affluence and increased education were partly responsible for more efficient central government and, although perhaps most of the personnel were in holy orders, albeit minor ones, this demanded and in turn created a growing number of clerical and administrative jobs. The establishment of royal exchequers, chanceries and law courts in the twelfth and thirteenth centuries meant that there were many more 'civil servants' to be fed. The widespread use of mercenary soldiers added still further to this category of non-productive men. The arrival and increase of these categories are ample proof of increased output. Had this output been used more productively, that is, had less of the surplus been spent on conspicuous consumption, war and administration and had more of it been ploughed back into the land, commerce and industry, the 'thirteenth-century boom' might have developed into a real breakthrough. But in the absence of inventions – and it is by no means certain that a better use of capital would have secured any in the face of inadequate education – such a breakthrough was not to be.

The boom brought about a significant change in the social structure in some parts of Europe. In areas of England, where until about 1175 great landowners, particularly monastic houses and cathedral chapters, had leased their demesnes, a movement in reverse started and demesnes were again directly exploited. As corn prices rose towards the end of the twelfth century direct exploitation became more profitable and fewer agricultural works were commuted. This trend led to considerable discontent among villein-serfs, as the numerous thirteenth-century cases in the king's courts amply demonstrate. But in many parts of Europe such a movement was absent and those who had obtained their freedom were not brought back to servile status. In fact whereas pattern maintenance had been secured by the knights and other landowners of similar status until the late tenth or early eleventh centuries with the cooperation of the serfs, this pattern maintenance probably became more difficult between the eleventh and the thirteenth centuries. The cooperation of the serfs had been secured because lords had provided essential protection which was no longer necessary. Certainly the class structure of the later Middle Ages was very different from that of the early Middle Ages.[1]

It is clear that the growth of the eleventh and twelfth centuries did not follow the more usual pattern of more modern epochs in which, firstly, comes a decline in the death rate to be followed by a decline in the birth rate, for the decline in the birth rate did not materialize. The population pressure continued to mount in the thirteenth century and the English peasantry was pushed nearer to the edge of the Malthusian precipice.[2] No new crop, like the potato, which would have yielded a larger return of calories to the acre, was available and no new method of intensive farming was devised to support the rapidly increasing population in England. There are signs that the balance between livestock and crops was affected and also some indications of soil exhaustion, erosion and of the upsetting of the hydrological balance because of the ploughing up of unsuitable land lying on steep slopes. It has been said that the destruction and impairment of the fertility of the soil is not solely or even primarily determined by the physical and chemical characteristics of the soil but by the manner in which it is used;[3] in thirteenth-century England some land was probably over-tilled. Why the birth rate did not decline must remain largely a matter of conjecture but the patterns of the birth rate, especially in pre-industrial societies, tend to change slowly. To some degree, large families gave prestige in the Middle Ages and those in higher income groups increased their family size by earlier marriage. Socially valued goals were attained through kinship and family ties rather than through other social relationships; nepotism rather than the old school tie provided jobs in the medieval period.

Such growth as there was in the economy came as the result of a fair measure of freedom of competition. It was an economy, unlike that of the later fourteenth and fifteenth centuries, which was open to market forces; it was planned to some extent but not to the degree that occurred from the 1300s on. Navigation acts, hosting, exchange control, the staple, price control, the tightening up of regulations concerning the methods of production, belong in the main to the

---

[1] Rushton Coulborn (ed.), *Feudalism in History*, p. 16.
[2] R. J. Chorley and P. Haggett (eds.), *Models in Geography.* p. 204.
[3] ibid. p. 199.

last two centuries of the Middle Ages. The twelfth and thirteenth centuries were an era when the economy was buoyant and growing trade required a larger volume of currency to finance it. International trade was supported by a gold currency, of which the Florentine florin minted in 1252 was effectively the first gold coin in western Europe,[1] apart from the Iberian peninsula and southern Italy, since the eighth century. England (1257), though not permanently, and Venice (1284) followed suit. Genoa also issued the *genovino* in 1252.[2] Internal trade was growing to such an extent that the silver penny became an inconveniently small unit and so Venice, Verona, Florence and Milan minted the *grosso* in the first half of the thirteenth century while north of the Alps Louis IX issued the *gros tournois* in 1266. Aragon, Castile and the Low Countries copied the French example but in England where the penny had not deteriorated to the same extent as had the *denier tournois*, the groat was only worth four old pennies instead of twelve of the old *deniers* as in France and Italy. Edward I's attempt did not succeed and the English groat did not become permanent until 1351, but this was largely because of the way in which the penny had maintained its value.

The story of European currencies in the thirteenth century reflects the growing intensity of international trade. It has been said that the extent of an economy's monetization is undoubtedly the most important single index of the mobilization of its resources, and hence of the flexibility of their allocation from human and natural resources to finished consumption goods and services.[3] The increased monetization of thirteenth-century European economies certainly demonstrates the truth of this assertion. In this thriving atmosphere it was unnecessary to put up barriers to trade and it was not until trade stagnated that various interests sought at all costs to protect their own position by creating quasi-monopolies. Economic growth, limited though it was, and in so many ways different from its nineteenth-century counterpart, was nevertheless a fact and it had to face similar constraints to those confronting underdeveloped countries in our

---

[1] W. A. Shaw, *The History of Currency* (London, Clement Wilson, 2nd ed. 1896), pp. 4 ff.

[2] *The Cambridge Economic History of Europe*, III, p. 590.

[3] 'Systems', 'Analysis', and 'Social systems' by Talcott Parsons, in *International Encyclopedia of the Social Sciences*.

own day. Considerable advances were made but lack of capital, and above all lack of any technological breakthrough, prevented medieval societies from achieving the take-off to sustained growth; but economic changes did something to effect some changes in political and ritual roles in society.

CHAPTER 9

Medieval Transport

Although the causes of trade revival and the organization of international commerce with its refined techniques such as partnerships, insurance and the credit mechanisms developed by a precocious banking system are of prime importance, the geographical difficulties and physical problems that medieval transporters had to face should not be overlooked. Roads in the Middle Ages were perhaps not so inadequate as some scholars at one time imagined. It is not true that all goods were carried on packhorses because road surfaces were insufficient to take wheeled vehicles. At some periods and in some places we have plenty of evidence of the use of carts. They were of course used to carry agricultural produce from one manor to another, and tenants had carting services laid upon them as an obligation, but evidence of carts in commercial use is abundant. The technical improvements, especially the introduction of the horse collar and the modification of the harness, enabled far greater loads to be carried. In fourteenth-century England, regular arrangements were made to cart wool to a river and thence to send it to a seaport for export[1] and the Brokage Books of Southampton illustrate for the fifteenth century the daily movement of goods into and out of that port in carts.[2] These carts were going not only to places such as Winchester and Salisbury but as far afield as Coventry, over 160 kilometres distant, and, while exceptionally bad weather might stop traffic then as now, it does not appear that the carting of goods was undertaken only in the summer months.

The great fairs of Champagne received many of the goods sold

---

[1] J. F. Willard, 'Inland transportation in England during the fourteenth century', and 'The use of carts in the fourteenth century'.

[2] O. Coleman, 'Trade and prosperity in the fifteenth century: some aspects of the trade of Southampton', *Econ. Hist. Review*, 2nd ser. XVI (1963), 9–22.

there by land routes. It is true that most of the towns were on rivers, Bar-sur-Aube, Chalons and Lagny on the Marne and Troyes on the Seine, but Provins was not on a river and merchants brought some goods by land even to those towns with river connections. The merchants from Flanders used land routes and the Italians crossed the Alps mainly by the Great St Bernard Pass, continuing thence by Dijon or Langres although they also used the Mont Cenis Pass and came through Lyons. A road followed the Rhone-Saône rivers and another crossed the Massif Central via Le Puy and Clermont Ferrand which was used by merchants from the Provençal ports. The Alpine passes had heavy traffic throughout the Middle Ages, although it is reasonable to suppose that here pack animals rather than carts were employed. The two St Bernard passes, a road by Mont Genèvre, the Septimer and Splügen passes, the Brenner, the Pontebba and Birnbaumer passes were all regularly used and there is evidence of medieval roadmaking and bridge building and of the construction of hospices. Roman roads were not simply allowed to run down in the Middle Ages, for there were many incentives to travel in the medieval period, both religious as well as commercial. In the western Alps the most frequented passes were the Mont Genèvre (1825 metres), the Great St Bernard (2433 m) and the Mont Cenis (2068 m). The question of elevation was less important than that of convenience and it is interesting to note that the relatively low Argentière (1963 m) and Tenda (1843 m) passes were unimportant because they were situated too far south to serve international traffic between Italy and north-western Europe; moreover, the Argentière route had no advantage over the sea route to the Rhone delta or over the littoral route through the Genoese Riviera and Provence. The other three routes, by contrast, stood in a fairly direct line between Piedmont and Champagne, Flanders and the Rhineland where trade and industry were concentrated. The Great St Bernard carried the heaviest weight of traffic, for those travelling between Basle and Lombardy, whether pilgrims, traders or soldiers, used it. The Simplon route was not much used before 1250 but, because it connected Milan with Dijon and although the route involved another pass, the Jougne through the Jura, it became popular in the later Middle Ages.

As Milan rose in commercial pre-eminence, the passes of the

central Alps, the Septimer and the St Gotthard, became more important. The latter could not be much traversed before the removal of
certain physical obstacles on its northern approach. A bridge had to
be constructed at the Schöllenen gorge and a valley road along the
Urserenthal into the Reuss valley; this was achieved in the early
decades of the thirteenth century.[1] It then became popular, since it
was on the direct route from Milan to Basle and avoided the detour
via Chur which was necessary for those travellers who took the
Septimer Pass. The Brenner assumed greater significance from the
later thirteenth century when eastern Germany was being developed; its low elevation (1548 m), the ample food supplies and the
wide choice of routes it commanded, all combined to make it a
much-used pass in the later Middle Ages. These Alpine passes played
an important part in the communications system of medieval Europe
and for that reason road transport cannot be ignored, although it
must be stressed that merchants preferred, wherever and whenever
possible, to send goods by water. Efforts were made to build hospices, to construct bridges and to improve roads so that men and
their beasts of burden, chiefly mules and asses, could get through.
Evidence has been brought forward to show that in the case of Mont
Cenis transport of goods did not cease entirely in winter for efforts
were made to clear the snow.

Traffic on the roads shared with water-borne traffic the increasing
curse of tolls levied upon the passage of goods. In the years of
anarchy between *c.* 850 and 950 to 1000, local lords had demanded
tolls from passers-by, even from those not engaged in commerce.
England remained remarkably free from tolls and where such payments were made they were usually small and used to defray the cost
of constructing or maintaining a road or bridge; France and
Germany on the other hand were plagued with service tolls. There,
no major road was entirely free from duty. The much-frequented
road route from Flanders to France in the thirteenth century had
numerous tolls upon it, many of which, on the stretch in northern
France, could not be avoided. The rivers were similarly burdened;
travellers on the Loire, Somme, Oise, Rhone and Garonne were all
heavily taxed and on the river Seine the toll charges on the grain
shipped over a distance of 320 kilometres equalled more than half its

[1] J. E. Tyler, *The Alpine Passes, 962–1250*, pp. 88–90.

selling price. In Germany, some roads like the great Hanseatic routes to the east were relatively free but others were 'expensive' to travel upon while the German rivers were notorious for their charges. The height of idiotic restriction was reached along the Rhine, which had about nineteen tolls at the end of the twelfth century, over thirty-five at the end of the thirteenth, nearly fifty a hundred years later and over sixty at the end of the fifteenth century. Although tolls were not sufficient to stop the great international traffic, they did fall heavily upon the local traffic and may to some extent have reinforced the particularism and self-sufficiency of local economies. But the ill effects of tolls may well have been over-estimated, for it must be remembered that a variety of routes often presented a choice to the trader. Apart from the choice that was sometimes offered by an alternative sea route, a possibility taken by the Italians in bringing wool from England rather than overland, a choice between different land routes was sometimes available and ways round the toll points were not infrequently taken. If one ruler became too oppressive in his demands, new routes would be nego-tiated: the Venetians for example developed the Bavarian route to the Alps through Nuremburg as an alternative to the French route.

Transport in the Middle Ages was a costly service and often pro-vided the main element of cost. Transport was wasteful of time, equipment and manpower. A thirteenth-century tariff of Péronne in northern France shows that local traffic was served by 'colliers' who drew barrows and other small vehicles by their neck (*collum*) and it is also clear that packhorses were used. Much traffic seems to have been carried in the *bronnette*, a two-wheeled cart; thirteen cloths or more required a *car* or *carrette*, a four-wheeled cart capable of carry-ing about three times as much as the *bronnette*. Stone, bricks, wood and charcoal were all carried in the carts. From the thirteenth century in England, common carriers undertook carting business and in London 'brokers of carts' existed who acted as middlemen between carters and owners of cargo. In the mid fourteenth century, the waggoners who transported wool from Flanders to Basle came mostly from the Saar and Alsace while the route from Brabant to the south was serviced mostly by carters from Lorraine. All this carting activity indicates fairly good roads. Often the roads followed the line of the old Roman ones but they were frequently re-surfaced.

A highway of cobbles or broken stones on a loose foundation was more suited to horse and cart traffic than the old blocks of the Roman roads, which had been designed primarily for marching troops. At the end of the Middle Ages paved roads were constructed particularly in the Low Countries and in Germany. The state took some responsibility for the roads and the *strata publica* in France and the king's highway in England had to be maintained; people were indicted for obstructing public roads, encroaching upon them or neglecting their duty in maintaining them. Of course there was much dereliction of public duty and work was usually confined to the upkeep of drains and ditches, for if a road was not actually flooded or barred it was regarded in English law, as passable. From England, instances of elaborate road works such as the causeway near Boston (Lincolnshire) made up of thirty stone bridges and a road laid across Sedgemoor near Glastonbury can be found. From Europe, hundreds of records of charitable gifts for the purpose of maintaining communications can be traced.

But when all has been said about roads and carting, the medieval merchant preferred to move his goods by water, either by barge along rivers or in larger vessels along the coasts of Europe or even, from time to time, beyond coastal waters. Then, as now, carriage by water was cheaper than carriage by land and traffic in weighty commodities was only possible where cheap water transport was available. In England it was cheaper to import timber from the Baltic to the south and east coasts than to bring it to those areas from the Midlands and the north-west of the country, and stone from Caen in Normandy was widely used in building the castles and cathedrals of southern England.

Sea transport was cheap despite the small size of the medieval boat. In northern Europe, a large round clinker-built ship with a single mast on which a square sail was erected, known as the cog, was most widely used. In order to be able to defend itself in some measure, raised platforms called castles were constructed at either end of the ship; hence the term forecastle – fo'c'sle. The stern post rudder is first found in northern Europe in the thirteenth century although it may have been used on Byzantine vessels earlier and probably came from China. The northern vessels eventually adopted the lateen sail for beating into the wind. Interesting borrowings occurred between northern and southern Europe, for the Italian merchants who had two-masted vessels with lateen sails adopted the cog with a single mast while retaining the lateen sails on their galleys until the sixteenth century. The round merchant vessels, clinker-built in the north but carvel-built in the south, were improved in the first half of the fifteenth century. The first stage was the addition of a second mast, a small foremast typical of the early carracks and as a result of the pressure exerted by the foresail on the rudder it was found necessary to provide some balance farther aft. This led to the addition of a third mast on the poop known as the mizzen mast. The first dated illustration of a three-masted carrack is of the year 1466. At the close of the Middle Ages some of these vessels were 60 metres in length with a beam of 15 metres and a tonnage of about 1400 tons.

River transport was undertaken in barges which in medieval Europe appear to have been of a standardized type. The river barge was built without a keel and usually six heavy planks formed the floor of the barge. Weirs on rivers proved a serious handicap to shipping and frequently goods had to be transhipped from one barge to another on the far side of an obstruction. Later, lifts were devised which took the form of inclined planes over which ships were hauled, and towards the end of the Middle Ages locks for lifting were developed in the Low Countries. This was a chamber with gates at either end which enabled the vessel to be transferred from one level to another. Canals and lift locks were constructed in Flanders and Holland from the late twelfth century on. Work was done at Damme in 1180 and we know of sluices on the river Reie serving the Bruges traffic in 1236 which were rebuilt in stone with a sea gate, a freshwater gate and a stone floor in 1394-6. The gates recessed in stone work slid up and down and were counterbalanced by massive lead weights. Spaarndam near Haarlem, in existence as early as 1253, was destroyed in 1277 and reconstructed between 1285 and 1315. The fifteenth century saw many refinements: paddles were used, as today, to control the flow of water in and out of the lock chambers through sluices which were cut in the gates or in the sides of the lock. Filippo Visconti of Milan used this system from 1440 onwards and it was well known and frequently described in the second half of the fifteenth century. Rivers formed a vital and integral part of the system of medieval trading routes. In eastern Europe the Elbe and the Oder were much used while in the west the rivers Seine, Somme, Oise, Scheldt, Meuse, Rhine, Main, Weser, Rhone and Garonne all carried long-distance traffic and were arteries of 'le grand commerce'. English rivers such as the Thames, Lea, Stour, Wye, Severn, Avon, Trent, Humber, Witham and the Yorkshire Ouse were all busy with barge traffic.

Sea-going trade increased between the twelfth and mid fourteenth centuries and, if the volume of trade declined in the century and a half before 1500, ships were at that time sailing much farther and venturing more frequently out of sight of land. The early Middle Ages had known the loadstone but in the fourteenth century a more sophisticated mariner's compass was employed and mariners sailed from north-western Spain to England and from England to Iceland out of sight of land and could make reasonably accurate calculations of their position. The great Venetian galleys came once a year, in a vast commercial armada to Southampton and Bruges and the Genoese carracks also made this journey. The increased size of ships deployed, especially by the Dutch, enabled them to lower freight rates and thus to enhance their sea power in the fifteenth century.

The costs of transport do not appear to have been excessively high. In England cartage added about 1·5 per cent to the cost of wool and 15 per cent to the cost of grain. Sea transport was generally cheaper. The cost of shipping a tun of Gascon wine at the end of the thirteenth century was about 8s. a tun or rather less than 10 per cent of its f.o.b. price at Bordeaux; wool freight from London to Calais at the same period was 4s. per sack or under 2 per cent of its f.o.b. price in London. A weigh (400 lb: 180 kg) of coal cost 2s. to transport from Newcastle to the south. But the amount added to the cost by transport obviously varied from trade to trade and from time to time and was also dependent upon whether the route was well served with plentiful and therefore cheap transport facilities.

CHAPTER 10

The Developed Areas of Medieval Europe: Byzantium and Córdoba

From the fifth century until the twelfth or even the thirteenth century, Europe from the North Cape to Constantinople and from Gibraltar to the Urals was divided into underdeveloped and developed areas, and two states that had extra-European links – the Byzantine Empire and the Islamic Caliphate of Córdoba – enjoyed standards that were superior to those of the rest of Europe. The former for many centuries had territory in Asia and the latter was controlled from Damascus, although from 756 onwards the emirate was independent of Damascus and Baghdad and became a fully independent caliphate in the tenth century; it nevertheless remained a vehicle for the transmission of Syrian influence. While it would be rash to assert that the entire population of these two countries shared in the general prosperity, the standard of living in the towns and even in parts of the countryside was far in excess of that enjoyed before the thirteenth century in Europe generally. Córdoba and Constantinople were cities that amazed the traveller by their size and wealth: the former had a population of about 200,000 and the latter of at least half a million. Consequently the greater wealth of these two states enabled them to maintain intellectual, cultural and artistic standards far more sophisticated than those in the rest of Europe where for many centuries after *c.* 400 such standards had been in decline.

The Sutton Hoo ship burial[1] which took place near Woodbridge in Suffolk in all probability in the 620s demonstrates, though it does not explain, the influence of Byzantium on European commerce. Among the finds in the grave were several silver objects only one of

[1] R. L. S. Bruce-Mitford, *The Sutton Hoo Ship-Burial* (London, British Museum, 1968), p. 57.

which, a great silver dish 68·5 centimetres in diameter, can be dated with certainty: it is marked with four stamps of the reign of Anastasius I, 491 to 518. The view has been advanced that the inferior quality of the workmanship argues against the silver having been a gift and in favour of its having found its way to England in the course of trade. Fairs were established in the territories of Frankish kings – a famous one at St Denis existed from 634 – and these were the most likely places at which Saxon traders acquired Byzantine articles made almost 3200 kilometres away from East Anglia. Degenerate and inferior in workmanship and artistic quality these silver vessels may be when compared with those of the Mildenhall treasure, produced probably some 150 or 200 years earlier, but they were certainly superior to productions of the barbarian kingdoms which had replaced the Roman Empire in northern and western Europe, even though these areas made some fine cloisonné enamel jewellery. But it was not only silver ware that the Byzantine Empire exported: carved ivories, silk and other precious textiles and mosaics found their way into many parts of Europe.

As is the custom of developed countries in the twentieth century, Byzantium exported technical know-how, not in manufacturing processes but in building design and decoration. It also exercised a profound influence upon European art between the fifth and the twelfth centuries; the technique of covering a square area with a dome which was really discovered by the Byzantine architects spread throughout Europe. Anyone who doubts this influence has only to look at the churches of Ravenna, St Mark in Venice, St Sophia at Kiev, the basilica at Aachen or at Kalat Seman in Syria without considering the less direct influence upon the Saxon and Romanesque churches of Germany or the domed churches of south-western France. The acquisition of this expertise in building and decoration did not always come directly from the capital and it may well never be settled whether the monks who were present at Hildesheim in Germany in such large numbers were Greeks or Armenians, for, as has been pointed out, it was the latter who were accustomed to building in stone and many medieval German churches bear a striking likeness to those of Armenia. However, the chapel of St Bartholomew at Paderborn is said to have been built by Greek monks. Another part of the Empire from and through which

Byzantine technical and artistic influence came, was Italy. The whole peninsula had been brought back within the Empire in the middle years of the sixth century and, even after the settlement of the Lombards, considerable parts of the north remained under Byzantine control until the mid eighth century, and parts of Sicily owed allegiance to Constantinople until about 900. It is not surprising, therefore, that after Charles the Great's descent into Italy the style of building within the Carolingian Empire was influenced by Byzantine architecture: the basilica at Aachen was modelled on San Vitale at Ravenna. Venice was an even more important centre of Byzantine art, for from the early tenth century onwards it had more direct links with Constantinople than any other area and, until the end of the twelfth century, Venetian art was essentially Byzantine in character. The church of St Mark is architecturally a rough copy of that of the Holy Apostles in Constantinople. Such was the prestige of the eastern empire that the overthrow of its authority, either by Moslems, Normans or Slavs, did not necessarily involve a curtailment of its influence: the cathedrals at Cefalù and Monreale in Sicily, although begun more than two centuries after the island had ceased to be ruled from Constantinople, had mosaic decorations that were entirely Greek in style and workmanship. The art and architecture of Christian Russia was firmly based on Byzantium for the church of St Sophia at Kiev was built and decorated by Greeks, and the introduction into Russia of a Byzantine icon, later known as 'Our Lady of Vladimir', marks the beginning of Russian icon painting. Byzantine influence on Italian painting until the time of Cimabue falls rather into the history of art than into social and economic history. In the Moslem world, however, the influence of Byzantium appears to have been limited for the Abbasids looked to Persia and India, and from the ninth century their main benefit from the Greeks was their use of Byzantine plans for their fortifications.

But, like developed countries of our own day, the Byzantine Empire not only exported technical know-how; its exports exceeded its imports as a general rule. Certainly its exports were nearly all *objets de luxe* but they were in great demand. Silk and other precious textiles such as silk brocades with gold or silver threads in them and fine woollen, cotton and linen cloths were in great demand at the courts of Germanic and Slavonic rulers and in the homes of great nobles and wealthy merchants. At first this had been partly a re-export trade, for the silk was imported from China and woven in the Empire or imported as silk cloth from Persia, which had obtained the raw silk from China. In one sense Justinian failed in his attempt to undermine the powerful grasp the Persians had on the trade because Byzantine shipping was inadequate and because the Axumites from Ethiopia, whom he had made his trade allies, were unable to purchase the silk in India and Ceylon as easily as were the Nestorian Christian merchants of Persia many of whom resided permanently in Taprobane (Ceylon). But two monks smuggled some silkworms into imperial territory.[1] Groves of mulberry trees were planted and factories for the weaving of silk stuffs sprang up so rapidly that by the reign of Justinian's successor Justin II (565–78) the industry was active and already supplying foreign customers. The Persians who had controlled the overland route from west China as well as the sea route from Ceylon to the Persian Gulf had lost their stranglehold over the Byzantine market and also a considerable revenue. On the other hand the economic gain to the Empire was enormous for high prices were paid for silk stuffs and purple cloth even while the Byzantine government sought to prohibit the export of goods of the highest quality.

Silk stuffs, purple cloth and gold embroidery were the attributes of imperial majesty, which the emperor was from time to time prepared to share with foreign rulers who needed them as symbols of political authority, and with the church which needed them for ecclesiastical ceremonies. The policy of the emperors was to maintain strict control over production, trade and export and they secured this by the continuation of a system prevalent in the undivided Empire. The old *gynaecia* became the imperial or public gilds which at first manufactured and dyed only for the emperor, his court and his friends and which made no second quality products for sale to the public, whose needs, within the limits of the sumptuary laws, were met by the inferior products of the private gilds. Later, in the reign of Justinian (527–65), all manufacture was concentrated in the hands of the imperial gilds for a time, but by the reign of Heraclius, and probably in the years between 565 and 610, some raw

[1] Probably in 553–4: see R. S. Lopez, 'The silk industry in the Byzantine Empire', p. 12.

silk was made available to private dealers. From that time it was the private gilds, the merchants of raw silk, the silk spinners, the clothiers and dyers, the merchants of domestic silk garments and merchants of imported silk fabrics who supplied the public both within and beyond the Empire, although occasionally small pieces of the imperial purple cloth were sold to the public. This was done by Leo VI between 888 and 899. The chief aim of successive Byzantine rulers was to prevent cloths of certain size and specification from being exported; these were the *kekolymena* or forbidden materials which could only be given with the emperor's permission, but apart from this prohibition the export of silk and other cloths was allowed and even encouraged. As we have seen, the Venetians were specially privileged and so were the Syrians for whom the emperor allowed a mosque to be built in Constantinople. The subjects of Islamic states were specially privileged, for the emperors regarded the caliphs almost as their equals and, also, such states could manufacture the first quality cloths which almost reached the standards of the *kekolymena* although even in the Caliphate a demand existed for Byzantine textiles.

About the other articles exported from the Byzantine Empire information is not so full. Carved ivory diptychs and triptychs, chairs and book covers are found throughout Europe: they were articles of great value and splendour which were used either to impress the owner's power upon the onlooker or to induce in him a sense of awe and reverence when they were displayed in church on the altar. Some of these carvings may have been sent abroad as gifts by the emperors and some may have entered into the normal export trade, but it is usually impossible to ascertain how these carvings reached countries outside the Byzantine Empire. A similar difficulty presents itself with jewels and enamelled jewellery and with manu-scripts and miniature paintings. From Liudprand of Cremona's account of the difficulties he encountered when he tried to smuggle out some purple cloth in 968, we know that exports were tightly controlled. Byzantium felt that it must guard these coveted treasures and to release or withhold them became an instrument of state policy which might be used to further its foreign policy and to wring con-cessions from other nations. On occasion after a diplomatic or mili-tary defeat the government was compelled to supply a specific quantity of cloth or other valuables to foreign rulers as a tribute which was, nevertheless, politely described as a gift. The Empire did not export any foodstuffs, with the exception of some wine, which was sold to the peoples of the steppes north of the Black Sea as a consequence of treaties made with Russia in the tenth century.

The insatiable demands for these Byzantine exports gave, in general, a favourable balance of trade to the Empire. Certainly the state imported commodities from abroad – the principal import was human beings. As more research is done, historians are increasingly stressing the importance of the slave trade not only in the early Middle Ages but right down to the twelfth century. Despite the pronouncements of many leading ecclesiastics and the practical steps that were taken by them to dissuade citizens from buying and keeping slaves, the practice of slavery continued. It is true that the enslavement of Christians by their fellow-Christians, being strongly condemned, tended to die out but there were hosts of captives in war who were sold into slavery and, especially between the ninth and eleventh centuries when slaves were cheap, their lot was probably worse than that of the most penurious among the free population. Victorious rulers such as Romanus I (920–44), Nicephorus II (963–9) and John I (969–76) flooded the market with cheap human merchandise and it was only the defeat of the Byzantine arms in the twelfth century with its consequent decline in the number of prisoners that gradually closed the slave markets and brought about the beginning of the end of slavery. At this same time a diminution in the wealth of individual Byzantine citizens occurred which made it impossible for them to afford slaves. Vast estates which had begun to take a more prominent part in the rural economy from the ninth century were cultivated by slave labour, for human porterage was needed in a period when draught animals were dear and the lack of a proper harness made their use inefficient. This demand for human merchandise could not be met within the Empire itself despite the fact that it was possible for freemen to sell themselves into slavery[1] and so large numbers of Slavs, from whom the word slave is derived, and of peoples from the steppes north of the Black Sea and even some Germanic peoples, were imported and sold as slaves. Customs

[1] G. Ostrogorsky, *History of the Byzantine State*, p. 393.

duties were levied upon imported slaves[1] which probably added, on average, about 10 per cent to their price, which varied from 20 to 50 *nomismata*. Some of the male slaves were castrated, since eunuchs played an important role at the imperial court and in the households of the nobility and even rose to high rank in the army, but it was only lawful to buy and sell eunuch slaves who were not Roman citizens and who had been emasculated outside Byzantine territory. As eunuchs fetched a higher price than other male slaves in Constantinople, castration took place outside the Empire and it appears frequently to have been done at Verdun. Apart from slaves, furs, dried fish, leather, Baltic amber and honey were the chief imports which came, in the main, from Russia. Cherson in the Crimea was the great entrepôt for furs, slaves and dried fish although some Russian ships from the river Dnieper berthed in Constantinople and furs and metals came to Thessolonica and were distributed from there by Greek vessels.

The Byzantine economy was strong and rigidly controlled. Its strength can, at the same time, be gauged by and attributed to the soundness of the imperial currency. The severest restrictions were placed upon the export of gold. It had been general policy to impose an embargo upon the export of any commodities, for example, wine, oil, salt, corn, fish sauce, whetstones, implements or arms, which might strengthen an enemy and this prohibition was made more specific by Leo VI (886–912) who laid it down that gold was not to be exported even to purchase slaves. Merchants were ordered to pay for imported slaves by exporting commodities. Governmental control over the economy was strictly enforced, for customs supervision was competently imposed with posts covering the approaches to Constantinople at Abydos and Hieron in operation at least from the second half of the fifth century. The favourable trade balance, which resulted in part from the silk monopoly, and the success of imperial supervision maintained the value of the Byzantine *solidus*, also known as the *nomisma* and *hyperperon*, century after century. What the U.S. dollar and the Swiss franc are in the twentieth century, the Byzantine *nomisma* was from the fourth to the eleventh centuries. The gold content of 4·48 grammes to the *solidus*

[1] H. Antoniadis-Bibicou, *Recherches sur les douanes à Bysance*, Cahiers des Annales No. 20 (Paris, 1963), p. 42.

E

which Constantine had fixed remained virtually unchanged for eight hundred years and thus the coin was the dollar of the period, the currency in which international trade was conducted.

Trade treaties were made with foreign states in which Byzantium always sought and usually obtained advantageous terms, and the imperial government used its armed might to defend its territory and its interests. Like the super powers of the twentieth century, Byzantium had armed forces that were far superior to those of their enemies both in equipment and in devices such as Greek fire, a form of explosive invented by Callinicus which would burn even on water. Their armed forces, though they lacked the uniting bonds of nationalism or religion were on the whole remarkably well led and successful and provided adequate defence of imperial territory until the twelfth century.

The buoyancy of the economy, secured by a sound currency and by fairly easy methods of raising capital at reasonable rates of interest, enabled the emperors in Constantinople to provide for their subjects a higher standard of living and 'social services' far in advance of anything found elsewhere in Europe at that time. The provision of 'social services' was shared between the church and the state. It is true that at all times administrative and military costs were high and these together with the upkeep of roads and bridges could only be met by heavy taxation. The *annona* or land tax was the essential basis of governmental income and the imperial tax gatherers were noted for their rapacity: even at times, such as the tenth century, when the Empire was extremely prosperous and order was good, those who could not pay their taxes were treated with extreme harshness so that many of them commended themselves to lords. The poorest peasants existed on barley bread and pulse eked out with fish, olives and honey, while the diet of the richer ones certainly included pork, mutton, poultry and wine; but beneath even the poorest were the slaves. It is clear that the 'social services' benefited the inhabitants of the towns, and above all those of the capital, more than the dwellers in the countryside. In a measure the old imperial policy of *panem et circenses* was continued. The gladiatorial shows were discontinued in the fifth century and in their place foot and horse races were substituted in the Hippodrome. These races enthralled the metropolitan crowds who were also amused by parades of elephants, tigers, giraffes and bears. The loss of Egypt between 638 and 641 put an end to the wholesale distribution of free bread but the emperors were still able to keep the price of wheat stabilized at the equivalent of 4s. a bushel and of barley at about 2s. 8d. A daily ration of peas or beans cost ½d. as did green vegetables; wine was 6d. and oil 1s. a quart and fish was cheap: it was therefore possible to support life on 6 to 8 halfpence a day and to secure a varied diet for 12 to 15 halfpence. The average pay of the humblest worker was 15 to 16 halfpence a day but a beggar on a good pitch could make twice that amount. Lodging and clothing prices were relatively higher than the cost of food and many were compelled to sleep out of doors, but the consensus of opinion among scholars is that the living standards at least of those in the capital and perhaps of those in other Byzantine cities exceeded those in other parts of Europe.

Moreover, much Christian charity was given to the poor, and organized charity maintained hospitals, orphanages and hostels. The chief guardian of charitable funds was the church but the state also helped in providing free distributions of bread, vegetables and fish at the time of the games celebrating the foundation of the city. An excellent water supply was available to the citizens which was secured by the provision of underground reservoirs, the remains of which may still be seen in the vast cistern known as the Yere Batan Sarnici. The economic prosperity of the state enabled all these bene-fits to be bestowed upon the underprivileged in the capital. This high standard remained as long as Byzantium continued to be a super power and it endured as such until the twelfth century. Its influence was felt as far away as Iceland and the Orkneys where young men were keen to serve in the Varangian guard and upon their return home to tell tales of the wealth and splendour of the 'great city'.

The other super power was the Islamic Empire, represented first by the Arabs and then, from the later eleventh century, by the Turks. Only a small part of the Moslem world established itself in Europe, in the Iberian peninsula; for a time its links with Damascus and Baghdad remained close. The two super powers were deadly rivals, threatening each other, and at intervals they were in fierce conflict, but often the 'cold war' thawed and trade between the two blocs became lively. It might be carried on officially or as contraband, or indirectly through Sicily and Venice on the one hand or through

Kievan Russia on the other hand, but trade links there were between
the two great powers. The Emperor Theophilus (829–42) urged that
Arab-Byzantine peace would promote trade and, in 969, a treaty
made between the two contained commercial clauses. Because the
Caliphate of Córboda had, like the Byzantine Empire, a buoyant
economy well managed by rulers who were generally powerful, it
could, like the Empire, secure standards of living for its citizens far
in excess of those obtaining elsewhere in Europe.

In Moslem Spain the town and its economic centre, the market
place, were more highly developed than in Europe generally. The
market place had adjoining *suks* which sold specialized goods and
had a regular system of police and porters together with a place
where currency might be exchanged. Frequently a mint and a warehouse (*funduk* in Arabic) for foreign merchandise existed near by,
with a mosque and its attached school or university in the vicinity.
Again, a sound currency, derived from and based upon the Byzantine gold coinage, was maintained. The gold dinar was an imitation
of the Byzantine *solidus* while the silver dirham was based upon the
Persian *drachma* and both coins maintained their value well. The
Moslem invaders of Spain, mostly Berbers but commanded by
Arabs, led by Tariq ibn Ziyad had landed in the Iberian peninsula in
711 and within three years almost the whole area as far as the Pyrénées had fallen to Islam. The peninsula was rich in minerals which
the Romans had intensively exploited and contained much fertile
land as well as barren plateau (*meseta*); it had been economically
prosperous under the Empire and its new rulers sought to maintain
that prosperity. By the second quarter of the ninth century, 'Abd ur-
Rahman II had an income of 1 million dinars a year, and a century
later 'Abd ur-Rahman III had 20 million dinars annually.

The emirs and, from 929, the caliphs of Córdoba aimed to promote both urban and rural prosperity. The state was part of a vast
Arabic Empire which stretched to the east as far as the river Indus
and had its centre in Syria and Iraq, and as a result of this the southern
part of the peninsula, known as al-Andalus, was open to Syrian
influence. Books, jewels, spices, fine textiles and furs were imported
by merchants most of whom were Jewish, for the Jews like the
Hispano-provincials had readily accepted Moslem rule. In fact the
Jews had welcomed the Moslems who did not persecute them as

vigorously as the Christians had done and who allowed them to work both as merchants and as craftsmen. Most Romano-provincials who had never liked their Visigothic conquerors accepted much of the Islamic 'way of life'; retaining Christianity but often speaking Arabic, these Christians soon become known as Mozarabs and formed a large section of the population which was often more loyal to the emirs and caliphs than were their Moslem subjects. Much intermarriage took place between the natives and the Arabs and Arabized Berbers and a high percentage of the population was bilingual, using Arabic and the Romance language indifferently not only in the streets but also in their own homes. Hispano-Arabic acquired many Romance words but Castilian obtained a greater number of words from Arabic. Within a short space of time a people of mixed racial origin created a Moslem Spanish state which was singularly united and which served to transmit Islamic culture to the peninsula and even to influence parts of Europe north of the Pyrénées.

It influenced Europe not only by the introduction of eastern flora and fauna and eastern industrial products but more importantly by the transmission of scientific and philosophical thought. The Caliphate preserved and handed on much of the learning of the ancient world, some of which had been embodied in the writings of its own scientists and philosophers and in the artistic works of its own decorators and architects. Gerbert of Auvergne, later Pope Sylvester II (999–1003) went to Córdoba to study geometry, mechanics and astronomy, and to him has been attributed the introduction of Arabic numerals into northern and western Europe and also of a clock with weights. Doubts have been cast upon the importance of the work of the Toledo school of translators as a centre from which Jews and Moslems influenced Christian thought[1] but it can scarcely be denied that the higher cultural level of the Jews and the superior technical skill of the Mudejars (Moslems in the parts of Spain that had been reconquered by Christian rulers) ultimately had some influence upon Christian society. Many works of Greek philosophers, above all of Aristotle, became available to the west through Latin translations of the Arabic versions of their works. Greek medicine as well as Moslem medical lore practised by Jewish physicians benefited

[1] J. Vicens Vives, *Approaches to the History of Spain*, p. 66.

northern and western Europe to some degree, as did inventions such as the compass and the windmill.

As in the Byzantine Empire, all this artistic and cultural activity could only be maintained by the establishment and by the continuance century after century of a prosperous economy. The zenith came in the early years of the tenth century when new Persian and Nabatean agricultural techniques, together with the development and improvement of the irrigation system, arrived in the Guadalquivir river valley, the Genil river depression and along the Mediterranean coast from Malaga to Tortosa. Some windmills, but more importantly, water mills, were built for grinding corn in the countryside along most of the length of the Guadalquivir. Cattle and goats increased in numbers and, as a result of improved irrigation, the crop yield of fruits, many of which such as figs, peaches, apricots, dates and pomegranates had been newly introduced, and of olives and Arab-introduced sugar cane and rice, rose. Irrigation was common during the Visigothic period but the Moslem rulers improved it. Certain areas began to specialize in certain products. As well as walnuts, almonds, saffron, flax and cotton, grapes were cultivated, for the followers of the Prophet in Spain appear to have drunk wine. The Persian geographer Ibn Khurdadbeh who visited Spain about the middle of the ninth century wrote with warm praise of its fruitfulness and others, such as Ya'kūbī and Makdisī ibn Hawkal, a century or so later, describe in glowing terms its social and economic life. The land was cultivated by a growing number of serfs and slaves and among the Arabs the primitive equalitarianism of the desert had certainly passed away by the ninth century. Slaves were imported in large numbers, as they were into the other developed country of Europe, and we are told that in the mid tenth century the slave market at Córdoba was second in importance only to that of Baghdad. Nevertheless, much land was farmed by sharecroppers who were better off under the Arabs than they had been under the Visigoths.

The more intensive mining of minerals also revived the economy: metals such as gold, silver, iron, mercury, iron sulphate, tin, lead, galena and salt and precious stones were found. The multiplicity of its towns distinguished the Caliphate from other parts of the Maghrib, as did the activity of its markets and the network of its roads. Córdoba in the tenth century had at least 200,000 residents, 600 mosques and 900 public baths; the streets were paved and houses were built around patios that contained fountains for which piped water was a necessity. Under al Hakim (961–76) Córdoba extended its control over north Africa when Morocco and parts of Algeria came under his domination. This led to the growing importance of Málaga (a town of some 15,000 inhabitants), which was the natural port for north Africa, although Almería (population 27,000), the place of transport to and from the Moslem and Christian east, remained the principal port. Ships from Syria, Egypt and Byzantium used it at least from the ninth century and at a later date Pisa and Genoa sent vessels there. It is said to have had 970 hostels where merchants could stay. This prosperity is all the more remarkable in view of the Córdoban government's policy, or rather lack of policy. At no time did the emirs or caliphs actively promote foreign trade and seek to attract foreign merchants to their ports; exchanges with the east most probably continued an ancient tradition of intra-Mediterranean trade. The natural commercial outlets for Spanish goods were overland to the north of the Pyrénées. The exports were principally textiles either for clothing or furnishing in wool, cotton or linen, but above all silk; brocades, gold thread, ceramics, glassware and mosaics (cubes of polychrome glass) were much in demand abroad. In the jeweller's art, in work in gold, silver and precious stones, Spain was the rival of Byzantium.

The towns specialized to some degree. Almería was noted for silk cloths, copper and iron utensils; Córdoba for jewellery, stones and carved ivories, marble, glass, crystal and other tableware, but above all for beaten and stamped leather, from which the English word cordwainer is derived. This leather, usually either goat skin or horse-hide, found its way all over Europe and shoes, scabbards, pouches and other articles were made from it. It was sometimes exported as plain or tanned leather but the famous *guadameciles* were processed in the city which was also famous for its carpets made in a royal factory, as was a brocade called *tiraz*. The Moslems of west Asia obtained the knowledge of paper manufacture from China and introduced it to Spain. Játiva specialized in its manufacture in the tenth century and Toledo in the eleventh. But Toledo was far better known for its steel which was made into weapons of the finest quality. All the principal towns had many people actively engaged in making goods or providing services that did not necessarily come into the export trade but helped to raise the standard of living; all had druggists, perfumers, booksellers, glaziers, carpenters, bakers, restaurateurs and fried fish merchants.

From these two developed countries the rest of Europe gained much advantage, although the benefits were sometimes slow in coming; paper, for example, was not known beyond the Pyrénées until the thirteenth century. It is true that in all probability they were not so highly developed at this period as was China, nor, if we are to judge by their art and supremely by their ceramics, as civilized, but down to the end of the twelfth century they were so far ahead of Europe generally that they stand in a unique position. The return which northern and Slavonic Europe made to these two giants was to provide them with raw materials and human slave power. Similarities exist between the developed and underdeveloped countries of our own era but it would be anachronistic to represent these areas as colonies either of the Byzantine Empire or of the Caliphate of Córdoba.

CHAPTER II

Industry in the Middle Ages: Building

In the Middle Ages the countries of Europe had economies that were primarily agricultural: almost everywhere in the continent, industry played a subordinate role to agriculture but the population had to be clothed and housed as well as fed. The European climate, except perhaps in the extreme south and south-east, made it essential that both the clothing and the housing should be solid and sufficient; neither could be as flimsy as was possible in some parts of the globe. Industry arose to supply the clothing and housing needs of medieval communities and to meet the demands of endemic warfare and spiritual devotion.

Some areas of Europe became, towards the close of the Middle Ages, quite highly industrialized. By this it is implied that so great a proportion of the population was in industrial employment that the labour force or the area of land remaining to agriculture was insufficient to feed the industrial population, which was compelled therefore to live by exporting its manufactured products and importing foodstuffs. Such districts were the cloth-producing areas of the Low Countries, particularly the towns of Ypres, Ghent, Bruges, Douai, Arras and Cambrai; the cloth producing towns of Italy, above all Florence; the metallurgical manufacturing areas, especially the towns of Namur, Dinant and Liège and the country around them. To these areas might be added individual towns which were so specialized in some or other industrial pursuit that they had to import foodstuffs not only from the immediately adjacent countryside but from a wider region. Such for example were towns like Lucca, which concentrated upon the production of silk textiles, or St Etienne, which specialized in fine steel. But even areas that were not heavily industrialized had a textile industry of some type and all areas had men engaged in the building industry, for everywhere houses, churches and castles were a necessity.

The documentation of the building industry has many gaps, particularly in the countries of continental Europe, but in England accounts of expenditure upon building operations exist in reasonably full series, as do contracts for the employment of carpenters and other building workers.[1] The King's works, as the castles and palaces that were built for the kings of England were called, are very fully documented,[2] as is the money spent upon London Bridge.[3] We have particulars from week to week or from month to month over several centuries as to what was spent on the Bridge, and these provide an invaluable record of changes in wages and prices over a long period. From the study of accounts and contracts, it is clear that, however architectural styles might change, the fundamental economic problems connected with building and the organization necessary to deal with those problems remained much the same in the principal countries of western Europe.

Apart from the basic need of housing the population, there were two great stimuli to building in the Middle Ages: firstly the needs of defence both of feudal lords, for each lord of a fief needed a place of defence, and of cities. To say nothing of sovereign rulers, thousands of feudal lords were scattered throughout Europe who demanded castles of differing size and complexity. Cities also, ranging in size from small ones like Aigues Mortes, the walls of which were only 1·6 kilometres round, to Nuremberg, which had 6·4 kilometres of double walling in the fourteenth century, needed defences. The second great stimulus was the medieval church. Early parish churches, with the exception of those in Scandinavia, were built from the eleventh century onwards of stone and from the previous century vast monastic buildings were being erected in stone. Already in the eleventh century, but more frequently in the subsequent one, bishops were renewing and enlarging their cathedral churches. The support of church building by the laity provided laymen both with an opportunity to gain spiritual merit and also with an occasion to show local pride, for the merchant class of one

[1] L. F. Salzman, *Building in England*, pp. 413 ff.
[2] R. A. Brown, H. M. Colvin and A. J. Taylor, *The History of the King's Works*.
[3] G. Home, *Old London Bridge* (London, Bodley Head, 1931).

town often vied with its opposite numbers in a neighbouring town in the size and lavishness of its church. Moreover, changes in style provided a continuing source of expenditure as churches were modified or, on occasion, completely torn down and rebuilt in the latest fashion.

The rising population from the eleventh to the mid fourteenth century and the demand for greater comfort among the wealthier classes were other stimuli to building. The building industry spent little of its time and resources on peasant housing, for all that was essential there was a carpenter and a thatcher to assist the peasant in putting up his own house, but in the towns domestic building was a more intricate and a slower business. Charters granted to some of the new towns in south-western France, the *bastides*, require settlers to have one third of the houses finished in the first year and two thirds of the total completed in the second year. At least in the larger towns a body of workmen would be occupied to keep pace with the building requirements of a growing population and to take care of the repair work. But these workers were carpenters and plasterers rather than masons, for in most towns throughout the Middle Ages houses were of lathe and plaster and thatched. Even in Caen, the centre of a stone quarrying district, timber houses were built as late as the early sixteenth century; in Hamburg stone houses were rare before 1350 and it was only after 1460 that slates were beginning to be substituted for thatch in that city. In London, however, we have evidence of stone building in the thirteenth century and even in the preceding one and the Jew's house in the Strait at Lincoln, dated *c*. 1170–80, demonstrates that the stone building of town houses was not unknown in England at a fairly early date although only men of great wealth could apparently afford it.[1]

In the cities public buildings called for the work and skill of stone-masons. The town hall, the bottom storey of which was often a market, and to which a belfry was frequently attached, was usually built of stone. In the countryside manor houses, most of which were built for comfort rather than security, were constructed quite early and in the fifteenth century their numbers mushroomed. Nearly all manor houses were of stone until the later Middle Ages when some

[1] Margaret Wood, *The English Mediaeval House,* p. 4.

building was done in brick in certain parts of Europe, notably England and the Low Countries.

What were the technical problems of medieval building? So far as is known there was no manual giving information on the strength of materials or what the stresses and strains were, but a body of expert knowledge existed which could be consulted by those commissioning building work. In case of doubt it was not unusual to call in master masons to check and approve the plan which a master mason had submitted. The term master mason was the name applied to the man who in effect was the architect and we know that the master mason was familiar with the practice of driving in piles to make foundations. He was consulted about the suitability of sites and the safety of structures, although in many instances his expertise was inadequate and severe cracking might occur or even the total collapse of a central tower.

The names of many English master masons are known, especially of those who worked for the Crown.[1] Walter of Hereford, called the master mason (*magister cementarius*) or the master of the works (*magister operacionum*), built the abbey of Vale Royal (Cheshire) between 1278 and 1280 and was in charge at Caernarvon in 1288–9 where, in 1315, he was succeeded by Henry de Elerton. Walter was a skilled man, for his pay was 2s. a day payable seven days in the week although he certainly would not have worked every day in the week: at this time a skilled ordinary mason working under him had a weekly wage of 2s. 6d. As to training, little is known although it seems likely that master masons were drawn from the skilled designers and carvers of tracery rather than from the ordinary masons who cut and laid blocks of stone. The master mason drew up the plans, supervised the construction of the building and, in all probability, hired masons, decided upon their rates of pay according to their skill and dismissed them if necessary. Henry Yevele, a master mason of the second half of the fourteenth century, was held in high esteem as an architect. He was closely associated with the work at Westminster Abbey as early as 1356, in 1397–8 he was master mason there and in 1395 he was 'consultant architect' for the rebuilding of Westminster Hall. In this enterprise the master carpenter was also in a sense an architect and the rebuilding of

[1] *Engilsh Mediaeval Architects*, compiled by John Harvey.

Westminster Hall offers a good example of the master mason and the master carpenter working together, for Hugh Herland the king's carpenter was responsible for the roof while Yevele designed the foundations and the walls. The Crown also employed a clerk of the works who, although not necessarily architecturally trained, had to know something about materials and supplies of them to a site. The most famous of these clerks of the works was Geoffrey Chaucer who in 1389 held that office to supervise works at Westminster Palace, the Tower, the castle of Berkhampstead, the manors of Kennington, Eltham, Clarendon, Sheen and Byfleet and other places. Masons and quarrymen had knowledge of the 'cleaving grain' of stone and of the way in which stone ought to be bedded in a building. Further, building workers were familiar with the block and pulley for lifting stone and with the windlass; they knew also how to construct an inclined tramway in the scaffolding along which heavy stones were wheeled to the top of the work. To master masons was left the task of surveying the site and measuring with rod and line and of making geometrical drawings, of which those of Villard de Honnecourt are the most famous.

The art of stone building was never completely lost in the period after the fall of the Roman Empire in the west, for in the remote Wearmouth Benedict Biscop was able *c.* 675 with the help of craftsmen from Gaul to build a church in stone, but in general between 400 and 800 building in stone was rare. Timber was widely employed for the centring for arches, doors, screens and partitions and, where vaulting was not used, for beams and other parts of the roof. The discovery of the vault resting upon a series of piers with pointed arches permitted the building of the roof without timber which greatly reduced the danger of fire. This was the real revolution in building which brought in the Gothic style. The new style of pointed arches and pointed vaults was first used in England in the rebuilding of Canterbury Cathedral after the disastrous fire of 1174, but it was introduced by a Frenchman, William de Sens, who had been working in the Île-de-France from the mid twelfth century onwards. These arches were built with wedge-shaped pieces of stone called *voussoirs*. The stones that formed the ribs of the vaulting were probably known in England by their French name, *ogives*, and the stones filling in the vaulting between the ribs as pendants, while the intersection of the ribs in a simple quadripartite vault was designated the key in the Middle Ages, although it is now called the boss. This new discovery enabled a larger space to be spanned and the centre of the vault could be carried to a greater height. It also permitted far more window space in the walls so that more light might flood into the church. With buttresses against the outside walls to carry the thrust of the roof it became possible to insert really large windows and to increase the height so much that the choir at Beauvais, built in the second half of the thirteenth century, reached 45 metres. Born in the Île-de-France, this new style appeared at Vézelay in Burgundy between 1160 and 1180 and before 1220 it had reached Toulouse. It did not reach Germany widely until the second half of the thirteenth century but it spread far afield, eventually to Burgos and Toledo, to Cologne and Bamberg, north to Upsala and south to Cyprus.

The Gothic style continued in fashion from the late twelfth to the middle of the sixteenth century in some parts of Europe although the rediscovery of the classical tradition in architecture, as well as in art and literature, brought about its abandonment in Italy from the 1440s on. Before the invention of the pointed arch and vault the style of church building had been much heavier. The roof had generally been of wood, although it was possible to use stone for smaller churches: such a stone roof was known as a barrel or tunnel vault, and groin vaults over square spaces were attempted. Large circular pillars decorated with a variety of mouldings supported the roof and gave an enormous strength and solidity to the building, a solidity which to William de Sens and his successors appeared dull and heavy. The windows compared with those in the Gothic style were small and rounded at the head: they could not be large because the walls had to take the downward and outward thrust of the roof. This style was known on the continent of Europe as Romanesque,[1] for it developed from the architecture of the late Roman Empire (*roman* from *romain* in French), but in England it is called Norman because it was introduced by William I's supporters after 1066. The pre-Conquest style of building in stone, examples of which can be seen at Earl's Barton (Northamptonshire), Bradford-on-Avon (Wiltshire), Escomb and Jarrow (County Durham) and Barton-on-

[1] Gustav Künstler (ed.), *Romanesque Art in Europe*.

Humber (Lincolnshire), was of the same Romanesque style as on the continent of Europe although it had certain national characteristics such as the bulbous pillar in the centre of the window and strips of stone work and arcading on the outside of the building. This Romanesque was in vogue in Europe from the ninth century until the mid twelfth in France and even in the thirteenth century in parts of Europe, notably in Germany and southern Italy.

Gothic lasted for four centuries in some regions but it developed and changed during that period and nowhere more markedly than in England. In the early transitional period from Norman to Gothic the windows tended to be long and narrow and are known as lancets, for architects did not dare to make large windows since all development was empirical in an age without manuals on materials and stresses. The fourteenth century saw really large broad windows that might take up the whole of the east or the west wall of a church, and at the same time ornamentation in carving became more elaborate. In England, historians of architecture have termed it the Decorated style. It was also an era of much painting in churches: the morbid introspection that was intensified by the Black Death led to the painting of the 'Danse Macabre' round the walls of many late medieval churches. Late Gothic was further developed in England towards the close of the fifteenth century into a style unique to this island, the Perpendicular. Characterized by ogee curves, intricate tracery and fan vaulting with large pendants, this style reached its full flowering in the chapels of Eton College and King's College Cambridge, in St George's Windsor and the Henry VII chapel in Westminster Abbey. Outstandingly, England was a country of regions and the truth of this assertion is nowhere more clearly illustrated than in the differing styles of its churches. The position or shape of towers, the presence or absence of steeples, the type of carving and many other details distinguish churches of one region from those of another.

In the building industry the problems of the supply of materials and of labour were very great. Medieval builders tried to use local stone if it was available, but if money was plentiful, stone such as the oolitic limestone of Caen might be brought in for building, especially where convenient sea or river transport existed. Stone for ornamental work was transported long distances, for example the alabaster from Chellaston (Derbyshire), which was found all over Europe in the fifteenth century. Stone was acquired either by buying or leasing a quarry or by buying it partly or fully dressed from the quarry owner.

The unskilled labour, such as hewers, mortar mixers and barrow-men, was always obtained locally but the skilled labour had to be imported. A body of skilled masons existed which was prepared to go anywhere throughout the country and even to other countries. They had to be accommodated on the site and hence lodges were erected in which they lived until the work was completed. These masons were divided into two categories: those who built walls and other works of solid masonry, who were known as setters, wallers or layers, and those called hewers or free masons because they worked free stone. The latter shaped or carved separate blocks of stone, making arch mouldings, window tracery, capitals and similar parts of the fabric, and they enjoyed a status superior to the setters or wallers. The sudden demand for labour first in one part of the country then in another (at Windsor in 1344, for example, about 500 men were employed for many weeks and in one week the figure reached 720) made it difficult for a craft gild to be established in any one town. Certainly in London between *c.* 1356 and 1376 a builders' gild existed, but in most towns there were insufficient masons to form a gild of their own and they united with the pavers, tilers, plasterers and brickmakers. But the masons were organized through the lodges on the site. These buildings housed the drawing office of the master mason, the 'trasour' or 'tracying house' where the plans were kept, and the masons retired thither for their meals and for their midday nap.

The York Fabric Roll for the years 1352, 1370 and 1409 has preserved for us the rules for the conduct and the control of work-men at the York lodge and from this document it appears that from Easter to Michaelmas the masons worked from sunrise till a bell rang for a twenty-minute breakfast break; then work was resumed until an hour's break was taken for dinner, followed between May and August by half an hour's sleep. Then work continued until the first bell for vespers when the masons broke off for a drink and, returning on the third bell, they worked on until sunset. In winter the masons worked from dawn to noon when dinner was taken, and then with only a drink at vespers they continued until dusk, and from 1 November to 1 February their wages fell from 5*d.* to 4*d.* a day because of the shortness of the working day. To offset these long hours, however, they performed no work on Holy days, probably about thirty-five a year in number, and on the vigils work ceased at noon and no work was done on Sundays. These lodges, of which the York lodge is but one example, became the centres where skilled craftsmen met and here they worked together for the benefit of their fellow masons in a way that was regarded as conspiratorial by their contemporaries. If we are to believe Wyclif, the masons of his day knew as much about restrictive practices as some twentieth-century employees and would not have been nonplussed in a modern 'who-does-what dispute', for he says that a free mason would do nothing but cut stone even though his master might ask him to lay a wall for one day, which work he could have done without any inconvenience to himself and to his master's profit.[1] The early free masons were a close-knit group which elected masters wherever building operations were in progress. These lodges, which certainly existed in England, Scotland and Germany in the fourteenth and fifteenth centuries and probably also in France, received strange masons, gave them work and, if none were available, fed them and passed them on to places where work might be found. Doubtless there were secret signs whereby mason recognized fellow mason.

The building industry was capitalist in its organization. The masons did not own the material with which they worked, nor in many cases even the tools of their trade, for the manager of the building operations frequently supplied tools and, at least, he provided the means to sharpen them, smiths being employed for that purpose, and a *portehache* was provided to carry tools between the smithy and the work. Some of the free masons doubtless owned some of their tools, but in general they had only their labour and their skill for sale. Owning neither their own materials nor the means of production they remained wage earners. On the other hand, they did not work in isolation like weavers, tailors and saddlers and their conditions of labour approached more nearly towards factory conditions than did those of any other group of workers in the medieval period. They were certainly in a better

[1] Quoted by D. Knoop and G. P. Jones, *The Mediaeval Mason*, p. 132.

position to bargain over wages and conditions of labour than were most groups, for they were frequently able, when dissatisfied, to pack up and go to another site. It is true that sovereigns compelled masons to work on royal buildings, and this royal impressment of labour continued throughout the Middle Ages, but nevertheless the power of the withdrawal of labour from ordinary employers placed the free mason in a fairly strong position. In the towns, builders were subject to a number of regulations drawn up by the municipality, by-laws were enacted in London as early as 1189 and other restrictions have come down to us from several towns. In many ways the building industry was untypical of medieval industry in general; it was capitalist in its structure from the start and depended upon a great mass of wage earning craftsmen.

CHAPTER 12

Industry in the Middle Ages: Textiles

In countries that are becoming industrialized, the textile industry is usually the first to develop. Warm clothing was and remains an essential for the overwhelming majority of the inhabitants of the European continent. How many people throughout the Middle Ages were dressed in homespuns – literally in cloths spun by themselves at home – is not known and never will be known but it may be confidently asserted that more were clothed in homespuns in the ninth than in the fifteenth century. The textile industry of medieval Europe was principally the woollen cloth and the linen cloth industries, for, although cotton and silk cloths were made, the output was small and such textiles were worn by a relatively tiny section of the population. Towards the end of the Middle Ages worsted cloth was made from the long-haired wool, which was prepared by combing rather than by carding, and a mixture of linen and wool fibres produced a fine light-weight cloth known as linsey-woolsey. Cloths made of mixtures of cotton and linen and cotton and wool were also produced though they were not perhaps widely available.

The making of woollen cloth varied little from the process employed in classical times with one important exception. The invention of the fulling mill in the late twelfth century, an invention that replaced fulling by the tread of men's feet by the beating of hammers upon the cloth, was a great step forward. Water power drove the hammers by means of a revolving drum attached to the spindle of a water wheel. Whole series of hammers could be set to work with one man to see that the cloth was kept properly moving in the troughs. This invention, which has been investigated by Professor E. M. Carus-Wilson, has been regarded by her as instigating the industrial revolution of the twelfth and thirteenth centuries.[1] The

[1] E. M. Carus-Wilson, *Medieval Merchant Venturers*, pp. 183–201.

process of cloth making started with shearing the sheep and washing the wool to get out some of the natural grease. Then the short-haired wool was carded – that is, worked between two implements like butter pats covered with leather into which nails or sharp hooked spikes were fixed and this action straightened the wool. Long-haired wool was not carded but combed; a process which consisted of lashing it on to a post and combing it down with a comb that contained several rows of teeth of varying length. There followed the process of spinning the wool into yarn, work done traditionally by women – the spinsters. Use of the distaff and spindle enabled women to work as they supervised other tasks but the spinning wheel was also employed in the later Middle Ages. The latter was probably invented in the thirteenth century: it was a major invention of the textile industry, although little is known in detail about its origin. Dyeing might be undertaken at this stage for the process could be carried out either in the wool, the yarn or the woven cloth.

From the spinner the weaver took the yarn to be woven into cloth. It was prepared for the weavers by the warpers who sized and wound the warp thread which, because it has to be stronger, had been differently spun from the woof thread. Warping was not an easy task since the full-sized broadcloth contained between 2000 and 3000 warp threads each 27 metres or more in length. The spoolers wound the woof thread on to the bobbin which was inserted into the shuttle. The broadcloths, some 183 centimetres wide, were woven by two workers sitting side by side at a double horizontal loom; narrow cloths were woven by one weaver on a single loom.

When the cloth was woven it was sent to the fullers. Despite the invention of the fulling mills, this process throughout the thirteenth century was still largely performed by men treading on the cloth which had been covered by fuller's earth and placed in shallow troughs filled with water. At this stage any unnecessary oil or grease was taken out of the cloth but the main purpose of fulling was to shrink the cloth so that the lines of warp and weft were no longer visible: it was thereby closed together or felted. After fulling, the cloth was hung out to dry on a tenter, an upright wooden frame to which the lists of the cloth were fastened by many tenterhooks. By this operation workers stretched the cloth to the correct length and breadth and the weight of a broadcloth when wet was such that many workers, especially if they were women, had to be employed. If it had not already been dyed, at this stage dyeing in the piece would be undertaken.

The final processes were raising and shearing. Teasels set in rows on a wooden frame shaped like the ace of spades raised the nap which was then shorn. This was done when the cloth was dry and the operation was performed with huge shears at least three to four feet long which were flat at the ends. They had a cutting edge of 46 centimetres and if badly ground the shears could damage a cloth. Shearing required great skill and after its completion the cloth was brushed, pressed and folded ready for the market.

Frequent complaints were made about the standards of cloth. English legislation in the fifteenth century provided severe penalties for those who stretched the cloth too much on the tenters. Over-stretching was a perpetual temptation to those who wanted short cloths to come up to the required measurements, and the results of over-tentering were to strain the cloth to such an extent that it might be thinned, almost to a hole, in some places. These deficiencies were cloaked by putting glue on the thin patches and covering them with chopped pieces of wool known as flocks, which operation hid the damage until the garment was worn in the rain when it buckled up. Mending, to make good a fault in one or two threads, and burling, to remove knots, were legitimate but the methods used to conceal over-tentering were not.

The medieval cloth industry, certainly in the closing centuries of the Middle Ages, was organized on a capitalist basis: artisans in the different branches of the industry were dependent upon an entre-preneur. The importation of the raw material (wool) into many areas of European cloth manufacture, the combination of the many processes of manufacture and the marketing of the cloth all called alike for entrepreneurial expertise. Certainly by the second half of the thirteenth century these entrepreneurs had joined together in merchant gilds in many cities, and weavers, dyers and fullers, men who soiled their hands at their work and were consequently called 'blue-nails', could not become members of these gilds. Leicester, Beverley, Winchester, Oxford and Marlborough all had merchant gilds which had rules stating that if weavers, fullers or other

craftsmen wished to join the gild they might be admitted on condition that they ceased to engage in a craft. The members of the
merchant gild were responsible for the purchase of the raw
material, for putting it out to artisans who specialized in the various
processes and finally they were instrumental in marketing the cloth.
Because of their control of raw materials and of the sale of the
finished article, the entrepreneurs controlled the great industry in
some detail. Control of the industry was rather by individual
entrepreneurs than by the gild merchants as a body corporate, and
intervention by the state began early. In England the Assize of Cloth
of 1197 fixed the statutory dimensions of cloth and clause 35 of
Magna Carta laid down that it was to be two ells in width between
the lists. Such statutory regulations were even fuller in Flanders than
in England: there, prohibitions included the mixing of different
kinds of wool in the same yarn or piece of cloth, the use of teasels
on dry cloth and the use of certain specified dyestuffs. State legislation simplified the task of the entrepreneurs in their supervision of
the work done on the artisans' own premises. It helped a town to
maintain the reputation of its cloth by ensuring uniformity of size
and quality. Inspectors, appointed by the municipal authorities and
usually having several merchants among their number, enforced
these regulations. Premises upon which work was done were open
to inspection, as were private homes if spinning was performed in
them. The inspectors' duty was to prevent fraud and trickery and
also to prevent discord between entrepreneurs and master craftsmen
or between the masters and their servants.

One of their most important functions was to take part in wage
negotiations. Evidence from Douai in the 1220s and from St Omer
in the first half of the fourteenth century shows that wages rose and
fell in accordance with the cost of living, but it is reasonable to
believe that this principle was followed generally. Wages were
frequently fixed as a result of a conflict between employer and
employee which often ended in a strike. The city authorities intervened to settle strikes and the employers usually were well placed
because of their influence in city government. The humbler craftsmen such as carders, combers and spinners who frequently worked
on the entrepreneurs' premises were in a less favourable bargaining
position for they were not organized in their own fraternities as were

weavers, dyers, fullers and shearmen, neither did they have separate inspectors for their branches of the industry. Piece-rates were paid for work in most branches of the industry, notably in weaving, fulling, tentering, shearing, and for dyeing when it was done on the dyer's premises. Weavers were paid by the yard according to the width of the cloth, fullers by the cloth reckoned according to the number of days fulling required by different types of material. The rates paid for dyeing depended upon the dyestuffs used and the dyer was compelled to show samples of standard colours giving the statutory prices for each dye. Not only were the rates of pay to be given by the entre-preneurs to master craftsmen fixed by the city authorities but they also settled the rates to be given by the master craftsman to his journeymen. Here payment was sometimes at a daily rate and some-times at piece-rates. Hours of work were also fixed; no one might work more or less than the specified hours, which were the hours of daylight with a break of one and a half hours in the middle of the day. A bell which served the purpose of a modern factory siren was rung four times a day, sometimes from a belfry specially built for the purpose as was the one over the Cloth Hall at Bruges. Thousands of people in Douai, Ypres, Bruges and Brussels went out of their homes to the workshops at dawn and filled the streets at midday and returned to their places of employment until dusk. The working day varied from between about eight hours in winter to about thirteen and a half or fourteen hours in summer, and wage rates varied accordingly. No work was allowed on Sundays or on the vigil of Sunday (i.e. Saturday afternoon) so that normally weekly hours of work were about sixty to seventy in summer and forty to forty-four in winter. Holidays were frequent, since all Sundays and all Holy Days, probably amounting to some thirty to thirty-five annually, were days of rest and, since work stopped at midday on the vigil of the feast, the total yearly holiday leave was longer than is common for industrial workers at the present day.

One of the three great centres of the woollen textile industry was Flanders where from the eleventh century clear signs of a surplus population are discernible. Some inhabitants of the region joined the Normans in their conquest of Sicily and England; others went on Crusade and others rushed from the countryside into the towns. Virtually every town in the county of Flanders was a textile town importing foodstuffs in exchange for cloth. We know that tolls were levied at Arras in 1024 and at St Omer in 1043 on wool, dyestuffs and teasels, and that by the end of the eleventh century Flemish cloth was praised as having a finish superior to any other. Dyers and fullers made agreements as to the use of streams, and fraternities of workers in various sections of the textile industry were probably formed in the twelfth century. Why the industry moved into the towns and did not stay in the countryside has been the cause of some controversy among scholars, but the view expressed by H. van Werveke, that it was because the towns had merchants not very skilled in accounting who could run the business side of the growing export industry only if they were in direct contact with the crafts-men, is the theory that currently holds the field.[1] Flanders in the twelfth century vastly increased its output and its range of cloth. Not only were the native plants woad, weld and madder used by the dyers to produce blues, yellows and reds, and by combination greens, but kermes commonly called grain imported from Asia Minor and from Spain was employed to dye cloth a brilliant scarlet. Brasil wood and vermilion, red crystalline mercuric sulphide, found by the Red Sea, gumlac, the resin exuded from the bark of a tree in southern Asia, and saffron from the stamens of the autumn crocus were also used. Even more important was alum, one of the principal mordants in the fixing of dyes, the chief source of which was at Phocaea in Asia Minor where it was exploited and controlled by the Genoese.

From the late twelfth to the late thirteenth centuries the Flemish industry was at the height of its prosperity. At first Ypres was the most famous town and its cloths appeared in the Mediterranean market in the early twelfth century; by the early thirteenth those of Ghent and Bruges were coming to rival those of Ypres. This cloth-producing area included other Flemish towns such as Poperinghe, Dixmude and Courtrai and in adjacent regions Arras, St Omer, Douai, Lille, Tournai, Amiens, St Quentin, Beauvais, Cambrai and Valenciennes were all important producers. These towns and many more stretching across modern Belgium and northern France, although in the territories of different feudal lords, had common

[1] H. van Werveke, 'Industrial growth in the Middle Ages: the cloth industry in Flanders', *Econ. Hist. Review*, 2nd ser. VI (1954), 240.

interests and common problems to face in the pursuance of their business interests, and by the end of the twelfth century they had come together in an association or 'hanse' to which the name of 'The Seventeen Towns' was given. This body regulated the conduct of their merchants at the Champagne fairs. Within the area considerable specialization developed; Picardy, for example, concentrated upon the growing of woad, so supplying the dyers of both Flanders and England from the ports at the mouth of the river Somme. In 1237 the woad merchants secured privileges to sell dyestuffs in London, Norwich and Bristol, and the importance of Amiens was based upon the woad trade. South-western France also produced vast amounts of the dye and in the later Middle Ages the area around Toulouse, Albi and Montauban (being under English influence) became the principal source of supply for the English textile industry. A lichen known as orchil imported from Norway yielded a purplish red dye.

In addition to dyestuffs, mordants had to be employed to fix the dyes: the two chief ones were potash and alum. The former was used with woad for the finest blue cloth and, as wood became insufficient both in England and Flanders, pot ashes were increasingly imported from northern Germany and the lands round the Baltic. Fuller's earth, a type of clay, and teasels for raising the nap were other essential raw materials, both of which were found near the chief sites of the industry in the Low Countries and in England.

Not until the close of the thirteenth century did the Italian woollen textile industry assume international importance, although as early as 1222 Genoa played a significant part in the cloth-finishing industry. In Florence merchants who dealt in imported cloth dwelt in a place of ill fame called the Calimala and when they joined together their association was known as the Calimala gild (*Arte di Calimala*). By the end of the thirteenth century the members of the *Arte* were engaged in finishing cloth as much as in dealing in imported northern cloth. Dyers and finishers were closely controlled in their work by the *Arte* which fixed their rate of pay and prohibited combination on the part of the craftsmen. Also several Italian towns were making cloth from the initial stages to the finished article: the *Arte della Lana* in Florence was certainly doing so in the early thirteenth century. But at that time Italian cloths were cheap articles compared with those of the north, as the Venetian tariff on imported cloths of 1265 clearly demonstrates. Italian wool was poor in quality and it was not until English wool was imported that fine cloth could be made, and made at a profit that covered the high cost of transport of the raw material. By the beginning of the fourteenth century the Italians were the principal dealers in English wool.

Italian textile production received its impetus from the difficulties of the Flemings, against whom the English frequently placed embargoes. This interruption in the supply of raw material together with the interference of the kings of France in the Champagne fairs made things difficult for the Flemish textile industry. More serious were the severe labour troubles of the closing years of the thirteenth century which culminated in a general revolt of the workers against the capitalist entrepreneurs who had dominated the cloth industry in Flanders and who also dominated the politics of the towns. At the battle of Courtrai (1302) the cause of democracy triumphed, but at Cassel (1328) artisans and peasants were defeated. The troubles of these years caused many skilled cloth makers to leave Flanders, either of their own accord or banished by the ruling class, and some of them went to Italy where they helped the growing industry. Italian towns raised tariff barriers against cloth imported from other Italian towns. Venice especially did so and also prevented Venetian subjects from going to work in the woollen industry of Treviso or Padua. Thus a keen rivalry emerged between Italian towns in the development of their woollen textile industries at the end of the thirteenth century.

The first half of the fourteenth century saw a phenomenal rise in Italian cloth production. In Florence the *Arte della Lana* outstripped the merchant *Arte de Calimala*, for, although in 1338 Florence still imported some 10,000 cloths a year, it was making about 80,000 in the city itself. Other Italian cities, all of which had made coarse cloth, were by the early fourteenth century producing fine cloth suitable for export. Milan, Brescia, Verona, Padua, Parma, Como, Monza, Bergamo, Vicenza, Treviso, Mantua and Cremona were all in the trade, some to a greater extent than others. The importance of the Tuscan towns of Pisa, Prato and Lucca must not be forgotten, although it has been overshadowed by the Florentine industry which in the 1330s was employing 30,000 persons.

The organization of the industry was, as in England and Flanders, capitalistic. The *lanaiuolo* was, like the English draper and the Flemish *drapier*, an entrepreneur who belonged to the *Arte della Lana*, which exercised the same control over cloth making as did the gilds of the north. But the *Arte* in Italian cities differed from the merchant gild of northern European cities in one respect: its members took no part in the export trade nor did they concern themselves with foreign trade in any way. Cloth for the foreign market was disposed of to export firms; neither did woollen merchants import wool themselves but they purchased it from large importing houses or from middlemen. The highly developed banking system played a part here. Large-scale organization in the woollen industry tended to increase as the *grande industrie* prospered: the number of manufacturing firms in Florence contracted from 300 to 200 in the thirty years after 1308. Some branches of the industry, for example the wool washers and the dealers in yarn, who had been independent, became mere employees of the wool merchants. The growth of large firms implied the growth of an urban proletariat, for small craftsmen were no longer able to acquire raw material or to dispose of the finished product, and they were thus compelled to work for members of the *Arte*.

The combers and carders, having only their labour for sale, worked in the entrepreneur's shop and were forbidden to assemble together or even to combine in a religious gild without the permission of the consuls of the *Arte*. At times of slump massive unemployment threatened them but after the attacks of the Black Death their bargaining power was increased. The gild intervened to abolish free contracts between employer and employee and it established fixed rates of wages which were mostly by the hour or by the day. In order to secure an adequate labour force in times of boom, entrepreneurs during times of short working advanced money to be repaid by workers later in labour. This system was not favoured in the early fourteenth century but it was approved later when rules of the *Arte* were enacted which forbade the repayment in money and insisted that it should be in labour. Spinners also were entirely dependent and became tied to a single entrepreneur whose wool alone they might spin, but they continued to work in their homes in the town or in the countryside. The entrepreneurs could arrange matters to suit themselves and to suppress craftsmen who made difficulties. Weavers also became increasingly dependent, some not even owning the tools of their trade, for in bad times many pledged their looms for money on which interest of 50 per cent per annum was not infrequently paid. Even the dyers and fullers were dominated by the wool merchants who owned dyeing and tentering equipment and let it out to the dyers and fullers of cloth. It is true that the dyers were admitted to the *Arte* as lesser members but the *membra majora*, the merchants, made policy and kept control. The *Arte* invested in equipment for all branches of the industry and in pursuance of its policy of controlling the workers it had its own inspectors and a court. Those found guilty of contravening the regulations were punished by deprivation of wages, flogging, loss of a hand or by death. The rising of the *Ciompi* in 1381 demonstrates how hard pressed the lower workers had been, for, led by a carder Michele di Lando, they rose in revolt only to be crushed when they were deserted by the workers' gilds of the *Tintori* and the *Farsettai*. Italy and above all Florence was the second outstanding area of woollen textile production in the Middle Ages and its rise was partly due to the troubles of the Flemish industry, although those troubles were a symptom of trade decline in the Low Countries rather than a cause of it.

The third great area in which the textile industry flourished in the Middle Ages was England. Only slowly did England shake off its 'colonial status' as a supplier of raw materials and became a 'developed' industrialized country which provided the clothing needs of vast areas of Europe and even of parts of Asia and Africa. English production received something of a setback as the Flemings rose to pre-eminence between the late twelfth and the beginning of the fourteenth centuries, and the overwhelming predominance of English cloth in European markets after *c.* 1350 tends to make us forget that it played a not insignificant part at an earlier period. The cloaks that had entered into Anglo-European trade in the eighth century, as is evidenced by Charlemagne's letter to king Offa, were probably part of a trade in woollen cloth of which traces are to be found in the preceding century and which continued until the Norman Conquest. The closer connection with the continent that resulted from the Conquest most probably brought about an expansion in woollen cloth exports, and Stamford and Lincoln cloths were entering into that trade in the twelfth century. England was as well endowed as Flanders to compete in the woollen industry for it had good sheep-rearing land and also produced such essential ingredients as fuller's earth, teasels and dyestuffs such as weld, woad and madder. The importance of this English industry can be seen from the importation of woad and the legislation on cloth in the last decade of the twelfth century. Organization arose among the merchants, who were responsible for the finishing processes and for marketing the cloth, and also among the craftsmen who wove it. The Pipe Roll of 1130–1 records the existence, through payments made by them, of weavers' gilds in London, Winchester, Lincoln, Oxford, Nottingham and Huntingdon. But the fine cloths that were exported to the Italian peninsula and Spain came mostly from eastern England, and Beverley, York, Lincoln, Louth and Stamford were the most frequent producers. The high-priced scarlet cloths, dyed in the grain (kermes), came mostly from Stamford and Lincoln; Lincoln green may well be a corruption of Lincoln in grain but the cloths, of whatever colour, were well known in southern Europe and are mentioned in the Venetian tariff of 1265.

But despite the prominence of some English cloths, England remained in the thirteenth century primarily a supplier of raw material. Flemish merchants scoured the country to purchase wool in competition with the English clothiers and the high prosperity of the Flemish industry rested upon the superior quality of English wool, especially that of Lindsey, produced on the Lincolnshire Wolds. However, they and the Italians who succeeded them went to all parts of the country, since the short wool used to make cloth of heavy texture was grown on the Welsh and Scottish borders, on the Yorkshire moors and on the chalk downlands of the south, especially between the river Severn and Wales, while the long wool came from the Lincolnshire Fens, Leicestershire and the Cotswolds and from the vale of Taunton, a small area in Somerset and north Devon of which the town of Bampton was the centre. Pegalotti, in his treatise already referred to, listed fifty-one different grades of wool valued at between £9 7s. 6d. and £2 10s. a sack of 364 lb (163·8 kg). The wool came both from the demesne and from tenant farmers, and the clip of great monastic houses, especially

Cistercian and Premonstratensian, was often sold up to twenty years ahead by advance contracts. They and other great lords, both lay and ecclesiastical, had in the late twelfth and thirteenth centuries vast flocks of sheep (the bishop of Winchester in 1259 owned 29,000), but small tenants were also important producers.

The latter marketed their wool in different ways. Sometimes they brought it to fairs or had it collected by agents while some made contracts with their landlords to sell the wool for them, so giving it something of a guarantee. We know this was done because the General Chapter of the Cistercian Order forbade the practice by their houses. But above all it was purchased by middlemen or wool-mongers who certainly existed by the middle of the twelfth century and who, in the middle of the following century, were complaining that monks, by collecting the wool of small traders, were ruining their trade. The *collecta*, as the wools of the smaller men were called, never fetched as good a price as that of the large monastic houses because its quality was not consistently so good but it was an important source of supply as villagers owned large numbers of sheep. On the Glastonbury manor of South Damerham in 1225 there were 570 sheep on the demesne farm and 3760 belonging to the tenants.

In the export trade Flemings took the lead from the last quarter of the eleventh century to the last quarter of the thirteenth, when they came increasingly under a royal ban, and embargoes were placed on the export of wool to the county in order to further the political aims of Edward I. Then the Italians who had come to England as papal tax collectors in the mid thirteenth century entered the wool trade and dominated it in the fifty years after 1280. The Riccardi of Lucca and the Frescobaldi, Bardi and Peruzzi of Florence were at the height of their power and exporting wool was one of their principal activities. It has been estimated that only one third of the trade in wool was in the hands of the natives in 1273, whereas by 1362-76 between two thirds and three quarters, and in the fifteenth century four fifths, of the export business was in English hands. Indeed the business methods of the English export trade in wool were completely transformed between the late thirteenth and the early fifteenth centuries, for, whereas in the former period the merchant gave credit to the wool producer, in the latter the producer gave credit to the buyer. A remarkable record of business letters, the Cely

Papers (1475–88), shows how the purchaser paid only one third of the purchase price down and the remaining two thirds were paid by bills falling due at a later date. The woolmonger bought on credit from the sheep farmer, while the Celys in London bought on credit from the wool dealer and Dutch and Flemish customers in Calais bought on credit from the Celys. These bills fell due six months later but in practice the Celys would sell them at a discount to a mercer or merchant adventurer who wished to import goods into England. In due course the Celys paid the Cotswold woolmonger on the stated date and he was then in a position to settle his debt, the remaining two thirds of the purchase price, with the wool grower. This was a very different procedure from the advanced contracts of the thirteenth century by means of which monastic houses had been able to mobilize capital.

The reason for the growth of the English share in the export trade is not to be sought in the view that in the twelfth and thirteenth centuries Englishmen were unskilled as traders but in the hard fact that artificial state regulation secured a virtual monopoly of the trade for native exporters. This state regulation resulted in the creation of the Staple. Edward I, in order to finance his wars with Wales, Scotland and France, was compelled to increase taxation and he appreciated that taxation upon wool was a profitable source of revenue. In furtherance of that policy and as a means of simplification of tax collection, Edward I directed in 1294 that all wool should be sent to a fixed place, first Dordrecht and then to Antwerp. This was the origin of the Staple system whereby one town was designated through which the export of wool was compulsorily directed but it was not as yet a true Staple for some wool was still going to Bruges. The crown employed two methods to raise revenue: direct appropriations of wool and loans in wool. Loans in wool were not so much objected to as export taxes on wool although even these became more acceptable as merchants appreciated that they could hand them on by lowering the price paid to the wool producer. From 1275 the king had enjoyed a custom of 6s. 8d. on every sack of wool exported,[1] between 1294 and 1297 a *maltote* of 3 marks a sack was levied, then abandoned; but from an agreement made with

[1] See N. S. B. Gras, *The Early English Customs System* (Cambridge, Mass., Harvard U.P., 1918).

foreign merchants which resulted in the *Carta Mercatoria* of 1303 foreign exporters paid an additional 3s. 4d. on every sack of wool which they sent out of the country – a total of 10s. In addition, subsidies on wool were granted either by the merchants or by the magnates or imposed by the king-in-council; these were levied at differing rates and always for a specific period of time. The idea of direction of trade on the part of the Crown was increasingly accepted and between 1313 and 1336 a Staple was established at a number of towns, of which the principal ones were St Omer, Antwerp and Bruges, while in 1326–7 and 1332–4 it was at home. From the 1360s Calais was frequently fixed as the Staple town and, although in the fourteenth century home towns were again named, from 1399 onwards Calais became until 1558 the site of the Staple with its company of Merchants of the Staple. Through it all wool, woolfells and other commodities were compulsorily exported. Aliens, with the exception of the Italians who accounted for about one fifth of the trade and who took wool directly to Italy and the Mediterranean via Gibraltar, were excluded from the wool export business which was entirely in the hands of the English Merchants of the Staple. This method satisfied the Crown, the quasi-mono-polistic Staplers who could squeeze the foreign consumer hard and the English woolmongers and clothiers who no longer had foreign merchants going up and down the country pushing up the cost of raw material against them.

It was against this background of English domination of the supplies of raw material plus the great taxative benefits which the English cloth industry acquired that England ceased to be a supplier of raw material and became the leading woollen textile producer of the later Middle Ages. While the export duty on wool was about 33⅓ per cent *ad valorem*, that on cloth (and native exporters did not pay it until 1347) was only about 2 per cent. With the difficulties of the Flemish industry at this period, and those that overtook the Florentine clothiers in the later fourteenth century, it is not surprising that the export of wool declined from 35,000 sacks per annum in the early fourteenth century to 19,000 sacks at the end of it, and shrank still further by the mid fifteenth to only 8000 sacks and continued thereafter to dwindle.

On the other hand the number of cloths exported, which had only been 4422 between Michaelmas 1347 and Michaelmas 1348, rose to an annual average of 16,000 cloths between 1366 and 1368, to 43,000 between 1392 and 1395, and by the mid fifteenth century exports were running at a rate of 54,000 a year. This figure at the end of Edward IV's reign had risen to 63,000, in the early years of Henry VIII it was 84,000 and by the mid sixteenth century the average annual export of cloths was 122,000. More and more wool was being diverted into the home industry. It may well be that overall production of wool declined in the fifteenth century although the inadequacy of the aulnage accounts prevents any firm judgement on that; but about the fact that less was sent abroad and more used at home there can be no doubt.[1] From 1353 a payment known as aulnage was levied on all cloths made for sale but the returns are so unsatisfactory that we cannot assess accurately the amount of cloth woven for sale on the home market and, of course, the amount of homespun can never be measured, although with the rising standard of living in England it was probably less. Neither can there be any doubt that the English woollen textile industry captured the European market in the second half of the fourteenth century with a dramatic rise in exports. The help given by Flemish workers was not the cause of this English success but rather symptomatic of it. As early as 1271 some foreign workers had immigrated and had been encouraged by grants of freedom from taxation and of royal protection, and after the battle of Cassel (1328) about 1000 workers, equally divided between weavers and fullers, left Ypres alone, while in 1344 certain weavers from Poperinghe were condemned to exile in England; but although they may have had great skill their numbers and influence were insufficient to account for the transformation which took place.

Despite the many subsidiary helping factors the growth of the English industry was due to a technological revolution which carried with it consequentially many other growth factors. Of the consequences of the introduction, probably in the thirteenth century, of the spinning wheel little is known, but those that followed the introduction of mechanical fulling can be clearly demonstrated. Cloth, like grapes, had from time immemorial been trodden or

[1] E. M. Carus-Wilson, 'The aulnage accounts: a criticism', *Econ. Hist. Review*, No. II (1929), 114–23.

F

walked in the process of fulling, a process that was designed primarily to felt the cloth, and therefore men stamped up and down upon it as it lay in the troughs. It was a wearisome and time-consuming task which required long hours of work from men of above average stamina, so that the introduction of fulling mills worked by water power brought about considerable economies. The first English fulling mills, one at Newsham (Yorkshire) and another at Barton in the Cotswolds, are mentioned in a survey of the property of the Templars in 1185, but such mills were not in wide use before the later thirteenth century. The machine consisted of two wooden hammers which were raised and dropped on to the cloth in the trough on the tilt hammer principle and all the labour that was required was that of one man who saw that all areas of the cloth were properly beaten by the hammers. Because the mills were driven by water power, fulling mills were constructed on upland streams which had swifter currents than those in low-lying towns such as London, York, Winchester or Northampton, and once the fulling process had been moved to the countryside it made economic sense to move other processes there also.

Another incentive for the capitalist clothiers to move out of the cities was to be found in the municipal and gild restrictions. In Leicester in 1264 and in 1275 respectively the weavers were accused of restrictive practices against members of the merchant gild and the fullers were accused of holding an illegal meeting. The fullers likewise in Norwich were accused in 1293 of having an illegal gild and the London burellers complained at the end of the thirteenth century that weavers were asking for more than double their previous wages, laying down conditions of work such as a minimum time of four days to weave a cloth and seeking to increase their holidays by doing no work between Christmas and Candlemas (2 February). It is little wonder therefore that capitalists established the textile industry in the rural areas where labour was plentiful, at least down to the 1360s, and in no way organized. The third technological invention, the gig mill, a roller set with teasels which was rotated by water power, was certainly in use in the fifteenth century and again, as with the fulling mill, required an upland site.

These inventions led to the decline of the urban woollen textile industry which had played so important a part in the English economy of the eleventh and twelfth centuries. Lincoln, Stamford, London, Oxford, Leicester, Northampton, Beverley and Winchester were all declining in the second half of the thirteenth century and a change took place in the location of the textile industry. It would be wrong to portray it as an industry totally in decline which was rescued by the fiscal measures of Edward III and the know-how of Flemish immigrants, as was common at one time.[1] In fact it became a rural industry, centred in the West Country, in East Anglia and in the West Riding of Yorkshire.

The first of these areas which produced the English broadcloth *par excellence* was centred in the southern Cotswolds in the Stroud valley and around Bradford-on-Avon in Wiltshire. It was a district that supplied first grade wool, fuller's earth was available and good water power was secured by the streams and rivers. West of England cloth of superb quality was woven and finished in places like Stroud and Castle Combe, Wickwar, Dursley, Wootton-under-Edge, Trowbridge, Bradford-on-Avon, Bath, Cirencester and Malmesbury. Kerseys and other cheaper and lighter fabrics were produced in the area from Bridgwater into Taunton, Barnstaple, Tiverton and Exeter, as they were along the Wylie and Kennet valleys to Salisbury, Marlborough, Newbury and Reading. The second area had a long-established woollen industry but activity increased along the Stour valley in the fourteenth century. Small towns such as Dedham, East Bergholt, Stratford St Mary, Nayland, Sudbury, Long Melford, Glemsford, Cavendish, Clare and Haverhill prospered exceedingly, as did Hadleigh, Kersey, Lavenham, Boxford and Great and Little Waldingford. A little farther away from the Stour valley, Bury St Edmunds, Halstead, Braintree and Coggeshall flourished. The Paycockes of Coggeshall and the Springs of Lavenham are two families of clothiers about whom we know something and there were many like them whose houses remain and whose gifts to churches are still to be seen. Farther north an industry flourished which was technically not the production of woollens but of lighter weight cloths, known as says, serges or worsteds. For this material the long-haired combed wool was used and, in addition to the small

---

[1] Cf. E. Lipson, *The History of the English Woollen and Worsted Industries* (London, Black, 1921), p. 11; and L. F. Salzman, *English Industries in the Middle Ages* (Oxford, Clarendon Press, 1923), p. 203.

town of Worsted, it was produced at villages such as Honing, Tunstead and Scottow as well as in Norwich itself which was the marketing centre for these cloths. The third major area was the Aire and Calder valleys in the West Riding of Yorkshire. Leeds, Bradford, Wakefield and Halifax rose to great prominence as towns manufacturing kerseys, cheap but hard wearing cloths, and the areas around Ripon and Barnsley and the city of York itself, though surpassed in output, remained of considerable significance as centres of production. Apart from these areas, Westmorland was well known for its 'Kendals', and the Welsh Marches with the highest quality wool produced fine cloth at Ludlow. Coventry was outstanding for its 'blues'.

This rural industry flourished because the English clothier was subject to fewer controls than his Flemish and Florentine counterparts. Men of villein status, such as William Haynes of Castle Combe, acquired great wealth as cloth makers and others, such as the Springs of Lavenham rose to become landed gentry. The English clothier was freed from the expenses of liveries and pageants that plagued his urban colleagues both native and foreign, and also from the gild and municipal regulations that restricted their enterprise especially in the Flemish cities. Apart from legislation as to measurements and standard – legislation which, to judge from its repetition was frequently disregarded – the clothier was subject to little restraint except from the occasional commissions to enforce standards. There was no regular system of state inspection and during the fifteenth century frequent complaints were made about English cloth. But the inordinate demand for it would indicate that for the European market it was the right commodity at the right price. Cloth was increasingly exported from the east coast ports with London acquiring a growing share of the trade. Every year the great St Bartholomew's fair held at Smithfield, commencing on 23 August, provided a venue for clothiers, as did the weekly market held from 1396 at Blackwell Hall in Basinghall Street where cloth was on sale between noon on Thursday and the same hour on Saturday.

The industry was organized on a capitalist or quasi-capitalist basis with the clothier purchasing the wool, putting it out to be sorted and spun, taking in the yarn and having it woven into cloth, then sending it out to be dyed and finished. Few of the workers owned the means of production although some weavers with their own looms were able, from time to time, to show some independence of the cloth-makers. Weavers' notoriety for the outspokenness of their views was proverbial in the Middle Ages and beyond and this independence of opinion was probably based upon some measure of economic independence: but for the most part workers in the industry had nothing to sell but their labour and their skill. The capitalist clothiers, we have reason to believe, were working for high, possibly outrageous profits, from the early fifteenth century, although their margins were probably sometimes curbed by the exporters, the Merchant Adventurers, who acquired a stranglehold over the export market from that same period.

Despite not being incorporated as a chartered company until 1505, the London Merchant Adventurers, great mercantile capitalists, had been active from the late fourteenth century as they separated from the Staplers and it has been estimated that by 1479–82, about 58 per cent of the import and export trade was in their hands. They had formed a fellowship of adventurers within the Mercers' Company as early as 1443–4[1] and a similar fellowship is found in Bristol, probably as early as 1467 and certainly ten years later. Of course other commodities went through their hands but woollen cloth was the principal article of their export business. These men took no part in cloth manufacture nor in the retail trade, neither were they engaged merely in the carrying trade, but they confined themselves to buying cloth wholesale and to shipping it and selling it abroad. Gradually no English subject not of their fraternity could export cloth and separate groups, trading one to the Low Countries, another to the Baltic and another to Scandinavia, emerged. They aimed, by regulating trade and avoiding gluts, at maintaining a high price for English commodities and they entered into a long struggle with the Hanseatic merchants who were their main competitors in foreign trade. Italians also maintained an active part in English foreign trade in the later Middle Ages but they did not antagonize the native merchants to the same degree. It was the long struggle between the Merchant Venturers and the Hanse that had so profound an effect upon the English export trade in the

[1] E. M. Carus-Wilson, *Medieval Merchant Venturers*, p. xxvi.

fifteenth and sixteenth centuries. The trade was subject to annual fluctuations, which were often violent, and the prosperity of the English woollen textile industry often depended on the prosperity or lack of it in parts of Europe far distant from East Anglia and the Cotswolds; it was at the mercy of the international market.[1] But the trend was clearly one of increasing cloth exports with a slightly increasing proportion of the business going through native rather than through alien merchants in the fifteenth century, although early in the following century aliens tended to increase their proportion of the export trade for a time. The complete transformation that had taken place, the replacement of 'colonial status' by the building up of a vast textile industry controlled by Englishmen, led to the creation of an industry in the later Middle Ages which surpassed that of Flanders and Italy in earlier centuries.

[1] For details of the export of wool and cloth, see E. M. Carus-Wilson, *Medieval Merchant Venturers*, p. xviii and passim.

CHAPTER 13

Mining and the Metallurgical Industries in the Middle Ages

From the abandonment of many of the mines of the Roman period it appears that the production of metals was probably less in the thousand years after A.D. 300 than it had been in the 500 years before that date; but iron seems to have been less affected by the down-turn than other metals. At many places in Gaul, the Rhineland, Saxony, Bohemia, Tuscany and Spain, and possibly in the eastern Alps, iron was mined in the early Middle Ages. Roman Britain had produced much tin and lead, copper and coal and, while the first two metals were still obtained in the early medieval period, the latter two were apparently not mined.

The first real growth in European mining after the fall of the Roman Empire did not come until the end of the ninth century or even the early tenth century when Germany became the main centre of increased output. Rich deposits of copper and lead ore were worked at the Rammelsberg, a hill rising 360 metres above the town of Goslar in the Harz mountains. In the eleventh and twelfth centuries mining grew in the mountains (so that in German the same word was used for miner and mountaineer); in the Harz, the Vosges, the Jura and especially in the eastern Alps workings for gold, silver, lead, copper and iron became numerous. From 1168 mine working extended still further with the discovery of rich silver-bearing ores at Freiberg in Saxony, and this period of expansion probably lasted for 150 years after that date.

Growth of population and the increasing need for the use of gold, silver, iron, lead, copper and tin for commercial, industrial and artistic purposes were the driving forces behind the development of mining, and men went out to Freiberg to mine for silver in a spirit not unlike that which inspired those who took part in the gold rush to California or the Yukon. Traders everywhere were on the look out for mineral ores, especially those containing gold or silver, and such veins were discovered in Saxony, Bohemia, Silesia and Hungary; these areas together with the Harz and the Black Forest became the suppliers of silver, copper and a little gold. In the valleys on the lower slopes of the mountain ranges and in the Carpathians, the Erzgebirge and the Sudeten mountains the thick woods provided timber for building and charcoal for the fuel that was needed in the smelting processes, while the streams provided water power for hammers to crush the ore or for blowers to pump air into the fires. The geographical accident of the location of these ores mainly in German lands made the Germans dominant in mining from the twelfth to the sixteenth centuries, although their dominance did not extend to the mining of ores containing only base metals. By the fourteenth century the copper mines of Stora Kopparberg near Falun in Sweden rivalled those of the Rammelsberg, and English lead mines in Somerset, Durham, Cumberland, Flintshire, Shrop-shire, and above all Derbyshire, were very important in the thir-teenth century when a growing export trade in lead arose and the Continent was as dependent upon Devon and Cornwall for its tin as it was on Saxony and Bohemia for its gold and silver. Between the mid twelfth century and the year 1338 the output of tin rose tenfold and the figures for the decade 1330 to 1340 were not surpassed until the later seventeenth century.[1]

Iron deposits were more widely spread than were ores of other metals, yet an international trade in iron ore developed as the demand for metal rose. More ploughshares, tools, axles, cauldrons, more anchors, keels and nails in shipbuilding, more armour, spears, swords and daggers, were all required by the growing population from the early twelfth century onwards. Styria, Carinthia and the Basque provinces of Biscay and Guipuzcoa were the principal exporting areas, and to a lesser extent Hungary, Sweden and Westphalia. But this growing demand should not mislead us into thinking that output was high: it has been estimated that the whole province of Styria turned out only 2000 tons a year at the beginning of the fourteenth century. The use of coal was also very restricted. There is no authentic record of its use before the 1190s but the

[1] G. R. Lewis, *The Stannaries*, pp. 252-5.

following century saw increasing use of it and shallow pits 6 to 15 metres in depth were dug in the coalfields of England near Newcastle, in Scotland, in the Low Countries at Liège and Mons, and in parts of France such as Lyonnais, Forez and Anjou. Limeburners increasingly used it in their work.

Mining in the Middle Ages was organized according to rigid laws and customs. Landowners on whose territory mineral-bearing ores were situated had every incentive to throw open the mines on their lands to all comers and to claim as large a share of the output as possible. The origin of the landowner's right to the *Bergregal* (such rights were not recognized before the late tenth or even the eleventh centuries) came somewhat late, but by the 1300s lords were successfully claiming a share in the produce from veins of ore found under their estates. These rights varied from place to place but might include a share of the ore, usually one tenth, in addition to which the lords often received coinage dues and the right of pre-emption over the entire output of the best metal, i.e. the right to buy all of it at a price lower than it would have fetched on the open market. But as the mines had to be worked and as many lords either did not wish to or could not exploit the ore themselves by direct labour, they were forced to moderate their demands and allow the miners deductions to meet the cost of sinking, draining and ventilating the pits.

The Holy Roman emperors in the twelfth century had attempted to enforce the view that all mining rights belonged to them, not as lord of estates but as sovereign, but in the following century they were unable to maintain this legal doctrine and Charles IV conceded by the Golden Bull of 1356 that the regalian rights to mines went with the lordship of the territories. This did not prevent the princes from delegating their rights to their vassals or even to their rear vassals if they chose but it did prevent mining rights and miners from being the sole prerogative of the emperor. But the princes could not and did not always enforce their rights in the case of all metals and many lords of the land carried on mining without the permission of the prince and made no payment to him. Especially was this so as regards coal and iron ore, and the princes tended to limit their regalian claims to ores containing substantial quantities of gold and silver. Private landlords who were not territorial princes were usually compelled to allow miners who had obtained the prince's permission to mine for ores on their estates and to grant them rights to use the streams for washing ores and driving crushing mills. Also the miners generally had a title to at least part of the timber that they needed for building and for fuel to fire their kilns and furnaces. Though the miners had to pay for these privileges, landlords could not refuse to grant them. They did, however, sometimes share the regalian rights of the territorial prince and they set up officials to supervise the mines. In some areas of Bohemia two sets of officials worked side by side, those of the lord of the soil and those of the territorial lord.

In countries where the power of the sovereign ruler increased instead of decreased, as it did in the Holy Roman Empire, kings obtained a firmer grip upon mining rights. During and after the reign of Philip Augustus the kings of France began to assert regalian rights over mines in the lands of their vassals, although they made claims less bold than those of the emperor or the king of England. It was not until 1413 that it was made illegal for any lord except the king to collect the royalty on mines in France. In England the Crown controlled all gold- and silver-bearing ores and it collected a royalty on the produce of gold and silver mines. It also regulated through its possession of the Earldom (later Duchy) of Cornwall the right to grant concessions to miners in the tin mines of Devon and Cornwall. In these counties miners were free to search for tin without the permission of the landlords on whose land the tin might be. The Crown also had the right of pre-emption and charged dues for stamping the blocks of tin.

The Forest of Dean, one of the most productive areas both of iron ore and of coal, was largely royal demesne and the Crown claimed a part of all metals obtained there. The finder of ore there, as in Europe generally, staked out a claim and the lord's principal officer – in Germany the *Bergmeister* – or his delegate invested the miner for an indefinite period with the right to exploit the staked-out section of the seam. Sometimes the right to work ores was limited to inhabitants of the locality. Except for iron and coal, the miners of other metals and their families usually formed a separate community apart from the cultivators of the soil and they enjoyed a status usually as high as that of the citizens in the rising towns of the twelfth and thirteenth centuries. Indeed a way to free status was to become a miner or a craftsman or trader in the towns. In places the new mining communities were so large that they established towns such as Liège, Freiberg, Iglau (Jihlava on the Bohemian-Moravian border) and Schemnitz (now Banska Stiavnica in Czechoslovakia).

The regulations governing the methods of sinking and supporting pits, of raising the ore, the hours of work and the division of profits and losses were determined by consultation between the lord's officials and the representatives of the miners. The miners usually had their special courts which dealt with disputes over mining or over the making of metal, and the customs which grew up in the mining industry gave to the workers considerable privileges and powers. All over Europe men drew up mining codes, many of them modelled on the code issued in 1185 by the bishop of Trent, or more frequently on the codes drawn up by the king of Bohemia for Iglau from 1249 onwards. The mining and metallurgical industries attracted venturing spirits into areas where there had been little or no cultivation and it was inevitable therefore that miners should be free men with no taint of servile status.

By the fourteenth century the mining industry had reached a crisis because the surface and shallow seams had become exhausted and continued successful exploitation rested upon sinking deeper shafts, which in turn depended upon better draining and better support of the walls. This called for greater capital investment in the industry. Attempts were made to drain mines by open ditches dug from the bottom of the shafts down into the valley and also with leather buckets filled with water which were wound up from the bottom of the pit by a windlass which was hand operated. Because the soil of the Alps and countries to the north was much damper than that of most Mediterranean lands flooding could be a serious danger at 18 to 30 metres, and the only way to deal with this successfully was to dig long tunnels; these adits as they were called were apparently first constructed in Bohemia at the beginning of the fourteenth century. Some of these adits were over one and a half kilometres long before they reached an opening in the valley below the level of the shaft bottom or the level of the sump in which the waters collected, but seepage of the water back into the mine resulted unless the adit was maintained in a good state of repair. In Saxony, the Harz and southern Bavaria at this time, miners experimented with water- and horse-driven machinery to draw water from the pits but this was not really effective until the late fifteenth century as more substantial wheels, axles and gears came into use.

The preparation and smelting of ores became significantly more efficient in the fifteenth century. Washing, breaking and crushing were done by hand to a large extent before the close of the Middle Ages. Smelters invented different varieties of hearths, trenches, pots, ovens and furnaces but their equipment remained basically simple. Iron ore was heated at tiny forges equipped with hand- or foot-driven bellows. Forges and hammers were constructed near the pits but like the pits they were easily abandoned: little in the way of permanent equipment existed. The extraction of silver was a more complicated and expensive process than that of either gold or the base metals and it was in the preparation of silver that the first really large capital investment was made. The silver-bearing lead yielded silver by oxidizing it in a cupelling hearth so that the lead or litharge was removed. Already at the beginning of the thirteenth century in southern Tyrol water wheels drove both the hammers for crushing ore and the bellows that raised the temperature of the smelting furnaces, and by 1300 water power was in common use to power the machinery that crushed the ores. Then gradually water-driven wheels were introduced for operating the bellows and hammers in the chief iron making regions of Styria, Carinthia, Bohemia, Lorraine and Dauphiné. The heart-shaped bellows with a flap valve may have appeared in the early twelfth century but by the fourteenth century a double bellows which produced a constant rather than an intermittent blast was in use. The hotter flame from the new and longer water-driven bellows produced large pigs of metal, and as a consequence large furnaces had to be devised while power-driven tilt hammers were needed to reduce the pigs to blooms of wrought iron.

The old bloomery forges widely in use until the fourteenth century were slowly being replaced in that same century by furnaces of three types: the Catalan forge in France and Spain, the Osmund furnace in Scandinavia and the *Stückofen* in Germany. The last of these three was the most effective and spread most widely in central Europe, eastern France and the Alps. This *Stückofen*, from which the blast furnace derived, unlike the small woodland bloomery forges that rose only 1 or 1·2 metres from ground level, was a substantial structure of brick and stone usually built close to the streams to make use of water power for the bellows. It was about 3 metres high and consisted of a circular or quadrangular shaft about 0·5 metres across at the top and bottom and widening out to about 1·5 metres in the middle. Such a furnace could produce 40 or 50 tons of iron a year. It transformed the manufacture of iron but it was only used in the principal mining centres of Germany, eastern France and, above all, in the region around Namur and Liège, and it was not introduced into England until the sixteenth century. Not until the second half of the fifteenth century and the first half of the sixteenth was research done into metals and their qualities, which investigations had a profound effect upon metal production. Agricola's *De Re Metallica*, the standard treatise on metals, did not appear until the mid sixteenth century.

Considerable finds of new veins of ore occurred in the mid fifteenth century. The discovery of calamine in the Tyrol and Carinthia and especially at Moresnet near Aachen led to the revival of extensive brass production; brass, an alloy of zinc and copper, had been little manufactured in the Middle Ages. More importantly, the discovery was made that silver could be obtained from argentiferous copper ores by the use of lead. Johannsen Funcken appears to have introduced this method into Saxony in 1451. Both these discoveries led to more intensive mining of copper ore in the later fifteenth century and at the same time more powerful drainage engines were introduced and more skilful adits constructed so that mines of far greater depth yielded their ores. Improved methods of ventilation allowed more effective dispersal of noxious gases. At Schemnitz water from the bottom of the pit was pumped up three flights before it was sufficiently near the surface to be led off by an adit. The rotation of a large horse-driven wheel set each pump in motion and the horses employed reached the wheel by corkscrew-like passages down which they were led.

At the very close of the Middle Ages the blast furnace enabled cast iron to be made; this was the most important invention in the metallurgical industry. Bronze, a compound of copper and tin, with its much lower melting point than iron, had been cast since the early twelfth century and used in the making of bells and statues, but the hotter blast of the fourteenth century enabled even iron ore to liquefy. Guns were at first cast in bronze but by the mid fifteenth century cannons appeared which were made of cast iron and even small cast iron objects were becoming common. Men in the areas in and around Namur and Liège, in the domains of the duke of Burgundy, were the first to cast cannons, and Italy soon followed that lead, but the real development of cannons was made in south-eastern England near Robertsbridge in Sussex in the 1540s. Because the ore was in contact for long periods with carbon, it absorbed much carbon. The molten metal ran out into moulds of sand and the shape was known as a sow, while small branches leading off the main mould were called pigs. But this iron was unsuitable for wrought products such as tools, weapons and armour because it was too brittle and it had therefore to be treated to decarbonize it. Re-heating under oxidizing conditions gave an unlimited spongy mass, which by continued forging became equivalent and even superior to the old directly reduced iron produced by the bloomery process. Blast furnaces were more powerful than the *Stückofen* and were equipped with powerful bellows while the adjacent forges had more powerful hammers. All countries contributed to these technical advances, but in general experts from Hungary, Bohemia, Saxony, Tyrol and the Low Countries led the way in the technical development of mining and metallurgy, although Italy and France were also in the forefront of improvements in iron manufacture. In coal mining northern England was in the van with shafts 45 metres deep, although silver ore was obtained 180 metres below the surface in Saxony, Bohemia and Hungary. Yet in the main mining was remarkably shallow and coal and iron ore were mostly found on the surface, and the processing of metals had not been revolutionized by the introduction of water power.

Greatly increased silver production, which was necessary to finance the expanding commerce of the late fifteenth century, occurred in Germany. The high point of production was reached at Schneeberg between Zwickau and Aue in Saxony in the 1480s and at Freiberg in the same region in the 1540s. Between 1515 and 1540 silver production increased considerably, perhaps in the longer span between 1460 and 1530, as much as five times and annual output reached a figure that was not surpassed until the 1850s. Copper output also rose phenomenally and, here again, Germany took the lead especially in the Erzgebirge. Mercury production at Idria in Carniola and at Almedén in Spain also rose, as did the output of alum from deposits found in 1461 at Tolfa in the Papal States.

But above all the warlike activities of the rising nation states and the expansion of industry provided the insistent demand for iron and steel. Areas that had long been producers of iron (Styria, for example, probably increased output fourfold between the 1460s and the 1560s) stepped up their tonnage. A similar rate of increase was almost certainly achieved in the valley of the Meuse where the forests of the Ardennes suffered as a result of this expansion. Westphalia, the Harz, Lorraine, Champagne, Dauphiné, Tuscany, Piedmont and the Basque provinces paralleled the increase made elsewhere. Water power was used to drive bellows and hammers and fuel had to be brought to the furnaces and forges. These installations became far more permanent than they had been when iron had been produced by the bloomery process. Already we hear complaints of the countryside being spoilt and of pollution of rivers if not of the atmosphere. Coal could only be used by limeburners and for the production of crude iron, but as the timber shortage grew it was increasingly employed and one centre in Europe, Liège, began to thrive almost entirely on mining and selling it, and the sea coals of Newcastle had even earlier been condemned for the pollution they caused.

CHAPTER 14

Medieval Agrarian Society at its Zenith: Tenurial Relations

In earlier chapters (chapters 2 and 3) the development of agricultural techniques, which led to a divergence in the cultivation patterns of northern and southern Europe and the emergence of dependent tenures, creating the manor, has been traced down to the eleventh century. We must now look at the manor at its zenith and discuss the relations between lord and tenant during this period. The whole weight of historical research in the last fifty years underlines the dangers of generalization: land was not exploited everywhere throughout Europe under 'the manorial system', which was the economic base on which 'the feudal system' rested. These 'systems' were the inventions of eighteenth-century writers and yet it would be wrong to deny that European civilization between the eleventh and early thirteenth century was not going through a feudal period. The method of granting land on certain conditions to fighting men, which Charles Martel had pioneered in the middle of the eighth century, continued in western and eastern Francia and later in France and Germany, and the descendants of those vassals who had originally but a life interest in their estates converted them into hereditary fiefs. These conversions of the *beneficium* into a hereditary fief (*feudum* or *feodum*) began to take place in France in the ninth century, whereas it did not arise in England until the late eleventh or early twelfth century and in the Holy Roman Empire until about 100 years later. In writing about medieval agrarian society it is necessary to say something of the feudal structure of society, if only to point out the difference between the two 'systems' for, closely interrelated as they were, they were not one and the same thing. True it is that a fief is a landed estate and that that same estate might be cultivated in such a way, by dependent labour, as to call it a manor, but there were many such estates similarly cultivated, and therefore correctly termed manors, that were not held by feudal tenures. Moreover, those tenants, both villein and free, who worked on the lord's manor must be excluded from the feudal 'chain of tenure' for if a strict view be taken of feudalism only those who held by knight service or by tenures closely analogous to it, such as serjeanty, truly held by a feudal tenancy. The peasantry, although they sometimes served as fighting men, certainly did not hold their strips on condition of performing war-like services and so must, in order to avoid confusion, be excluded from the ranks of feudatories; at the same time their labour underpinned the entire feudal hierarchy. It has been estimated that the labour of fifteen to thirty peasant families was required to keep one knightly household.

The manor, with its division into three parts – the peasants' holdings, the demesne and the common or wasteland – though not universal, was widespread over the European continent. Over large areas of France, Germany, Italy, Spain, England, Scotland, Ireland, Poland and the Low Countries, the lord of the manor with his dependent tenants was the rule. And not only was he to be found in western Europe, for, from the second half of the eleventh century, powerful landowners in the Byzantine Empire, the *pronoetes* had the peasants (*paroikoi*) living on the land handed over to them with the large estates with which emperors endowed them. The *pronoia* system by which they held did not confer on the grantee a hereditary fief but in many ways the tenure was similar to that of the western feudal magnate and, with the Latin conquest of large parts of the Empire after 1204, the fief, as known in the west, was introduced.

Certainly the time at which the system of land exploitation by manorial estates reached its zenith varied in different parts of Europe. It reached its height in France between the ninth and early eleventh centuries and in the following century, there, as in England, the practice of cultivating the estate by a mixture of free, servile and hired labour was undergoing radical change. In Germany the manorial estate was not fully developed until the period of decline had started in France, while in eastern Europe the colonizing movements of the twelfth and thirteenth centuries created conditions in which servile tenure was virtually unknown and it was not until the late fifteenth and sixteenth centuries that vast estates employing servile labour appeared. Here exploitation of the land by serfs lasted well into the nineteenth century. The timing of the rise and fall of manorialism was influenced by political as well as by economic factors. In general, weak central government enabled lords to exploit their tenants more rigorously than was possible under a firm ruler, both because weak rulers were more generous in their grants of immunities to lords and because widespread disorder would put the peasants into a state of insecurity in which they would be more willing to accept a lord's protection. However, on occasion, a firm ruler might follow a policy of establishing his domination by strengthening the authority of feudal lords; Frederick Barbarossa pursued such a line. In eastern Europe, where estates cultivated by the labour of serfs was impossible because only free men could be attracted into the region between the twelfth and fourteenth centuries, only the upheavals of the Prusso-Polish wars, the Russo-Lithuanian and Russo-Tartar wars and the Hussite wars in Bohemia brought about conditions of insecurity which enabled lords to create huge estates with enserfed tenants. An economic factor, the demand for Baltic grain, helped this movement since large estates were more profitable units of production for the market.

The powers a lord exercised over his tenants may be classified under two heads, economic and jurisdictional. Both had financial implications. In general terms the economic demands that the lords made tended to decline between the ninth and the twelfth centuries. The three days of week-work on the lord's demesne that had been demanded from a full holding (*manse* in French, *Hufe* in German, hide in English) gradually diminished in many areas as the manses disintegrated, either by division among heirs or by alienation, and the growing population, at least from the eleventh century, was another cause of the diminution of demand. As the labour force on the manor grew it became more profitable for the lord to commute services for an annual rent and with the money thus acquired to hire labour which would be more efficient and reliable than the grudging service given by the customary tenants, whose main interest was the cultivation of their own land and who resented every hour that they had to spend on the demesne. Arable services were sold rather earlier than were 'industrial' services and the obligations to cart goods on the lord's behalf. The burden of labour services a tenant had to perform on his lord's demesne varied in detail from estate to estate and in general from region to region.

This fact is amply affirmed by the eleventh-century English treatise *Rectitudines Singularum Personarum* whose author wrote 'this land-law holds in certain places, but elsewhere, as we have said, it is heavier or lighter, for the institutions of all estates are not alike: let him who is over the district take care that he knows what the old land-customs are and what are the customs of the people'.[1] In the main, heavier labour services were demanded on estates with large demesnes that concentrated upon grain production than upon the estates where livestock husbandry played a more prominent role, and, because geographical and climatic factors favoured corn growing in some regions and animal husbandry in others, labour demands would tend to vary regionally. On the plain between the Rhine and the Loire, large corn and wine producing estates existed which made heavy demands on peasant labour. They were so large that they comprised a whole village and occasionally several villages. But even here the size of demesnes varied. Geography was not the only factor, for decisions on the size of the demesne and the amount of labour required might be taken in the light of economic advantage; a great lord might find it profitable to cut down carting costs by limiting the direct exploitation of demesnes on estates far distant from his principal residence. Such a consideration would apply with even greater force to the distant estates of monastic houses, for the monks could not travel from manor to manor to eat up the surpluses as did the magnates. Such a limitation occurred on the estates of Saint-Germain-des-Prés where, even in the ninth century, only 11·5 per cent of the total arable at Villemeux was under direct cultivation, as compared with 35·7 per cent at Palaiseau, and on many German monastic estates in the eleventh century the demesne holdings were only between 13 and 20 per cent of the total arable. We know that Suger, the twelfth-century abbot of St Denis, advocated and carried into effect a policy of deliberately reducing the size of the demesnes on his monastic estates by means of leasing. Thus the demands made for labour services upon the peasants varied according to their status, to the size of their holdings, to the

[1] E. Lipson, *The Economic History of England* (London, Black, 7th ed. 1937), vol. I, p. 14.

type of husbandry predominantly employed on the estate, to the region in which they lived, to the economic policy of the lord, to the strength of the central administration. All these variables changed over the five centuries between 1000 and 1500.

The regular burden of week-work, frequently, though by no means everywhere, consisting of three days' labour, was increased at certain times of the year, notably at harvest time, by the so-called boon works. Week-work became by the twelfth century one of the surest tests of villein tenure and, although in many places free tenements owed that service, the owners of free holdings often only performed boon works and such obligations as carting for the lord. In France, western Germany and England these labour services, in general, decreased in the later eleventh and twelfth centuries and in some areas, notably England, increased again in the thirteenth.[1] The demand for labour services was a direct reflection of the extent to which the demesne was or was not directly exploited by the land-owner. Perhaps the most important long term reason for the abandonment of domanial exploitation by labour services was the passive resistance put up by the peasants to working on the lord's *réserve*. Little direct evidence of this opposition is available before the thirteenth century but we know that the conversion of labour services to money dues, though it might primarily have been under-taken because it was economically beneficial to the lord in so far as he could obtain hired labour for less than the tax paid by the peasants to be free from the duties, was sometimes attributable to an element of passive resistance. In 1117 the abbot of Marmoutier in Alsace suppressed the week-work on the abbey's demesnes on account of 'the negligence, the uselessness, the slackness and the idleness of those who serve'.[2] This suppression was undoubtedly because of an excess of unskilled labour but also because that labour was slack and inefficient: the lord's steward (*villicus*) could not be everywhere in his supervision of the works. Secondly, the fragmen-tation of the manse made it more difficult for the lord to impose fully the services owing from the holding, just as the fragmentation of the demesne implied a diminishing need for labour services upon

---

[1] M. Postan, 'The chronology of labour services'.
[2] G. Duby, *Rural Economy and Country Life in the Medieval West,* trans. C. Postan (London, Edward Arnold, 1968), p. 207.

it. Moreover, the speed-up in ploughing made possible by more developed ploughs and better harness – the Île-de-France went over to the use of horses for ploughing *c.* 1200 – meant that work on the demesne could be done more quickly and hence fewer labour services were required. It was to the lord's advantage to obtain fixed payments in return for unwanted services and, at this same time in the twelfth century, the revival of trade and the expanding corn and wine market put money into the hands of peasants so that those desirous of avoiding the obligations of servile tenure had the where-withal to commute those services and, above all, to rid themselves of week-work.

This reduction in labour services was connected with a certain slacking of interest on the part of lords in the direct exploitation of the demesne in the twelfth century and a return of interest at the end of that century and in the succeeding one. This movement can be most clearly demonstrated in England. Economic and political factors cannot be separated – indeed, they are closely interdependent. The period from *c.* 1130 to *c.* 1175 in England saw many years in which unrest and disorder made it unprofitable for a lord to cultivate his demesnes directly, especially those at a considerable distance from his main residence. On the evidence of the prices paid for purchases for the king's court contained in the Pipe Rolls of the Exchequer, it would appear that prices differed widely from one region of England to another and this would argue imperfect interregional traffic. Such imperfection is not surprising when we consider the uncertainty of securing safe passage along the highways, at least in the middle years of the century, and this difficulty must have in-duced many lords to abandon the direct cultivation of their demesnes and to lease them out. Many twelfth-century documents testify to this leasing.

In the last quarter of the century, however, the beginning of a price rise, which continued well into the next century, made corn growing a much more profitable business than it had been during the previous fifty or more years. So lords took back the demesnes into their hands and accordingly, as wages rose, they demanded the labour services due from their tenants' holdings. This they could do in so far as the lords or their stewards had often merely sold the 'works', and in theory whether the tenant held *ad opus* or *ad censum* was at the lord's wish, although in practice it was virtually impossible to change the type of service after a period of time had elapsed. However, in the thirteenth century on many estates the process of commutation of labour services was stopped and on some it was reversed where the demesne husbandry was buoyant and where the lord therefore had need of additional labour, particularly for seasonal tasks such as ditching, carting and, above all, harvesting. On some estates, notably ecclesiastical ones,[1] attempts were made to redefine the labour services and to reimpose services upon those whose ancestors had converted them to mollands (lands held by rent service) and the king's court adjudicated on many cases concerning the obligations that attached to certain holdings.

Villagers sought to prove, usually unsuccessfully, that they held by money rents plus light services but they had a bad case in law, for many of the relaxations in the twelfth century had been 'illegal' in so far as they had been acquired without any formal charter of enfranchisement or manumission. So great was the land hunger of the thirteenth century that landlords were in a strong position to impose labour services upon pieces of land for which a queue of tenants existed. These movements of relaxation of labour services and of diminution in the direct exploitation of demesnes and the reversal of those trends may have their parallels on the Continent but they are most marked in England. Of course, in some regions of Europe demesne farming was buoyant in the thirteenth century, but in the main only on those demesnes where labour services had been retained or which had always been predominantly worked by hired labour; where demesnes had been diminished by trickery or by leasing, they were not built up again to the same extent as occurred in England.

Lords of manors exercised jurisdictional powers over their tenants and also over those in the neighbourhood who were not their tenants and these jurisdictional rights could be used to the economic advantage of the lord and to the disadvantage of the rural population. We have seen (Chapter 3) how lords obtained and used the *ban* (which was originally the right of the king and his representatives to judge, command and punish) to judge, command and punish on their own account. While the lord's economic demands upon his

---

[1] Those of the bishops of Worcester and Ely and of the abbey of Peterborough.

tenants were decreasing in the eleventh and twelfth centuries, his jurisdictional powers so far from declining in many ways grew stronger. For one thing the lords or their representatives, the *avoués* (lay stewards) on ecclesiastical lands were foremost in this respect, extended their authority to all on their estates whether they were their 'men' or tenants or not; for another, they extended it even beyond their estates to those who were under their protection. This jurisdictional right, first and foremost, involved the people of the countryside in the obligation to attend the manorial court and other courts which the lord might have and to be justiciable to them.

What other courts he might have depended upon what judicial powers had been delegated to him or his ancestors by the Crown or upon what powers he or they might have managed to assume over the years. We must distinguish clearly between the judicial rights of a lord as lord of the manor and his rights as the representative of royal power or as a substitute for the ancient public courts. In England the code known as the *Leges Henrici Primi* declared in the early twelfth century what was already a long established practice – that every lord was entitled to his own court. But also in England lords who had been granted a whole hundred (a division of the shire) acquired the public court known as the 'hundred court'. All infringements of the law that had previously been judicable in this public court were still tried in the hundred court but as a consequence of the grant it was in the hands of the lord. The twice-yearly view of frankpledge was frequently usurped by private lords, many of whom exercised leet jurisdiction; the residual jurisdiction in criminal matters, after more serious crimes had been reserved to the sole judgement of the Crown (although preliminary enquiry even into these took place in a 'court leet'), came into lords' hands. The 'court leet' was another court at which the people of the countryside were compelled to attend if they were between the ages of twelve and sixty years and before which they were justiciable. Magnates had baronial and honorial courts for their free tenants although these played a minor part after the legal reforms of Henry II gave freeholders a remedy in the king's court in disputes concerning their tenements. On the Continent the legal powers of landowners were more rigidly defined: some enjoyed powers of *haute justice*, some of *moyenne* and some of *basse justice*. The exercise of these varying judicial powers benefited lords in varying measure but the amercements or fines, as we should call them today, on occasion provided them with considerable revenues.

The use of the *ban* created, from the eleventh century onwards, a new type of *seigneurie*, known as *Bann* in German and *poesté* in French, and these rights of seignorial origin (*exactiones*) as distinct from those of tenurial obligation became increasingly important. New obligations were created which sprang basically from the seignorial authority of the lord and not from the fact that the tenants held their strips from a lord on certain conditions; so it came about that at the same time as labour services were diminishing new burdens fell upon the peasants. Some of the *banalités* have already been mentioned (see Chapter 3) but tallage and the creation of new *corvées*, such as carrying and mowing services, really sprang from the demands made by a lord in the exercise of his *ban*. Amercements for breaking the assize of ale, which were in theory punitive, were in fact regular licence fees for permission to brew, and chevage payments, payments for permission to marry off a daughter, pannage (a charge made to allow pigs to feed in the waste and woodland) and agistment (for the use of the lord's pasture for cattle) were all burdens that bore heavily upon tenants. In addition the 'capital' payments of 'heriot' – namely, the gift of the best beast of a deceased tenant – and the 'entry fine' made by the heir on taking up a holding were other onerous burdens. All these charges, together with 'pennies' and money rent, emerged in some degree from the exercise of the lord's *ban* rather than from the simple theory that a man was under obligation to work for his lord when he had granted his land to his superior and received it back again as a benefice.

In attempting to assess the burden that lay upon customary tenants, other obligations must not be overlooked. They had to pay 'church scot' and tithe. A full history of the origin and development of tithe has yet to be written, but we know that what started as voluntary contributions to the upkeep of the parish church grew into the heavy obligation of every tenth sheaf of corn, every tenth calf, lamb, chick and egg and a tenth of all wood cut. And many of these tithes were in the hands of laymen who refused to give them up even when the Gregorian reform movement gained sufficient strength to compel laymen to give up the actual churches;[1] other tithes were paid to large monastic houses which had appropriated the churches. Royal taxation, even although occasionally levied, added a further burden. Ecclesiastical and royal taxation fell, of course, on freeholders as well as upon customary tenants, as did many of the obligations arising out of the lord's exercise of his *ban*, but a customary tenant because of the villein incidents to which a freeholder was not subjected would want more land to maintain the same standard of living as his free neighbour. It has been estimated that the total charges upon a villein amounted to about 50 per cent of his gross output[2] and it has been cited in argument that leases *ad campi partem* frequently gave the lessor 50 per cent of the profits. The soil was, indeed, exploited in some places, at some times and for some peasants at very great cost to tenants and to the very great advantage of landlords.

Nevertheless, despite what might today be regarded as too generous a 'rake-off' for the landlords, they also faced at times severe problems. These arose frequently from the poor communications of the medieval period, which in turn caused difficulties in the control of distant estates. On these estates far from a monastery – for monastic houses, especially in the Low Countries and Germany, seemed to be the worst sufferers – the bailiffs (in Latin *villici* or *maiores*, in French *maires*, in German *Meier*) who had of necessity been put in charge by the lord, added pieces of the demesne land to their own *ex officio* holdings and their subordinates, provosts and foresters, emulated their example. These bailiffs who were forming and being assimilated into the class of *ministeriales*, whose holdings were *ex officio* and not true fees, were in effect filching land from their employers in considerable quantities between 1050 and 1200, for these stewards frequently took the manor house and a certain amount of land, paying to the lord only a quit-rent (*cens*). In theory they were managing the estate for their lord but in practice most of the benefits of its exploitation came to the *Meier* and the monastery eventually found that it had lost the usufruct of the land for an inadequate quit-rent.

Another way in which lords lost part of the demesne arose from

---

[1] G. Duby, op. cit., p. 213.
[2] M. M. Postan in *Cambridge Economic History of Europe* (2nd. ed.), I, p. 603.

the practice of cultivating part of the demesne not by week-work but by piece work (*riga* or *corvée aux pièces*). These pieces of the demesne, called *ansanges* in Lorraine and *petitorii iornales* along the lower Rhine, were tilled by the occupants of specific tenements who tended to convert them to tenements held on a quit-rent. In these various ways during the period from 1050 to 1200 pieces of the demesne were being removed from direct cultivation. In the same century and a half, parts of the demesne were lost by the creation out of it of small holdings for serfs whom the lord had originally supported and housed probably in his own courtyard or over his stables. The creation of these small holdings, known as *curtes* or *dominicales curtes* or as *Kot* in the Low Countries and *Haus* in Germany, reduced still further the acreage of demesne under direct cultivation. Unlike the policy of leasing, which was undertaken as part of a reorganization of the estate by lords such as the abbot of St Denis, these developments were accidental: lords did not intend to dismantle their demesnes, they were forced to it by difficulties that sprang either from inadequate supervision or from shortage of labour. Also among lay lords the division of estates among co-heirs, or more frequently among co-heiresses, led to the fragmenta-tion of the demesne and the break up of the *villa* or classical manor.

Having reviewed the heavy obligations upon tenants, especially upon customary tenants, and the difficulties that landlords might encounter, we must turn to a process, which, although it had its disadvantages, benefited all classes of society; the opening up of new lands to cultivation. Reclamation before the millennium was perhaps proportionally less in Europe than in England but from the eleventh century under the stimulus of growing population and of revived international exchanges great tracts of land were reclaimed.[1] Here again, as with other aspects of estate management, the timing of this reclamation varied from region to region. In Germany the twelfth century was the great age of *Urbarmachung*, which finished in the lands west of the Elbe *c.* 1250, but continued east of that river throughout the Middle Ages. In general the period between *c.* 1150 and *c.* 1325 saw large acreages of waste and forest land brought under the plough. Signs of this development have left their traces in place

---

[1] L. Génicot, 'On evidence of growth of population from the 11th to the thirteenth centuries'.

names all over Europe: Dutch names ending in *-rode* and French names ending in *-sart*, to say nothing of the 'Newtowns' and the 'Villeneuves', all point to expansion.

These reclamations, often undertaken by a lord who had waste going into partnership (*pariage*) with one who had capital, were hardly ever additions to the settled arable. The pieces taken in from the waste (assarts) were small enclosed holdings held by the tenant either for a money rent or on a *métayage*, that is a crop-sharing contract. Not only did the taking up of these assarts raise the status of the peasant, for they were free tenements, but the opportunities for settlement were so many that men might leave lands burdened by customary obligations, so forcing lords to lighten the burdens appurtenant to the old arable. In the eleventh century throughout the greater part of Europe the rural population, both serfs (*servi* in Latin, *Leibeigenen* in German) and non-serfs (*villani, hospites, manentes* in Latin, *Hörigen* in German) had restrictions placed upon the free disposal of their goods and persons, but under the counter-attraction of the new reclaimed lands lords were compelled to grant charters of enfranchisement called customs. Louis VI of France ceded the charter of Lorris whereby in the Gâtinais *chevage, main-morte* and *formariage* were abolished; in Normandy serfdom ceased to exist after the early twelfth century and in the districts around Paris and on the high, fertile plateau of Beauce it had disappeared before 1325. Grants of *villes neuves* and of *chartes lois* brought freedom to the peasants of the county of Hainault and serfdom (*Leibeigenschaft*) was on the decline in Germany between the eleventh and the thirteenth centuries. Those peasants living near large and growing towns could enrich themselves by the sale of surplus produce in the adjacent market and thus were in a position to purchase their freedom.

In England the reclamations of land in the twelfth and thirteenth centuries were only the end of a 600-year process of colonization which had already by that date brought under cultivation the cold heavy clays of south-east Leicestershire and west Northamptonshire, and those of the Weald, south Essex and the vale of the White Horse; they succeeded in settling the interior of Devon and Cornwall, in cultivating the eastern Cotswolds and the salt marshes of the west Midlands and north-west Staffordshire. The Crown made great profits by permitting assarts in the royal forests of Rockingham (Northamptonshire), Chippenham (Wiltshire), Sherwood (Nottinghamshire), Charnwood (Leicestershire) and Needwood (Staffordshire), and even the poor soil of the Breckland in Norfolk was brought under the plough. These reclamations for a time raised the status of the peasant and raised his standard of living until, in the thirteenth century, land hunger became so great that for a while reclamations merely kept pace with the growing population's demand for food and then failed even to do that, with a resultant marked fall in the standard of living of the small tenant. But just as they had initially benefited the tenants, so they were to the lords' advantage and they did not suffer from the insistent demand for land; on the contrary, they were the gainers. Although they did not enlarge their demesnes by the method of assarting, they did increase their incomes and as the land famine grew they were able to increase their entry fines or to shorten or alter the terms of leases to their advantage. The *Urbarmachung* helped to make landlords more rentiers and less lords. They had the power to relax terms in order to attract men to clear and cultivate forest and waste when many tempting baits of personal freedom and minimal obligations were laid before the settlers, or they could make harsher terms when economic conditions turned in the lords' favour as they did in most parts of Europe down to the last decade of the thirteenth century.

The warning that M. M. Postan has given with reference to England, about not attempting to assemble all the medieval agrarian institutions into a portmanteau model,[1] applies *a fortiori* to Europe as a whole. There are innumerable varieties of agrarian estates between the *Grundherrschaften*, manors where all the lands were let out to tenants and from which the lord received nothing but rents, and *Gutsherrschaften*, manors where all the land was in demesne which yielded all their revenue in the form of profits from domanial cultivation. The proportions and the manner in which these two elements combined varied regionally and in time. The degree to which a manor departed from the classical type depended also on the social structure of the inhabitants of the region or of their ancestors but it probably owed more to the type of landowner. The older Benedictine monasteries favoured the classical type of manor

[1] *Cambridge Economic History of Europe* (2nd ed.), I, p. 571.

because they were large families with need for food and fodder but on lay estates the large landowners with many manors tended to have smaller demesnes than the *agrarii milites* with one or two manors who lived off their own lands. Exceptions can indeed be found, but in general such knights had larger demesnes than did the magnates.

Another point at which the old model of the classical manor falls down is the realization of the falsity of the assumption that used to be made about the rough equality of holdings of the different groups. True it is that the bordiers and cottars held smaller holdings than the villein tenants, who might or might not be holders of a full virgate, and it seems likely that in the top layer of village tenants, that is to say those with two virgates or more (in many places 24 hectares or over), larger numbers of freemen than of villeins were to be found. But almost from the earliest records we find that, in England, families were rising and falling in the social scale by acquiring or by losing land, so that, by the time of the royal enquiry that produced the Hundred Rolls of 1279, large variations are evident in the size of holdings. This had occurred because not only freehold land was bought and sold but because villein land was also disposed of with (and sometimes without) the lord's permission. However, freeholdings underwent more rapid and thorough fragmentation because they were exposed to the action of the land market but even more because they were frequently subject to partible inheritance.[1] The intricacies of the rules of inheritance have not yet been exhaustively explored, but, whereas bond land had frequently to be left to a single heir, either the eldest or the youngest son, free land was usually divisible among all the heirs. We shall review later how this diversity in the size of holdings increased in the last 150 years or so of the Middle Ages, but already in the thirteenth century tenements varied from mere cottages to estates large enough to be regarded as submanors. That the peasant with the half virgate, say about 6 hectares, was the most characteristic of medieval England is an idealized notion based upon the assumption that the peasant was an occupying owner with a subsistence income; it would appear that the characteristic countryman was one with less than a quarter of a virgate who had to supplement his income by

[1] See B. Dodwell (ed.), *Feet of Fines for the County of Norfolk*, vols 27 and 32.

working for a lord or for the wealthier peasants or by undertaking various 'industrial' activities. At the other end of the scale, it would seem that many peasants were more interested in acquiring land than in purchasing their freedom, for, as in all peasant communities, a true appreciation that the fundamental thing was the size of the holding seems to have been firmly ingrained among the tenants in the top rank of village society. These wealthy peasants were not only buying land but they provided the money for smaller landowners to make purchases, for we have no record of men like the German *Wucher* or the French *usurier* operating in English villages; neither did the Jews or the Italians supply agrarian capital to small men.

The manor existed nearly all over Europe. It should not be implied from the considerable differences in estate organization between the lands to the south and those to the north of the Alps, between those to the east and those to the west of the Elbe, or between those on either side of the Pyrénéan divide, that unity existed in the areas of France, western Germany and England that we have already considered. But the differences between estate management in Italy and in eastern Europe as compared with the three countries already reviewed are greater than those within France, England and western Germany.

The history of the manor in Italy is far more closely bound up with the history of the growing towns than it is in other parts of Europe. In the late tenth and eleventh centuries land prices began to rise in Italy and this increased demand, which was obviously caused by a growing population and a heightened commercial activity, led to the improvement of lands and to widespread reclamation to provide new arable. Enterprising landlords reorganized their estates, and so great was the pressure upon the land that holdings were divided with consequent rural underemployment. Reclamation by the clearing of marshes and of scrub land was also under way, as the references to *essarta runci*, to canals and to irrigation works prove, and this movement is further attested by place names such as Ronco, Selva and Cortenuova. From the late twelfth century privileges to settlers *ad runcandum et laborandum* (to clear and to plough) exist in growing numbers. This was a great age of *défrichement* which continued into the fourteenth century and which despite its disastrous effect upon the woodland vastly expanded the arable. These assarts, as in other parts of Europe, were let out to individuals, and as early as 1118 the bishop of Asti granted land to the villagers of Vico for partition into lots (*sortes*) to be held for corn rents, and towns also undertook clearances and parcelled out the new land among families of free peasants. The manor with unfree peasants upon it was more unevenly spread in Italy than north of the Alps.

Great estates were formed by the Church in the eighth century, and records of the archbishop of Ravenna's estates at Padua demonstrate the existence of week-work as early as the mid sixth century, but by the 800s there were large numbers of dependent tenants known as *massarii, coloni, manentes* or *villani*. They were subject to manorial jurisdiction (*districtus*) and to restraints upon movement, upon the free disposal of their holdings and upon their choice of marriage partner, as were their like in France; in fact the Frankish descent into the peninsula must have helped to align their position with those of dependent tenants in other parts of the Carolingian Empire. But the manor was created in the north and a version of it existed in the south where cultivation by slave labour long persisted; in central Italy it appears never to have been known. But in Italy labour services were extremely rare; the typical charge upon the tenant was a rent in money or in kind.

The dependent tenant on an Italian manor was typically a leaseholder under a *libellus* or *livello*, which gave the grantee a tenure for a period of years, usually for twenty-nine years. Under this agreement he was compelled to reside and cultivate the soil and the landlord, who controlled the village economy to the extent of fixing the time of the corn harvest and vintage, sent round his agent to supervise the grantee's farming and he evicted him if he were negligent in his husbandry or if he failed to carry out his tenurial obligations. These obligations varied considerably; some owned plough oxen and performed ploughing works while others performed only manual services. As in Francia, servile tenants had holdings known as *case servile* while the free tenants (*commendati*) held *case massaricie,* sometimes performing only token duties. The manor in Italy showed signs of disintegrating very early; such signs of collapse are discernible even in the tenth century, but, in the eleventh, tenants became more difficult to obtain because they were flocking into the growing towns.

The construction of *castella*, small fortified towns, brought into existence a new type of tenant, the *castellani*, who were part peasant and part knight. They eventually became burgesses who held by rent service. As in parts of France, the period from 1050 to 1300 saw the decline of the manor. The great urban centres continued to attract serfs and others left for the small towns or *castra* with their mixed communities of peasants, tradesmen and craftsmen and, in the main, the lords let them go for they were busy reorganizing their estates and leasing them out on *métayage* arrangements. By 1300 the class of serfs had disappeared and the appellation *vilano* had taken on its modern meaning. The pace differed between the south and the north and the south was slower to end villeinage but it disappeared there also in time. Lords everywhere had recognized freedom of sale and free disposition of land as early as the twelfth century. In most ways the manor and serfdom went out earlier in Italy than anywhere else in Europe. The demesnes were no longer directly exploited; they were leased sometimes to the whole village community but more often to individuals and estates were exploited far more commercially than elsewhere: rents and sharecropping arrangements designedly gave the landlord a profit on assessed market prices of the various crops. This organization we would expect of the commercially minded Italians. But despite the wealth these methods gave to landlords, village organizations were strong and in Italy many of the *banalités*, which farther north benefited the lords, were run to the advantage of the village community as a whole and village life was regulated by codes of statutes. Many similar developments occurred, such as the disappearance of the *mansi*, which could be paralleled north of the Alps, but the main differences that stand out are the large numbers of *livellari*, the virtual absence of labour services and the sharecropping arrangements, the *mezzadria*.

Of the other Mediterranean country, Spain, little is known of the details of manorial cultivation. Slaves played an important part in the working of the ground and in the early fifteenth century an active market in humans existed in Catalonia. It would appear that most tenants paid rents in kind and that labour services were very light, only six days a year. The *banalités* were widespread. Serfs there were who were tied to the soil (*payeses de remensa*) and who complained of the evil customs (*malos usos*) whereby the lord took a third to a half of the peasant's land if he died intestate, but in general the impression is of much use of hired labour which was frequently remunerated in kind. Large areas of the country were devoted to livestock husbandry, especially to the rearing of sheep.

What of the manor in eastern Europe? The writing of its history in medieval Russia is severely hampered by lack of documentation. It is known that settlements were extremely small, often only four to six households. We know from an account of the monastery of Vladimir dated 1391 that their estates had tenants who performed labour services, threshing and making nets, but rents in kind were also paid and the slave labour force was an important factor. The enserfment of large numbers of the peasantry came very late, at a time when it had been abolished in western Europe. After the confiscation of Novgorod land in 1478 and the distribution of Tartar lands in 1480, grants of land were made on condition of performing labour services, and although the peasants opposed these additional burdens they could not easily move to other estates, and after 1497 they found themselves unable to leave the soil except during the week before and the week after St George's day.

Similarly in the lands east of the Elbe and in Schleswig servile tenure arrived late. Here in the fifteenth century the great landowners, the Prussian Junkers, were able to direct to their own advantage the obligations the population bore to the state. They were powerful enough to compel towns to return to their lords those who had escaped thither and in 1494 the Prussian Diet gave them authority to hang without trial fugitives from their estates. Economic circumstances in the shape of insistent demand from Holland for Baltic grain made demesne farming highly profitable and so tenants were turned out in order to enlarge the demesne and to enable the lords to form *Gutsherrschaften*. By the early sixteenth century conditions were so different in eastern and western Europe that a great divide was fixed between the methods of estate management and between the two forms of agrarian society in the two parts of the Continent. All this happened in a vast area where the manor and servile tenure had hitherto been virtually unknown, for in order to attract settlers they had been given holdings usually of two *Hufe* or about 32 hectares. These *Hufe* were heritable and only a quit-rent fell to the

G

lord; moreover, they could be sold provided the lord was given the first refusal. So it is apparent that wide variations existed between the lords and their tenants throughout Europe, but the predominance of manors and of dependent tenure, modified as both were over the centuries, was a salient feature of European agrarian society at its prime.

CHAPTER 15

Medieval Agrarian Society at its Zenith: the Working of the Land, Techniques and Crops

The manor and all that it involved profoundly influenced the pattern of agrarian society in all but a few regions of medieval Europe, but the trend of research in more recent years has been to look beyond tenurial relations, which occupied the attention of the founding fathers of economic history who were by training mostly legal historians, to the realities of soils and manure, of the types of plough and the shape of implements, of the crops and the balance of arable and livestock, and to the productivity of farming and the relative abundance or scarcity of food supplies. The interests of the economist and the agriculturalist now loom larger than those of the lawyer and the constitutional historian. The study of these aspects of medieval agrarian society is a more difficult task than the study of the manor because the documentary evidence facilitates the presenting of a study of the institution rather than the making of an assessment of crops and farming techniques.

It is true that the historian of medieval agrarian society no longer has to rely solely upon documentary evidence, for of late years aerial photography and archaeology have played an increasing part in supplying him with data about field patterns and abandoned settlements. Aerial reconnaissance during World War I produced innumerable photographs which interested scholars as well as soldiers and in the late 1920s O. G. S. Crawford and E. C. Curwen perfected and explained the techniques of taking photographs of the countryside, at certain times of the year and at certain times of the day when the correct shadows were cast, which showed up clearly the shape of earlier field systems and long disused roads and other features of the landscape as an X-ray photograph may reveal another painting beneath the one that is visible to the naked eye. This technique was an extension of the actual examination of the land which had been undertaken much earlier and upon which Seebohm had based many of his findings published in his pioneer work *The English Village Community* in 1883. The examination of lynchets on hillsides and of ridge and furrow in pasture land could give some indication of what lands had been cultivated and then abandoned or converted to other uses, just as the modern study of pollen analysis, which has developed in the last twenty years, has informed us about what crops were grown on a particular piece of land before it reverted to scrub or forest. Medieval archaeology, to which in England a special society with its own journal has been devoted since 1957, has done much to bring to light medieval implements and the ground plans of medieval farm buildings. But, important as all these techniques are, documentary evidence remains the most important source for the writing of medieval agrarian history for two reasons: these new types of evidence are difficult to interpret and as yet, and for the foreseeable future, they are less numerous than the considerable body of manuscript material.

This is not the place for an exhaustive survey of the documentary evidence upon which histories of medieval agrarian societies are based. English medieval sources in this sphere, as in so many others, are more numerous than those of continental countries. The documentation falls roughly into three categories: the corpus produced by central government, that produced which refers to the estates of a territorial magnate as a whole, and that produced locally on the manor itself. Royal surveys were not infrequently undertaken in the Middle Ages and their 'reports' in the form of such returns as the Domesday Book and the Hundred Rolls throw much light on agrarian society, although rather more on the institutional side than upon crops and techniques. Great lords had extensive surveys of their estates compiled; those of monasteries and bishoprics have mostly survived, from which some information on crops and techniques is obtainable. Such compilations as the Boldon Book of the lands of the bishop of Durham and the Domesday of St Paul's have contributed significantly to our knowledge in this respect, but the documents produced on the manor itself are of the greatest importance as source material from which the historian can reconstruct an account of some of the practical issues of medieval farming. In

England (the same is not true on the Continent) manors in general produced three types of document: surveys in the form of custumals or terriers, court rolls and account rolls. All these are useful sources, but the *compoti* drawn up year by year in which the bailiff rendered account of his stewardship usually contain details of the amount of corn and other crops sown and harvested thereby making some rough calculation of yields possible. Details of livestock are also recorded. The accounting period normally ended at Michaelmas and the bailiff was then called to account for rents, corn and stock and was given allowances for expenditure and for receipts which he had legitimately not been able to obtain. There was, so to speak, a fixed sum at which the account was supposed to balance so that even if a parcel of land was untenanted the rent was still regarded as due from the bailiff and an allowance had to be given him to reduce his liability. The dorse of the account roll frequently recorded the amount of seed corn and the number of animals purchased and also how much corn and how many animals had been sold. Using a terrier or survey, the historian can sometimes assess the acreage of demesne arable and so arrive at some estimate of the amount sown and the yield achieved. Terriers frequently provide evidence as to the number of fields and therefore offer a clue to the system of crop rotation.

Another documentary source and one that requires cautious treatment is the treatise on estate management. Several of these treatises were written in thirteenth-century England, of which Walter of Henley's *Husbandry* is perhaps the best known. In Europe Pietro de Crescenzia, a Bolognese who travelled widely through France, wrote a work, *The Twelve Books of Rural Economy*, which was translated from the original Latin into several vernaculars. These treatises either give an idealized picture of the rural economy of their day or they tend to repeat the nostrums of classical authors such as Varro and Columella; they are therefore unreliable guides to medieval agricultural practice.

As we shall see, the yield especially of some grains was minute compared with twentieth-century yields. Several reasons may be adduced to explain this; poor seed, inadequate working of the soil and above all lack of fertilizer. A poor balance between livestock and arable farming resulted in a chronic shortage of manure on much arable land throughout Europe in the Middle Ages. It is true that alternatives to farmyard manure, such as the application of seaweed on fields near the coast, green manuring, 'denshiring' – that is, burning the vegetation – and other methods of raising fertility were employed, but none of them was as effective a restorative of the land's fertility as a good dressing of manure would have been. As a result of this shortage, the arable land had to be kept fallow for considerable periods in order that it might regain heart. The same land could not support year after year cereals that took much nitrogen out of the soil unless yields were to become derisory.

Speaking in general terms the Middle Ages knew two methods for overcoming this exhaustion of the soil: intensive cultivation for a few years followed by a long spell of recuperation, a system called run-rig, or, alternatively, the regular resting of part of the arable every fourth, third or even every other year. It would be unwise to be more specific than to say that the former method of cultivation tended to be more common in the mountainous areas of scattered settlement while the latter predominated in the great plains and in districts of nucleated settlement, for many variations and combinations of the systems were prevalent. In the run-rig system all the manure which the community possessed was lavished upon an in-field which was cultivated intensively year after year, while the larger out-field, a clearing from the waste that was fertile because it was virgin soil and because the burnt wood and scrub made it even more fertile, was worked for a few years and then allowed to go back to scrub. On the great plain of northern Europe, however, and in the Midland plain of England, and indeed in other parts, the arable was commonly cultivated in large unhedged fields frequently divided into strips or furlongs and these vast fields would frequently be devoted to one crop then to another and then to fallow. The most prodigal use of the land was to allow half of it to lie waste every year – the so-called two-field system.

In the early Middle Ages, when the population of Europe was low and when, therefore, land was plentiful, and when means for adequate cultivation were limited, this two-field system was widespread although some evidence suggests that the arable was divided between winter grain, spring corn (*tramesium*) and fallow in Carolingian times on the lands of some abbeys between the Loire and the

Rhine. Twelfth-century documents suggest that the three-year course had been adopted in some fertile lands but that it could not always be maintained, and that peasants had some liberty in determining what sequence of crops they would grow and how often they would fallow their lands.[1] By the thirteenth century, however, the three-year course was becoming more widespread and the acreages devoted to winter-sown corn, to spring-sown crops and the fallow land were more nearly equal, although everywhere the nature of the soil and the demands of the lord either for wheat or for oats would influence the balance between the three. The classical 'three-field system' was much less common than scholars at one time supposed, and in some parts of Europe, even in England where landlords were keen to raise production, this desired goal of advanced farming was not reached until the fourteenth century. One of the great advantages of it was, of course, that it made more efficient use of the plough teams for their work could be spread more evenly over the year. Under the two-field system part of the field in cultivation had been devoted to spring-sown corn but with the three-year rotation and the more equable division in acreage between the three fields, ploughing could be more evenly spread.

If we devise what might be a typical annual work plan on a manor in champion country that is not to forget the innumerable variations which in fact occurred. On such a manor, in say 1300, which had three fields, field one having been sown with winter corn, wheat or rye at the end of September 1299, the plan of husbandry for 1300 would run along the following lines. In March, field two would be sown with the spring corn, either oats or barley, and then in May and June field three which was fallow would be ploughed. In August, earlier of course farther south than England, fields one and two would be reaped and at the end of the month or early in September the fallow would be ploughed for a second time and field two would be ploughed at the same time. At the end of September wheat or rye would be sown in field two and field one would be designated as fallow. The following year the spring corn would go into field three and field one would lie fallow, while in the third year of the cycle the spring corn would be sown in field

[1] G. Duby, *Rural Economy and Country Life in the Medieval West*, trans. C. Postan (London, Edward Arnold, 1968), pp. 93–4.

one and field two would be fallow. By 1303 the same fields would be sown with similar crops to those in 1300 and the rotation would thus have completed its course.

In some exceedingly fertile areas, known as one-year lands, a crop was taken annually from the soil; this happened invariably in parts of Norfolk and Suffolk but other areas were not fertile enough to bear crops even two years out of three and the great expansion in agricultural production between the eleventh and the early fourteenth centuries was more likely attributable to reclamations than to a diminution in the period of fallow. Indeed, it has been pointed out that in Alsace an abandonment of spring-sown corn occurred and agriculturalists there concentrated upon supplying the needs of the growing Rhineland towns for wheat which they grew on their two fields in alternate years.[1] But in some areas, with the introduction of more leguminous crops, a four-year course was emerging by the beginning of the fourteenth century. The open fields were widespread throughout Europe, whether an estate had two, three or even occasionally four of them. On many manors they were of considerable antiquity, for there has not been general support for the view that open fields with the obligatory rotation of crops and co-aration came only with the pasturing of animals on the post-harvest stubble when village wastelands had been ploughed up in the later thirteenth century. Examples of open fields in England certainly exist for the twelfth century and probably even earlier.[2] This pattern of the regular rotation of crops in different fields can be traced all over Europe, and in Italy both districts of open field and areas of enclosed arable produce examples. In parts of the peninsula where the arable was subject to common rotation, fallowing was enforced and frequently the arable was redistributed every year.

The increase in production from the land between the eleventh and the early fourteenth centuries, however brought about, was made necessary by the increasing number of mouths to be fed and made possible by more diligent cultivation. This better cultivation in turn resulted from improved implements and farming techniques. Judged by modern standards these improvements may well appear puny but the increasing use of iron after 1000 meant that many

[1] ibid., p. 97.
[2] M. M. Postan in *Cambridge Economic History of Europe*, I, pp. 572–3.

common agricultural implements, which had previously been made of wood, were from about that date made of metal and were therefore stronger and more durable; in this connection it must not be forgotten that some backward areas where the terrain was difficult hardly knew the plough. The growth in the number of rural blacksmiths manufacturing metal billhooks, saws, knives, scythes and ploughshares and their willingness to maintain the agricultural 'machinery' of the large landowners for an annual payment in corn testify to the increasing importance of metal tools. But it was the improvement in the plough and the more efficient way of harnessing animals to it that made more frequent cultivation of the arable possible, and the greater number of ploughings in turn influenced favourably the fertility of the soil.

The design of the plough perhaps did not change between the twelfth and the fifteenth centuries but experiments were made; in some areas wheels were added and probably everywhere the instrument became more robust. From the twelfth century the cutting edge of the share, even in backward areas, was reinforced with metal and the mouldboard came into wider use. The widespread adoption of the horse collar permitted horses to be harnessed to the plough instead of oxen, a change that occurred in the Paris region about 1200. Also more efficient use was made of oxen by the invention of the frontal yoke, probably in the eleventh century, for this harness gave them greater tractive power than the one previously employed which was attached to their horns. The shoeing of both horses and oxen added to their efficiency. Considerable controversy ranged among agricultural writers on the economics of using horses as against oxen, but undoubtedly the horse was a much speedier animal and equine ploughing allowed the work to be finished more quickly and in consequence more ploughing operations resulted. This greater number of ploughings undoubtedly increased the fertility of the soil and in so far as the horse population grew, a greater demand for oats arose. In some measure this may have effected a more even balance between the land devoted to winter-sown and that given over to spring-sown crops and to that extent facilitated the introduction of a three-year rotation. But not all regions went over to horses. In the Île-de-France, in the plains of Picardy and Flanders and in Lorraine horses replaced oxen but this was not so in Burgundy or in Mediterranean Europe generally where oats, the main fodder crop for horses, grew poorly. More intensive ploughing resulted from an increase in the number of draught animals which permitted more plough teams to be put to work in the fields: on nine manors of Ramsey Abbey the number of animals rose by 20 per cent to 30 per cent in the sixty years or so after the Domesday Survey. Moreover, the animals as a result of improved feeding and selective breeding may have been stronger. Another improvement in technique was the wider use of the harrow to cover sowings of seed, which operation helped to increase germination and to reduce loss.

Turning from a consideration of tools and ploughs to farming methods, we are made aware that our sources are scanty. Apart from the system of rotation of crops, attention was paid to marling and manuring, to terracing, irrigation and drainage. Marling, the practice of mixing light soils especially with a clay containing carbonate of lime, was well known and the obligation to dig and cart marl sometimes attached to peasant holdings. A chronic shortage of manure held down the yields of medieval agriculture and it is not surprising that those who exercised power in the countryside used it to secure the most plentiful supply possible. Tenants were compelled to fold their sheep and cattle on their lord's land, an obligation known in England as 'fold-soke', and lords usually had large flocks of their own, with the result that the demesne was frequently better nourished than the tenants' strips. A thirteenth-century English treatise recommended the mixing of dung with marl and demonstrated the benefit its application to sandy soil would effect. In mountainous country, terracing of the hillside to prevent wastage of soil was undertaken, and examples of this practice are to be found in Italy with the construction of embankments and of terraces retained by earth or stones.

Irrigation occurred in many parts of Europe and here again Italy probably led the way. Both pasture and arable were irrigated. The first record of a permanent water meadow, in a place near Milan, dates from 1138; by *c.* 1250 irrigation works existed in all districts north of the river Po and by the early fourteenth century had reached Parma, Modena and Bologna. At the close of the Middle Ages, the north Italian plain was the outstanding European example of successful irrigation. Water meadows existed also in France and in England and the rich crop of hay that they produced made them extremely valuable. Drainage of marshes added to the land suitable for cultivation and where applied improved land generally. But the method of ploughing up so that the middle of the strip was raised above the sides to permit drainage was not very satisfactory, for in wet years the sides of the slopes were waterlogged and in years of low rainfall the top of the ridge was dried out. Examples of hillside drainage occur in Italy, and in completely different terrain in eastern England the fen region was partially drained largely by the enterprise of village communities; and marshy areas of the Low Countries, particularly of the county of Holland, were converted to pasture or even brought under the plough.

Of more significance perhaps than improved techniques of working the land were the new methods of processing agricultural products made possible by the application of water and wind power. Flour mills operated by water power increased greatly in numbers in the twelfth and thirteenth centuries: by a stream in Rouen, two mills existed in the tenth century, five new ones were built in the twelfth century and ten more in the thirteenth. The abbot of Tavistock in Devon built water-powered mills in the twelfth century and many other examples could be cited. Moreover, water wheels could be used to work other machinery such as presses to extract oil, hammers for fulling cloth and flails for threshing. Another source of power, however, was being exploited from the twelfth century onwards, wind. Windmills are mentioned at Arles for the first time between 1162 and 1180 and at the very end of the twelfth century they appeared in Normandy, England and Flanders. This application of power, even in a simple way, freed manpower for other tasks in the countryside, tasks that helped to improve the productivity of farming. Man no longer had to grind his corn by hand and, indeed, the lord's *ban* frequently forbade him to use his hand-mills.

Before discussing any increase that might have taken place in the productivity of agricultural enterprises, we must first review what crops were cultivated. The grains remained in the main the same as at the earlier period (see Chapter 2), although the balance of one corn to another changed and some new crops emerged. Of course the climate and the soil remained the two basic factors governing the choice of crops grown. In Italy, for example, the leached soil and the summer heat were a constant threat to grain harvests and virtually prevented the growing of oats, but olives, almonds and figs could survive and do well under such conditions. On the other hand, in the far north, in Scandinavia, barley and rye had to be grown because of the lack of warmth and the excessive rainfall.

The demand for white bread, which grew in the Middle Ages especially among urban dwellers, led to an increased production of wheat in the last three medieval centuries. The soft varieties were found everywhere but the hard (*Triticum durum*) grew only in southern Europe and, as it was not very satisfactory for bread, it was probably used in Italy for the making of pasta as early as 1300. Also in Italy grew two husked varieties, spelt in the north and emmer in the south of the peninsula. But white bread was not the staple diet of the rural population of Europe in the Middle Ages, for rustics had to live on black bread made from rye or on bread made from a mixed corn, maslin – if, indeed, their staple was not porridge or gruel. In many parts of Europe peasants grew wheat for sale on the market while they themselves subsisted on rye or maslin, and frequently land that would have produced a better crop of rye was devoted to wheat because of the lords' and the townspeople's demand for the latter grain and because of the peasants' necessity to have money for the purchase of essential implements and for tax payments. The bread grains, rye and wheat (although in fact bread was made from almost anything including beans on occasion), were normally sown in the autumn and the drink grains and horse fodder, barley and oats, in the spring. Barley had been a widely grown grain in Carolingian times but it appears to have lost its popularity in later centuries, until at the close of the fourteenth and in the fifteenth century more land may have been given to it, as some evidence suggests an increased consumption of ale and beer at that period. The regions from which grain was obtained in large quantities changed also. In the eleventh and twelfth centuries northern France had been the bread basket of districts that could not indigenously meet their demands but from the late thirteenth century onwards the new lands of eastern Europe, the prairies of the later

Middle Ages, provided 'industrialized' regions with bread corns at low prices. The trade in corn undertaken mostly by the Hollanders in the fourteenth and fifteenth centuries was of vast proportions. The yield of oats was outstandingly poor throughout the whole of the medieval period, but with the increasing number of horses, both for use as draught animals and beasts of burden and for bearing knights to combat, more oats had to be grown, although in the Mediterranean region so difficult was it to prevent oats drying out that horses fed on barley. Other grains such as sorghum, first mentioned in the ninth century, and buckwheat, called in Italian *grano saraceno*, were grown in the lands around the Mediterranean although the latter did not appear in Italy until the fifteenth century.

Perhaps the outstanding change that took place in the pattern of cultivation from *c.* 1200 onwards was the increasing acreage assigned to the *leguminosae*. Peas, beans and vetches played an important part in human diet but a more significant role as animal fodder and they were also of vital importance as green manure. After they had been fed to the animals or after the animals had grazed off the plants they were dug in and thus provided a useful source of nitrogenous fertilizer. The range of vegetables grown undoubtedly expanded in the later Middle Ages and peasants put all their available manure on their tofts to produce herbs and vegetables. Master John Gardener, who probably came from Kent, writing about 1450 mentioned vegetables such as leeks, lettuce, onions, spinach, kale and cabbage, and as herbs he named among others mint, camomile, fennel, garlic, parsley, rue, sage and thyme. This concentration on legumes allowed some lands in Tuscany to grow pulses and wheat in alternate years with only a few months fallow in between during which time intensive ploughing and digging restored the land. Another important change was the increased growing of 'industrial' crops, above all of dyestuffs. As the textile industry advanced, the dyeing process required more and more woad, weld, madder and saffron and the finishing required more and more teasels. Lombardy produced massive quantities of woad, as did certain areas in the Low Countries. Although not so localized, fruit growing was concentrated in well-defined areas: apples in Normandy and parts of England, grapes for wine making in France, western Germany, Italy and Spain, and almost everywhere in Europe pears, peaches, cherries and medlars.

These fruits entered hardly at all into trade exchanges but nuts, particularly almonds, were exported from southern Italy.

In addition to sorghum and buckwheat other new crops which were even more important were introduced into the Mediterranean region; rice, sugar cane, cotton and mulberry trees. Either the Greeks in the sixth century or the Arabs in the tenth introduced them. Citrus fruits, lemons and bitter oranges, were brought to the south of the peninsula and tended to spread to the north where sweet oranges and other citrus were found around Lake Garda in the thirteenth century, and rice and even a little sugar cane appeared in the Lombardy plain. New varieties of vine were developed during the Middle Ages, the *trebbiano* in Tuscany, the *vernaccia* in Liguria and the *schiava* in the Po valley, and concentration upon wine production was such that Italian wines entered the export trade. In France most of the areas that today make the best wines were developed in the medieval period.

What was the effect of the advances, limited as they were, in agricultural implements and techniques? Did the introduction of new crops or new varieties and the development of more complex rotation systems make much improvement in the productivity of farming? The answer to these questions must undeniably be that these advances did not raise the level of yields very high. Columella had said that the yield of increase for Italy as a whole was about four times;[1] the earliest direct information on southern Italy dating from *c.* 1550 suggests that a normal harvest was ten times, a poor one eight, and a good yield twelve. However, these figures come from a very fertile area and it has been suggested that in other districts the average yield might only have been three to six times. Certainly the yield varied from one corn to another. Oats, a poor yielder, perhaps never gave an increase of more than six to one and documents from a Ramsey abbey manor show that on occasion the harvest barely exceeded the amount which had been sown.[2] Wheat yielded much better and returns from very fertile land have been recorded which match those from poor lands today, reaching fifteen to one in Artois, yet no English yield approached that figure. The English thirteenth-century agricultural treatises state an increase of eight for barley,

[1] See P. Jones, in *Cambridge Economic History of Europe*, I, p. 377.
[2] G. Duby, op. cit. pp. 99, 100.

seven for rye, six for *leguminosae*, five for wheat and four for oats, but it is difficult always to know what is being taken into account in the calculation – whether, for example, payments out of corn have been made. The returns from the well cultivated lands of the bishop of Winchester over a span of two and a half centuries from 1200 demonstrate that the figures of the treatises are over-optimistic. Wheat and barley yielded 3·8 to one and oats only 2·4 to one. The figures indicate a decline in yields on the Winchester estates in the second half of the thirteenth century, which may reflect a growing imbalance between arable and livestock farming, followed by a recovery when the average yield of wheat rose from 4·22 grains to one in the period 1300 to 1349, to 4·35 between 1350 and 1399 and to 4·45 in the following fifty years.

This improvement in yields, it has been argued by some economic historians, was the result of the abandonment of marginal lands which had been pressed into use during the land hunger of the thirteenth century, but M. M. Postan has cast doubt upon this interpretation by pointing out that the data come from Winchester demesne lands which had excellent cultivation and the best available supplies of manure.[1] He argues, probably quite correctly, that we cannot postulate a general increase in yields in England in the later Middle Ages. It is demonstrable that productivity varied enormously from place to place and from year to year but it can be said with tolerable certainty that yields were as high in the later medieval period as they were at any time before the agricultural revolution of the nineteenth century. The present-day yields of twenty to one or more were unknown in the period under review, but so were they in the first decades of the last century; this shows that the technical level of medieval farming was not improved upon until the nineteenth century. Nevertheless, the thirteenth-century yields were immensely better than those of Carolingian times and Walter of Henley's view that a three-fold increase was essential for the peasant and his family to survive was a level that was usually reached, and anything over that was available for sale on the market. However, that should not blind us to the fact that population pressure in the 1200s and the early 1300s was very severe, particularly in England, which had a rural population probably as great as it was in

[1] In *Cambridge Economic History of Europe*, I, p. 557.

the early eighteenth century, and that as a result of this pressure a sizeable proportion of the people was living on the margin of starvation. This in turn has been adduced as one of the causes of high mortality in years of bad harvests.

It was the demographic catastrophe coupled with the probably slightly improved yields that permitted a higher standard of living to the peasant. More meat and more dairy produce entered into his diet and some switches in consumer preference can be noted from the evidence of prices. In the main the diet of the later fourteenth- and fifteenth-century peasant, in many areas of Europe and notably in England, contained less bread, more peas and beans, butter and cheese and more meat, of which beef comprised an increasing and pork a diminishing part. In conclusion, despite the slowness of progress in arable and livestock farming, despite the disastrous crop failures and attacks of murrain, and in the absence of any far-reaching technological inventions, medieval agriculture succeeded, once the population explosion of the twelfth and thirteenth centuries had exhausted itself, in securing a higher standard of living to a greater proportion of the population in the late fourteenth and fifteenth centuries than it had previously done. To some extent the wealth was more equitably shared. This achievement of medieval farming was secured in the main by hard working of the soil, for medieval farming was labour-intensive rather than capital-intensive and aided by more efficient management of which the treatises on accounting are a sign.

CHAPTER 16

Decline and Change:
Rebirth and New Horizons

While the temptation to attribute all the changes in the economy and social structure of Europe in the second half of the fourteenth century and throughout the fifteenth century to the attacks of the plague must be resisted, it is undeniable that the Black Death and the demographic *sequelae* of it had a deep, far-reaching and long-lasting effect. The plague, which was carried by fleas whose host was the black rat, was of two types – the bubonic and the more deadly pneumonic – and it arrived in Europe in 1348 by way of the Levantine ports. Everywhere mortality was heavy but some areas of Europe escaped more lightly than others.

Statistical data upon which the demographer can base estimates of the population of Europe in the Middle Ages are generally highly unsatisfactory, since, with the exception of a few Continental town surveys, nothing in the form of a modern census was taken and consequently the researcher has to add a figure to cover categories that are not included in the survey, tax list or other type of return. The English Poll-tax lists well illustrate this difficulty, for here a hypothetical figure must be added to cover the children and the indigent who were not taxed, but an even more frequently found difficulty is the one arising from the conversion of heads of households into total population figures. So many medieval returns (Domesday Book is an outstanding example) list heads of households or landowners and the problem then arises as to what the multiplier should be: estimates for Domesday have ranged from three and a half to five times and various scholars have advanced opinions with more or less statistical backing to substantiate their arguments. J. C. Russell attempted to show that three and a half was a better figure as a multiplier than five on the grounds that if the latter figure were taken then only a third of the men would have been house-holders and that the average age of entry to their inheritance would have been between thirty and thirty-three years,[1] whereas according to the data recorded in the Inquisitions *post mortem*, surveys made on the death of a tenant of some note, the average age for succession was twenty-two to twenty-five years. But his calculations were based on a very small number of tenants who had inquisitions taken at their death and his figure has been seriously challenged by many, notably by J. T. Krause.[2]

The result of much labour in the field of demographic history is to leave us, in many ways, less certain than we were about the total size of the European population in the Middle Ages. In fact it is now realized that no figure that commands much respect can be arrived at, but that all the demographer can do is to indicate the trend; and the trend has more significance for the economic and social historian than the gross population figure. J. C. Russell argued for a rise in the population of England from 1·75 million in 1086 to 3·7 million in 1348, followed by a decline by 1377 to 2·2 million and a low of 2·1 million in the first decade of the fifteenth century, but most histori-ans are now inclined to think these figures too low and the highest estimate for 1348 is nearly 7 million; the possible variants in working out these estimates are so great that the exercise perhaps ought not be undertaken. But all are agreed on a steady rise in the population of England, at least until the 1320s, and a dramatic fall between 1348 and the early fifteenth century. Estimates have been made and repeatedly revised as to the mortality caused by the plague attack of 1348–50 in England and the most recent suggestion is that one third of the population died from the disease.[3] Attempts have also been made to assess the percentage of deaths to the total numbers in various age groups and to build theories on this analysis. It would appear that in 1348–50 perhaps only a fifth of those in the 25–30 age group died and it has been argued therefore that many of the survivors were able to enter into their inheritances at an earlier age and to marry (it seems that marriage rarely preceded entry into a

[1] *British Medieval Population* (Albuquerque, University of New Mexico Press, 1948).
[2] J. T. Krause, 'The medieval household: large or small?', *Econ. Hist. Review*, 2nd ser. IX (1957), 420–32.
[3] M. M. Postan in *Cambridge Economic History of Europe*, I, p. 569.

holding) and consequently to produce offspring to help correct the high mortality. In 1361, however, children seem to have been the principal victims; indeed the *Anonimalle Chronicle* refers to the outbreak as the 'children's pestilence' and two further epidemics in 1369 and 1375 took a heavy toll of the reduced population. Thereafter the disease became endemic in England until 1665.

On the Continent the plague also reduced population. Evidence about urban centres shows that few new towns were established in contradistinction to the urban growth of the twelfth and thirteenth centuries, and a decline occurred in the size of towns of which Toulouse affords a striking example: from about 30,000 in 1335 its population fell to 26,000 in 1385, 20,700 in 1398, 19,000 in 1405 and 8000 in 1430. Between 1346 and 1440–70 the population of the Île-de-France fell by a half and expansion ceased in the colonized lands of eastern Europe. On the other hand the population of the Tyrol rose by 50 per cent between 1312 and 1427, but this was not because of the absence of plague (although its incidence there may have been less severe) but because of the attractive employments offered by an expanding mining industry. Also the countryside of northern and central Italy appears to have filled up and this seems to have been attributable to a light visitation of the plague. Aragon and Lithuania escaped the worst rigours of the disease and if we judge upon the forest clearings that went on in Sussex and the Haut-Dauphiné, although such evidence is liable to several interpretations, it would appear that the population there was not too adversely affected.

Historians have ceased to attribute all the economic and social ills of the closing years of the Middle Ages to the Black Death because research has shown other causal factors at work. There is good evidence for thinking that the population explosion which probably started in the eleventh century was dying down before the arrival of the plague. In England, by using manorial surveys, which were mostly made on monastic estates, and comparing them with the returns of Domesday Book, it would appear that the rate of increase began to slow down certainly in the early fourteenth century if not a little before. Whether in England and in Europe generally the three famine years of 1314–17 were a watershed or not will perhaps never be ascertained but the second and third decades of the fourteenth century showed a down-turn in economic activity.

To judge from corn prices, demand after 1325 was not outrunning supply to the extent that it had previously done when population pressure on the food resources had been enormous. Price evidence may not be an infallible guide as to what was happening but it could be that such a large number had been killed by the famine that the labour force began to shrink, and a slight rise in wages at this period tends to confirm such a hypothesis. Catalonia, Scotland and Sweden seem to be exceptions, for in these countries the population increase appears to have continued until 1348, but almost everywhere else it seems to have ended between 1310 and 1320. Large landowners at this same period appear to have lost interest in the development of their estates, and families which throughout the thirteenth century had been adding acre to acre ceased to expand further and began to withdraw from direct cultivation of the demesne.

Another cause of the down-turn in some parts of Europe may have been the worsening climate of the fourteenth century, which had a delererious effect upon harvests and which completely prevented the cultivation of some crops. Meteorological statistics do not exist for the fourteenth century but from chronicle and other sources it is known that more summers had inadequate sunshine levels and increased rainfall and that temperatures were lower than in the preceding century. The results of these climatic changes were far-reaching; grapes which had been cultivated easily in southern England and northern Germany were no longer grown there. Wheat, judging by its violent price fluctuations, seems to have been more affected than barley, rye or oats by bad weather conditions and it is interesting to note that towns on the coast returned steadier prices, since they could be more easily supplied by ship. Forests in Europe could no longer be sustained to as great an altitude as previously and settlements in Greenland which had been able to supply themselves with grain first retreated southwards and in the fifteenth century were completely abandoned.

The increased taxation of the fourteenth century, mostly for war purposes, and the greater expenditure of the landowning classes on arms and the raising of armed bands ('bastard feudalism') decreased the money available for investment in land or for farming improvements. Neither did the clergy escape higher taxation, for not only were they more and more subject to the exactions of the state but papal levies were raised in the fourteenth century and they became especially severe during the papal residence at Avignon and during the Great Schism. The result of this inability or unwillingness to cultivate estates was a policy of leasing part or all of the demesne which was a growing practice even before the advent of the plague.

The full effect of increased taxation upon economic activity needs further investigation. Rising prices, administrative expansion and the decay of unpaid services, especially in the military sphere, had caused a steady rise in royal expenditure throughout Europe in the thirteenth century, but in the following 100 years the normal revenues of the Crown both in France and in England became quite inadequate. The receipts from the royal domain, from forests, from the profits of justice, markets and ecclesiastical patronage did not suffice to provide for the increased royal expenditure. Hence in England a national customs system had to be devised. The 'Great and Ancient Custom', as it was called, levied export duties on wool, wool fells and hides from 1275 onwards and in 1303 additional export and import tolls were paid by foreign merchants. In France, Philip IV raised money by taxes on income from property or chattels and introduced the hearth tax. Edward I was voted grants by Parliament known as the tenth and fifteenth and Philip IV also levied subsidies. Gradually these extraordinary levies came to overshadow the ordinary income from the hereditary revenues of the Crown so that in the tax year 1374–5 when Edward III received *in toto* £112,000, only £22,000 came from the traditional royal revenue and £82,000 from direct and indirect taxation. The remainder was derived from borrowing. In England this extraordinary income had to be sanctioned by Parliament and, in effect, by the House of Commons; in France this was not so. Charles V (1364–80) laid down the basis of the French financial system which allowed the Crown to levy the *taille*, a direct tax paid by non-nobles only in the north and centre of the country and levied on non-noble property in the south. Also he had *aides*, an internal sales tax, and the *gabelle*, the proceeds of the royal monopoly of the salt trade. All these were levied without the consent of the Estates. Because the nobles and the clergy were not liable to this taxation, opposition to it was leaderless.

Despite the vast increase of royal taxation in the later thirteenth and fourteenth centuries, monarchs were still short of money and much recourse was had to borrowing. The Italian bankers, especially the Riccardi and the Frescobaldi in England, religious orders such as the Templars and cities and native businessmen stepped in to loan money to various sovereigns. Towards the end of the fourteenth century, lenders were less forthcoming and some resort had to be made – more in France than in England – to forced loans. In the following century in England borrowing became still more difficult and under Henry VI a collapse in royal finances occurred. The demands of the monarchy, and especially of the kings of England and France, from the end of the thirteenth century were onerous and it has been suggested that the fall in the value of land in Normandy at this period was possibly due to heavy taxation. The slowing down of the economy from the early fourteenth century may have fiscal causes. The result of heavier taxation and of borrowing may have been to divert capital away from productive uses and from estate development several decades before 1348.

The results of the Black Death upon agrarian society were an intensification of those movements that had already been manifesting themselves in the previous twenty or thirty years. This is not surprising because if we can postulate that some of the changes were the result of a slackening of the population increase then the phenomenal population decline that took place after 1348 could only intensify the processes already in train. Let us look first at the effects upon the upper echelons of society, the large landowners – by which is implied in this context the holders of a manor and above. As a result of the high mortality a dearth of tenants occurred, which meant that many of the customary lands on the estate could not be cultivated, and in order to attract tenants to the land the lords had to concede more favourable terms: hence the policy of leasing spread from the demesne to the tenants' lands. The terms of the leases became increasingly favourable to the lessees and rents began to fall. The landowning classes were not too severely affected: before the 1370s rents seem to have kept up reasonably well and an adequate supply of tenants continued. This was probably caused by the absorption as tenants of large numbers of landless peasants and of those who had previously possessed inadequate holdings, but when those tenants who had been able to obtain holdings as a result of the high mortality of 1348–50 themselves began to die, many of them without heirs in the 1370s and 1380s, landlords found it more difficult to get their lands cultivated. Customary holdings were freed from the obligations that had formerly pertained to them and the services were commuted for small annual payments.

The process of commutation and above all its timing have been much disputed among historians but it is quite clear that the practice of substituting money payments for labour services did not commence with the Black Death. It was legally possible for the bailiff to retain or sell the works year by year as the demands of the demesne farm required, but in practice when the works had been relaxed for a number of years at a fixed rent it became virtually impossible either to reimpose the works or to increase the money payment *in lieu*. Very few years established a custom 'time out of mind' in the Middle Ages and any going back on it would have been met by the combined hostility of the peasantry. The most general consensus would appear to be that commutation was going on at all periods but that, in England, the process was speeded up by the Black Death so that villein tenure more or less disappeared in the fifteenth century. In other areas of Europe, however, villein tenure had disappeared much earlier, in some districts round Paris and in Normandy in the early twelfth century and in the Île-de-France and Beauce by the end of the thirteenth century.

The results of the Black Death were different upon different groups of landowners. The great landowners with hundreds of manors, the great honorial complexes of which the de Lacy and Lancaster estates were outstanding English examples, were not affected in the same way as the holders of a single manor with a demesne of perhaps 40 to 120 hectares. The large landlords were already, even before 1348 rentiers, the principal part of whose income was derived from rents, leases, the profits of courts and other incidents of feudal lordship, while the small ones in order to feed their own families continued to farm their demesnes directly and obtained little from rents and less from the profits of lordship or franchisal courts, for their jurisdictional powers were limited or non-existent. The former faced the problem of declining rents after the 1370s, the latter faced the problem of inadequate services on their demesnes and of high wages for hired labour. Wage legislation was passed by a House of Commons avowedly interested in those who '*vivent par geynerie de lour Terre e que nont seigneurie ne villeins par eix servir*'. Thirty years or so after the first attack of the plague the great lords were hit by vacant lands and reduced rents. In an effort to meet that situation, leasing became more common, the great monastic house of Ramsey started about 1370 to lease out manors previously held in demesne and by 1390 all of them had been leased. Lords followed a variety of policies. Some leased the entire demesne to one lessee while others divided it into small parcels and leased these to peasants. The former action was easier when the demesne had been to some extent consolidated and was not entirely in scattered strips commingled with the peasants' holdings. At first, landlords leased stock with the tenement, the so-called 'stock and land lease', but such arrangements were usually for a short term of years and were abandoned as the duration of leases became longer. In the fifteenth century, as tenants became increasingly difficult to find, leases for twelve, twenty and forty years were common and Chertsey Abbey granted leases for 99, 200 and even 300 years.

Rents were at the same time manifesting a severe downward trend. In the 1390s the Duke of Lancaster's council caused an enquiry to be made into the Duke's declining income from land. The manor of Leeds on the Duchy estates has left two rentals, one of 1400 and another of 1425, which illustrate how rents declined between 33·5 and 55·5 per cent over the figures obtaining in the 1380s. In Leicestershire some rents fell by a quarter between 1408 and 1477 and the average rent of $10\frac{3}{4}d.$ for an acre (0·4 hectare) of land at Forncett (Norfolk) in 1376–8 dropped to $6\frac{1}{4}d.$ between 1451 and 1460 and before 1500 never rose above 8*d.*

The decline in population, which the Black Death and the endemic nature of the plague together caused, led to a reversal of the thirteenth-century position. From the 1380s at the latest there was a surplus of land and a dearth of people to cultivate it. Hence much land went out of production. The *Wüstungen* of Germany and the deserted villages of England could be matched, although perhaps not so vividly, in other parts of Europe. In England nearly 1500 of these abandoned sites have been identified[1] and in Germany nearly a

[1] M. Beresford, *The Lost Villages of England*, and the Annual Reports of the Deserted Medieval Village Research Group.

quarter of the places inhabited in 1300 had disappeared by 1500. But the desertion was not only due to declining population (in fact relatively few deserted village sites appear to date immediately after 1348–50) but also to a change in land use. As rents for arable land continued to sag in the wake of stagnant corn prices, some landlords decided to convert the arable to pasture and to concentrate upon livestock production, for rents for meadow and pasture land did not fall to the same degree. The reason for the maintenance of these rents is to be found in the firm prices for meat and dairy products and the well maintained demand for English wool, which increased after the mid fifteenth century. Moreover, livestock and particularly sheep farming permitted a reduction in labour costs which appealed to landlords at a time when wages were rising and so, on those grounds also, enclosure and conversion of arable to pasture made sense to them. Such a policy was easily carried out where all or nearly all the inhabitants had disappeared and the land had reverted to the lord and it was not difficult to come to some agreement with those who remained. The height of the enclosure and conversion movement was reached in England between 1450 and 1485 and was specially prevalent in the areas of the champion country where the soil was as suitable for grass as for cereals – in particular in Lincolnshire, Leicestershire and Warwickshire and in the North and East Ridings of Yorkshire.

The results of the Black Death may well have been to alter the relative wealth and economic power of the whole class of landowners or of certain groups within it, to bring about a morphological change as contrasted with a metabolic change. The supporters of the metabolic change argue that the balance of economic power between the greater and smaller families (magnates and gentry) was more or less constant and that change was limited to the replacement of some great families by others, while the protagonists of morphological change assert that one group rose at the expense of another. The latter theory seems to fit the fifteenth century better, for the smaller men, whose labour costs were lower, who could live off their own demesnes and who were often the beneficiaries of 'bastard feudalism', were probably in a relatively better economic position *vis-à-vis* the magnates than they had been two centuries earlier.

However that may be, clear gain is demonstrable for the peasant farmers who acquired by purchase either customary or freehold land or who leased part of the demesne. Although here again the movement did not start at the time of the Black Death, the last century and a half of the medieval epoch saw a growing disparity in the size of holdings between one peasant and another. Many examples demonstrate that enterprising peasants took on more land; sometimes they sublet part of their own customary holding and leased a greater acreage elsewhere and it would appear that they had clear ideas about the size of holding that was most profitable to cultivate. The Randolffs of Wigston (Leicestershire) had built up an estate of 60 hectares by 1450; at Neufbourg the percentages of those in the total population holding 1·5–2, 2–4, 4–8 and over 8 hectares rose, while the percentage holding less than 1·5–2 hectares fell; and at Weedon Beck (Northamptonshire) there is some evidence that the number of those with large holdings had increased between 1248 and 1365. These thrusting farmers prospered mainly by increasing the size of their holdings but also through hard work, and success often depended upon a strong, healthy, vigorous and cohesive family which would exploit the land keeping labour costs to a minimum, although it is true that many of these men were able to employ landless labourers. These 'kulaks' of the later medieval agrarian scene were on the way to becoming the gentry of the late fifteenth, sixteenth and seventeenth centuries. Social promotion was typical of the period.

The lower classes in the countryside also benefited from the consequences of the Black Death. In fact the smallholders and the landless men profited perhaps more than any other group, for those with under 2·5 hectares, many of whom had had insufficient land to maintain their families, were in a position to acquire more and the landless benefited from the high wages and were often able to obtain some land. So short was labour that wages immediately after the attack of 1348–50 soared and in England statutory control at the pre-1348 levels resulted from the Ordinance and then the Statute of Labourers of 1351. Although not completely able to overcome the iron law of supply and demand, the act was not a dead letter, for the justices of labourers followed later by the justices of the peace did their best to enforce it; nevertheless, wages rose from two to two and a half times and when, in the following century, further legislation was passed, Parliament, recognizing the upward trend, set higher maxima in 1496-7 than it had done in 1447. Moreover, the maximum for wages was not observed. Another feature was the decrease in the differential between the wages of skilled and unskilled workers, a sure sign of labour shortage. But it was from steady and in some instances declining prices that wage earners gained more than through higher wages. Because of the inelasticity of demand for grains, prices fell more than proportionately to the excess of grain and so, for some corns and in some places – and the regional differences must be stressed – during several decades of the fifteenth century the price was only about 50 to 60 per cent of the average prices in 1401-10.[1] Wages on the other hand at the time of low corn prices hardly diminished, and hence the rise in the standard of living of many wage earners, in real terms, has been calculated at about 250 per cent. To what extent heavier state taxation fell upon the labourer is a factor that has not yet been thoroughly investigated; neither has the way in which he spent his increased income. This income was often considerable for it has been estimated that a plough-man's or a carter's wage plus the earnings of his wife and son would have been equivalent to the profits from the cultivation of an 8 hectare holding.

Despite or perhaps because of this considerable increase in living standards, the European peasant was not satisfied. While in large areas of Europe he had been freed from the tenurial burdens of villein tenure by commutation, he was not always free from the incidents that imposed upon him a social stigma. The peasants' objection to payments such as *formariage* or *leyrwite* or for permission for their sons to take Holy Orders sprang from the fact that these were galling reminders to many of them of their unfree status and their grievances must have been intensified by the fact that conditions were so varied. Such dues were enforced in one place while in another only a few kilometres away they were not, and those who were serfs of great monastic houses often bore the heaviest burdens. In Switzerland villeinage disappeared as a result of the struggle for national independence while in parts of France serfdom was attached firmly to the holding, the *servage réel* or 'serfdom of the air'. This

[1] L. Génicot in *Cambridge Economic History of Europe*, I, p. 684 ff.

occurred in Laon, Champagne, certain parts of Burgundy, Franche-Comté and Nivernais. While in the district of Entre-deux-Mers serfdom was virtually non-existent, in the neighbouring Médoc it was widespread. In Franconia serfdom was being abolished before the Black Death and the Count of Namur renounced all his rights over serfs, while in eastern Europe many were being enserfed. It would appear in England, however, that peasants spent their money on purchasing more land – for, as in most peasant societies, they realized that land was the most important asset – rather than on purchasing their freedom, but that does not imply that the incidents of villein tenure were not irksome to them. Royal taxation they vigorously opposed.

So the fourteenth and fifteenth centuries, although Scotland and Poland avoided them, saw many peasant risings, from Flanders in 1310 to the Jacquerie in France in 1358 and the Peasants' Revolt in England in 1381, to name only the more important uprisings. The egalitarian doctrines expressed by John Ball and others ('When Adam delved and Eve span, who was then the gentleman?') were indicative of peasant feelings about a society that had become anachronistic. Many centuries previously, peasants had been prepared to accept burdens and obligations to their lords in return for support in difficult times and for defence against enemies but society had changed to such a degree that food surplus rather than dearth was likely and lords were more often exploiters than protectors. At least in the states with increasingly strong central government, the lord was not needed as a protector and the country people appreciated that he was obtaining too large a 'rake-off' for the functions he was performing. Taxation was the other urgent grievance of the peasantry and it was the second levy of the Poll-tax within four years that sparked off the Peasants' Revolt. Theories, advanced by some scholars, which attributed it to the reimposition of labour services, have no serious foundation in fact since it was so easy for a villein tenant to run away from a manor and find employment and land elsewhere that only the most stupid lord would have attempted such a futile policy. The picture emerges therefore of a peasantry that was becoming articulate in its protest, voicing its grievances and demanding its rights, and which, although some at the lower end might be desperately poor, on the whole enjoyed a rising standard of living. Although the rise in wages came earlier in some places, although it varied from region to region and trade to trade and although the price structure varied from place to place, nevertheless in real terms wage earners enjoyed a substantial rise, often in the order of 200 to 250 per cent.

Finally in many areas of Europe the structure of estate management changed radically. The manor in many regions disappeared and the lord of the manor was replaced in importance in the countryside by the lessees and wealthy tenant farmers, many of them men who had made their money in commerce or industry. The landed aristocracy and gentry in some measure, in England at least, appeared to have abrogated their position as leaders in the countryside, and rural communities such as the *Schansen* in Germany emerged to be responsible for tax obligations and defence. The *Dorfgemeinschaft* played a prominent part in later medieval Germany. But even where all the demesne had been leased and the lord of the manor had become purely a rentier, he usually retained the profits of the court and his legal rights which were to enable his successors to reimpose their control over the land. By raising entry fines the lord could squeeze tenants off the land when he wished to enclose and convert an estate to parkland or pasture. But in the last century and a half of the Middle Ages the England of the manors became the England of the peasant cultivator – it was his diligence and initiative that maintained agricultural output. Whether production was as efficient as it had been on the great demesne farms of the thirteenth century is a matter of dispute among economic historians but the peasants were working their own land, often almost entirely with members of their own family, and it can be assumed that their interest and enthusiasm was greater than that which they had evinced when they worked the lord's demesne.

Of course the population decline of the fourteenth century, which continued into the following century, since population replacement rates were inadequate to raise the population to its pre-1348 level much before 1600, led to a reduction in output not only of agricultural produce but also of some other commodities. Much discussion has ranged over the question as to whether the economy stagnated at this period. It seems clear that a secular slump began in the 1320s and lasted for nearly 200 years until the second decade of the sixteenth century, but within that lengthy span periods of improvement and recession alternated. Many of the misunderstandings about this late medieval period would disappear if economic historians defined more precisely the terms they are using in their analyses. It would have been surprising if the output of some commodities had not been reduced, for had production continued at the pre-1348 levels, prices would have been so reduced as to make production completely unremunerative. This happened from time to time with the grains that on occasion fell to ridiculously low prices, which could only betoken a gross imbalance between supply and demand, though in this regard the inrush of cheap corn from eastern Europe and the fact that grain prices were highly sensitive must not be overlooked. Obviously the same amount of foodstuff does not need to be produced for a population that, to use rough generalizations, had been reduced by between one third and a half. Even if vast masses had been malnourished before the 1320s, great surpluses would have occurred if the same quantity of foodstuffs had been produced for such a reduced population. Many economic historians fail to point out this obvious fact.

Output of cloth, household articles, furniture, wooden and metal ware and the level of building are almost impossible to assess accurately. Whether the decline in cloth production in Flanders was offset by the developing English industry or not, or whether English production exceeded Flemish production or not, the overall impression remains that the decline in the production of commodities did not match that of foodstuffs and above all of grain. In fact there may have been no decline in the production of some commodities. Judging by the inventories attached to wills, it becomes apparent that more and more household articles were possessed by all ranks of society as the fifteenth century progressed. Undoubtedly also, this period was one of much building of town houses, as witness the city of Bruges, which the flourishing cloth industry had deserted, and of fortified and unfortified manor houses and of solid yeoman farmhouses.

In so far as production declined, the 200 years after c. 1320 may be said to be a period of down-turn in the economy as a whole. This decline may to some extent have been caused by a shortage of bullion. The shortage brought about a decline in prices which peasant proprietors tried to overcome by selling more produce on the market, which led to a greater disequilibrium between supply and demand and a further fall in prices. It is noticeable that, at least until the new German silver was circulating in the late fifteenth century, the frequent devaluations of several European currencies did not raise prices significantly or not at any rate for very long. An inadequate supply of the precious metals, particularly of silver, leading to a scarcity of money in circulation is a feature of the period and one that tended to depress prices. On the other hand the increased labour costs would tend to raise the price of goods with a high labour content. As the costs of basic foodstuffs remained low and as wages rose, many people would have more money to spend on higher protein foods and more drink, on clothes, furs and consumer durables, and the impression that we gain (it can be no more than an impression) is that the reduction in the production of commodities was slight, unlike grain output, and that in some commodities there was no reduction at all. Tin production in Devon and Cornwall was well maintained after the Black Death and so were English wool exports, either in wool or in cloth, although we cannot be certain as to whether this maintenance also applied to total wool production. The price of many industrial goods rose but it is almost impossible to assess whether this rise was the result of a reduction in supply or of an increase in demand. Complaints abound on the subject of declining output in established clothing centres such as the cities of Ghent, Ypres and Bruges and in English towns such as York but these cannot be arguments for postulating the stagnation of the clothing industry as a whole, for in England it had become a rural industry. Often towns pleaded poverty in an attempt to obtain a reduction of the levies placed upon them by the Crown. But the value of English cloth plus wool exports remained remarkably steady with the exception of the three decades between 1451 and 1480; though the population might have decreased by a third, the value of these exports did not fall in proportion.

Within this period not only were there recessions and improvements in overall trade but there were, perhaps more importantly, shifts in the patterns of European trade which brought relative prosperity to some countries and decline to others. England was a gainer in international trade in the later Middle Ages, as were the districts of Holland and Brabant; Flanders and some of the Italian cities suffered. These shifts in trade were sometimes the result of changes in demand patterns or in the sources of supply, as happened with the discovery of alum mines at Tolfa in the Papal States which made Europe less dependent on the Turkish-dominated supplies in Asia Minor, or they might result from political manoeuvrings like those of the dukes of Burgundy who favoured Antwerp as against Bruges, or from conquests like those of Tamurlaine which cut the Italians off from the overland routes to Asia. But the exchanges of corn, wine, wool, cotton, linen and woollen cloth between one part of Europe and another was a new type of trade far removed from the traffic in luxury goods, silks and spices which had been the staple of international trade before the early or mid fourteenth century. In this trade the monopoly of the Hanseatic League and the Italian maritime towns was challenged by Seville and Castile, England and Holland, Nuremberg and Ravensburg and other south German and Lombard towns. The impression obtained is of an economy that was shifting rather than stagnant but overall decline may be possible, perhaps even probable.

Certainly many restrictive practices emerged both in industry and commerce in the late medieval period. The gilds were largely successful in controlling output and highly successful in restricting entry to their trades: this was the time when seven-year apprenticeships were enforced in trades whose skills could often have been learnt in one or two years even by the dullest boys. Apprenticeship became a source of cheap labour for the master at a time of rising wage rates. Price fixing was also a prominent feature; avowedly in the interests of the consumer, it was sometimes, like the price ring in candles at Norwich, to the advantage of the producer. In international trade the English Merchant Adventurers provide an excellent example of the way in which trade was limited to members and such a restriction, forms of which existed throughout Europe, perhaps indicates that the volume of trade was limited and that had any merchant been allowed to partake in it, profits would have become too slender. Certainly the way in which the Merchants of the Staple shared out profits according to the number of sacks of wool a merchant had brought to Calais rather than by the number he had actually sold demonstrates a restrictive practice designed to benefit English nationals and the national economy. So-called 'mercantilist' theories were abroad in England from Richard II's reign and hazy views of the balance of trade induced the government to attempt to restrict imports and promote exports, and in the fifteenth century a number of 'hosting' laws endeavoured to restrict the freedom of action of foreign merchants. The Hanseatic League, following a similar policy, attempted but eventually failed to keep English merchants out of the Baltic. All these signs of restriction of trade are the surest indications we have of a down-turn in the economy at this time but they are not irrefutable proof of an overall falling-off in the volume of trade.

Was it then stagnation? In a sense it was, but the crucial question surely is 'to what extent could production and commercial exchanges be expected to remain at the same level in a population that had been reduced at least by 30 per cent and possibly by 50 per cent?' That there was some decline, though the degree of it may never be quantifiable, is what we should expect but strong evidence exists of an increase in *per capita* income for large sections of the people of Europe. Over-concentration on the English economy may produce a false picture, for England, like Holland, had a flourishing export trade and had, moreover, by the 1430s ceased to be primarily an exporter of raw materials and had become an exporter of manufactured goods in the form of unfinished and finished cloth. It has been estimated that four and one third cloths could be made from one sack of wool and yet the sale price of two cloths in Flanders was about the same as that of a sack of wool; so England obtained a greater return for its exports. Other parts of Europe were certainly less fortunate; the clothmakers of the Flemish towns, the impoverished peasants in French villages that had been decimated by war, the enserfed peasants of eastern Europe perhaps did not achieve any increase in living standards, but from these examples also it would be unsafe to argue generally. In some parts of the Continent the 'economic cake' was more equally divided than it had been in previous centuries: landlords suffered a decline in their incomes from rents (to what extent they offset this decline from other sources has as yet not been established), while wage earners achieved an advance in income.

H

How far this increase in *per capita* income was reflected in a growth in *per capita* consumption presents another difficult problem on which further research is necessary. We do not know to what extent or upon what commodities the English wage earner spent his additional income. It seems likely that he spent it on more ale and beer, on more meat and dairy produce, to judge from price evidence, and probably he spent more money on clothes, if the English sumptuary laws can be taken as evidence that people were dressing 'above their station'. So even in an era when the economy may have been in recession, life for a larger proportion of Europe's population was better than it had been in the boom period of demesne farming.

But man does not live by bread alone and in some ways the quality of life deteriorated during the period when men were living under the shadow of the pestilence. The appallingly high mortality had its effect upon man's religious beliefs. A morbid interest in death, which produced the paintings of *danses macabres* around the walls of many churches and the tombstones with carved skeletons upon them, is perhaps not surprising, but for many, religious belief descended into mere superstition. A new spirit of competition and commercialism became apparent although it would be unwise to assert that it had not existed earlier; capitalist organization of industry, again not new, became more widespread and the sources of local charity perhaps began to dry up a little. At the same time new blossomings in architecture and above all in painting and literature emerged to form a movement that has been known to generations as the 'Renaissance'.

Yet the European world to some extent, despite its contacts with the Moslem Near East and the Orient, was a world closed in upon itself ready for new horizons. This outward looking came first with the Portuguese voyages of discovery southward along the west African coastline under the direction of Prince Henry the Navigator and then at the close of the fifteenth century with the expeditions of Columbus. It was these voyages and the commercial outlets and sources of new imports they opened up that were to revolutionize the old trade routes. The traditional European routes from Italy to England and Flanders, from northern Germany to Scandinavia and the Baltic, from Italy into the Black Sea and the criss-crossing of the

Mediterranean gave way to the crossing of the Atlantic and Indian oceans.

And other portents of change arrived. The invention of printing in Europe was to open up vast opportunities for the spread of knowledge that had been unavailable to most men in the Middle Ages. The spread of gunpowder and the invention of cannon held a great potential for war-making on a vaster scale than had previously been known. The fifteenth century was an epoch of great promise but few living in that age could foresee what those new routes, those inventions and new techniques would bring forth. Nationalism was everywhere beginning to break down the underlying unity of European culture, a unity that had been fractured at the fall of the Roman Empire and then painfully reconstructed by the medieval church on the basis of Latin as the *lingua franca* of all learned men. The similarity in the way of life of a knight in Midland England or in northern France, of a merchant in Hamburg or in Venice or a villein serf in Somerset or Laon was so close that Europe from 800 to 1400 had been given a unity that it was not to know again until the twentieth century. Medieval Europe has been called 'the Europe of Latin and the horse'; from the fifteenth century it was no longer 'the Europe of Latin', although it remained until the nineteenth century 'the Europe of the horse'.

Bibliography

CHAPTER I

The Cambridge Medieval History (ed. J. R. Tanner), vols I and II (Cambridge U.P., 1911–13).

The Shorter Cambridge Medieval History (ed. C. W. P. Orton), vol. I (Cambridge U.P., 1952).

N. Åberg, *Die Goten und Langobarden in Italien*, Wilhelm Ekmans Universitetsfond No. 29 (Uppsala, 1923).

N. Åberg, *The Occident and the Orient in the Art of the Seventh Century*: Part 1 *The British Isles*, Part 2 *Lombard Italy*, Part 3 *The Merovingian Empire* (Stockholm, Vitterhets Historie och Antikvitets Akademiens Handlingar, 1943–7).

C. Dawson, *The Making of Europe* (London, Sheed & Ward, 1932).

M. Deanesly, *A History of Early Medieval Europe 476–911* (London, Methuen, rev. ed. 1969).

W. H. C. Frend, *The Donatist Church* (London, Oxford U.P., 2nd ed. 1971).

Glotz' *Histoire Générale, Histoire du Moyen Âge*, vol. I (ed. F. Lot, C. Pfister and F. L. Ganshof) (Paris, Presses Universitaires de France, 1928).

Gregory of Tours, *History of the Franks*, trans. O. M. Dalton (Oxford, Clarendon Press, 1927).

A. H. M. Jones, *The Later Roman Empire, 284–602* (Oxford, Blackwell, 1964)·

A. H. M. Jones, *The Decline of the Ancient World* (London, Longmans, 1966).

P. Krueger and T. Mommsen (eds.), *Corpus Iuris Civilis*, 3 vols (Berlin, latest ed. 1954).

M. L. W. Laistner, *Thought and Letters in Western Europe A.D. 500–900* (London, Methuen, 1931, 2nd ed. 1957).

R. S. Lopez, *The Birth of Europe* (London, Phoenix House, 1967).

F. Lot, *The End of the Ancient World and the Beginning of the Middle Ages*, trans. P. and M. Leon (London, Routledge, 1951).

F. Lot, *Les Invasions Germaniques* (Paris, 1935).

T. Mommsen and P. M. Meyer (eds.), *Theodosiani libri XVI*, etc. (Berlin, Societas Regia Scientiarum, 1905).

H. St L. B. Moss, *Birth of the Middle Ages, 395–814* (Oxford U.P., 1963).

M. Pacaut, *Guide de l'étudiant en histoire médiévale* (Paris, Presses Universitaires de France, 1968).

C. Pharr, *The Theodosian Code* (Princeton U.P., 1952).

Procopius, *De bello Vandalico*, with English translation (Loeb Classical Library, London, Heinemann, 1914).

E. A. Thompson, *A History of Attila and the Huns* (Oxford, Clarendon Press, 1948).

J. Vicens Vives, *Approaches to the History of Spain*, trans. J. C. Ullmann (Berkeley, California U.P., 1967).

J. M. Wallace-Hadrill, *The Barbarian West, 400–1000* (London, Hutchinson, rev. ed. 1967).

E. Will, 'Saint Apollinaire de Ravenne', *Publications de l'Université de Strasbourg*, fasc. 74 (1936).

CHAPTER 2

The Cambridge Economic History of Europe, vol. I (ed. M. M. Postan) *The Agrarian Life of the Middle Ages* (Cambridge U.P., 2nd ed. 1966). Hereafter called *The Cambridge Economic History*.

B. H. Slicher van Bath, *The Agrarian History of Western Europe, A.D. 500–1850*, trans. O. Ordish (London, Arnold, 1963).

G. Duby, *Rural Economy and Country Life in the Medieval West*, trans. C. Postan (London, Arnold, 1968).

A. G. Haudricourt and M. Jean-Brunhes Delmarre, *L'homme et la Charrue*, Geographie Humaine No. 25 (Paris, Gallimard, 1955).

M. Rostovtzeff, *Social and Economic History of the Roman Empire*, 2 vols (London, Oxford U.P., 2nd ed. 1957).

K. D. White, *Roman Farming* (London, Thames & Hudson, 1970).

L. White, Jr, *Medieval Technology and Social Change* (London, Oxford U.P., 1962, paperback ed. 1964).

CHAPTER 3

W. O. Ault, *Private Jurisdiction in England*, Yale Historical Publications Miscellany Vol. 10 (New Haven, 1923).

T. H. Aston, 'The origins of the manor in England', *Trans. Royal Hist. Soc.*, 5th ser. VIII (1958), 59–83.

M. Bloch, *Feudal Society*, trans. L. A. Manyon, 2 vols (London, Routledge, 1965).

M. Bloch, *Seigneurie française et manoir anglais*, Cahiers des Annales 16 (Paris, Colin, 1960).

R. Boutruche, *Seigneurie et féodalité*, vol. I, *Le premier âge des liens d'homme à homme* (Paris, Editions Montaigne, 1959).

J. Calmette, *La société féodale* (Paris, Colin, 3rd ed. 1932).

A. Dopsch, *The Economic and Social Foundations of European Civilization*, trans. M. G. Beard and N. Marshall (London, Kegan Paul, 1937).

F. L. Ganshof, *Feudalism*, trans. P. Grierson (London, Longmans, 3rd ed. 1964).

R. Grand and R. Delatouche, *L'Agriculture au Moyen Âge de la fin de l'Empire Romain aux XVIe siècle* (Paris, De Boccard, 1950).

L. Hauptmann, 'Colonus, Barschalk und Freiman', *Wirtschaft und Kultur: Festschrift zum 70 Geburtstag Alfons Dopsch* (Leipzig, Rohrer, 1938), pp. 170–90.

D. Herlihy, 'The agrarian revolution in southern France and Italy, 801–1150', *Speculum* (1958), 23–41.

D. Herlihy, 'The history of the rural seigneury in Italy, 751–1200', *Agricultural History*, XXXIII (1959), 58–71.

G. A. J. Hodgett, 'Feudal Wiltshire', *Victoria County History of Wiltshire*, vol. V (London, Oxford U.P., for the Institute of Historical Research, 1957).

A. H. M. Jones, 'The Roman colonate', *Past and Present*, XIII (1958), 1–13.

R. Latouche, *The Birth of Western Economy*, trans. E. M. Wilkinson (London, Methuen, 2nd ed. 1967).

A. Longnon, (ed.) *Polyptyque de l'Abbaye de St-Germain-des-Prés*, 2 vols (Paris, Société de l'Histoire de Paris, 1886–95).

F. Lütge, *Deutsch Sozial- und Wirtschaftsgeschichte*, part of the *Enzyklopädie der Rechts- und Staatswissenschaft* (Berlin, 2nd ed. 1960).

F. W. Maitland, *Domesday Book and Beyond*, with introduction by E. Miller (London, Collins, 1960).

G. Marten and K. Mäckelmann, *Dithmarschen* (Heide in Holstein, 1927).

F. Seebohm, *The English Village Community* (London, Longmans, 1883).

J. W. Thompson, *An Economic and Social History of the Middle Ages (300–1300)*, 2 vols (London, Constable, 2nd ed. 1959).

P. Vinogradoff, *The Growth of the Manor* (Newton Abbot, David & Charles, reprint 1968 of 1911 2nd ed.).

See also the bibliographies of Chapters 1 and 2, especially the works of F. Lot, A. H. M. Jones and M. Rostovsteff and the first volume of *The Cambridge Economic History*.

CHAPTER 4

The Cambridge Economic History, vol. II (ed. M. Postan and E. E. Rich) *Trade and Industry in the Middle Ages* (Cambridge U.P., 1952, new ed. forthcoming).

The Cambridge Economic History, vol. III (ed. M. M. Postan, E. E. Rich and E. Miller) *Economic Organization and Policies in the Middle Ages* (Cambridge U.P., 1963).

J. B. Bury, *History of the Later Roman Empire, 395–565*, 2 vols (London, Constable, 1923).

R. Doehaerd, *Le Haut Moyen Âge Occidental: Économies et Sociétés* (Paris, Presses Universitaires de France, 1971).

Tenney Frank, *Economic Survey of Ancient Rome*, 5 vols (Baltimore, Johns Hopkins Press, 1933–40).

P. Grierson, 'The relations between England and Flanders before the Norman Conquest', *Trans. Royal Hist. Soc.*, 4th ser. XXIII (1941), 71–112.

A. F. Havighurst (ed.), *The Pirenne Thesis: Analysis, Criticism and Revision* (Farnborough, Heath, 1958).

H. Jankuhn, *Haithabu, ein Handelsplatz der Wikingerzeit* (Neumünster, Karl Wacholtz, 4th ed. 1963).

S. Lauffer, *Diokletians Preisedikt* (Berlin, de Gruyter, 1971).

A. R. Lewis, *Naval Power and Trade in the Mediterranean, A.D. 500–1100* (Princeton U.P., 1951).

A. R. Lewis, *The Northern Seas: Shipping and Commerce in Northern Europe, A.D. 300–1100* (London, Oxford U.P., 1958).

R. S. Lopez, 'Mohammed and Charlemagne: a revision', *Speculum*, XVIII (1943), 14–38.

H. Mattingly, *Roman Coins* (London, Methuen, 2nd ed. 1960).

H. Michell, 'The edict of Diocletian: a study of price fixing in the Roman Empire', *Canadian J. of Econ. and Pol. Sci.*, XIII (1947), 1–13.

H. Pirenne, *Mohammed and Charlemagne*, trans. B. Miall (London, Allen & Unwin, 1939).

See also the bibliographies of Chapters 1, 2 and 3, especially the works of A. H. M. Jones, M. Rostovtzeff and A. Dopsch, and O. M. Dalton's translation of Gregory of Tours's *History of the Franks*.

CHAPTER 5

The Cambridge Economic History, vols II and III.

Z. N. Brooke, *A History of Europe, 911–1198* (London, Methuen, 3rd ed. 1956).

C. M. Cipolla, *Money, Prices and Civilization in the Mediterranean World* (Princeton U.P., 1956).

R. H. C. Davis, *A History of Mediaeval Europe from Constantine to St Louis* (London, Longmans, 1957).

F. Dvornik, *Les Slaves, Byzance et Rome au IXe siècle* (Paris, Institut d'Études Slaves, 1926).

F. Dvornik, *The Making of Central and Eastern Europe* (London, Polish Research Centre, 1949).

E. Ennen, *Frühgeschichte der europäischen Stadt* (Bonn, Rörscheid, 1953).

P. Grierson, 'Commerce in the Dark Ages', *Trans. Royal Hist. Soc.*, 5th ser. IX (1959), 123–40.

T. D. Kendrick, *A History of the Vikings* (London, Cass, 1962).

T. Lewicki, 'Il commercio arabo con la Russia e con i paesi slavi d'occidente nei secoli IX-XI', *Annali dell'Istituto universitario orientali di Napoli*, VIII (1958), 47–61.

G. Luzzatto, *An Economic History of Italy from the Fall of the Roman Empire to the Beginning of the Sixteenth Century*, trans. P. Jones (London, Routledge, 1961).

B. Lyon, 'L'oeuvre de Henri Pirenne après 25 ans', *Le Moyen Âge*, LXVI (1960), No. 4, 437–93.

A. Mawer, *The Vikings* (Cambridge U.P., 1913).

L. Musset, *Les peuples scandinaves au Moyen Âge* (Paris, Presses Universitaires de France, 1951).

H. Paszkiewicz, *The Origins of Russia* (London, Allen & Unwin, 1954).

P. H. Sawyer, *The Age of the Vikings* (London, Arnold, 1962).

F. Vercauteren, *Étude sur les civitates de la Belgique Seconde* (Brussels, Académie Royale de Belgique, 1934).

F. Vercauteren, 'Die europäischen Städte bis zum 11 Jahrhundert', in W. Rausch (ed.), *Die Städte Mitteleuropas im 12 und 13 Jahrhundert* (Linz, 1963), pp. 1–13.

C. Verlinden, *L'esclavage dans l'Europe médiévale, I: Péninsule ibérique, France* (Bruges, University of Ghent, 1955).

G. Vernadsky and M. Karpovich, *A History of Russia*, vols I and II (New Haven, Yale U.P., 1944, 1948).

G. Vernadsky, *The Origins of Russia* (London, Oxford U.P., 1959).

See also the bibliographies of Chapters 1 and 4, especially the works of R. S. Lopez and A. R. Lewis.

CHAPTER 6

The Cambridge Economic History, vols II and III.

J. Beloch, *Bevölkerungsgeschichte Italiens*, 3 vols (Berlin, de Gruyter, 1937–61).

P. Boissonade, *Life and Work in Medieval Europe*, English translation (London, Kegan Paul, 1927).

J. Brutzkus, 'Trade with eastern Europe, 800–1200', *Econ. Hist. Review*, XIII (1943), 31–41.

E. H. Byrne, *Genoese Shipping in the 12th and 13th Centuries*, Medieval Academy of America Publication No. 5 (Cambridge, Mass., 1930).

R. Doehaerd, *Les relations commerciales entre Gênes, la Belgique et l'Outrement*, 3 vols, Institut Historique Belge de Rome Études d'histoire économique et sociale vols 2–4 (Brussels and Rome, vol. 1, 1941).

A. Doren, *Italienische Wirtschaftsgeschichte*, Italian trans. by G. Luzzatto with additional bibliography (Padua, 1937).

W. Heyd, *Histoire du Commerce du Levant au Moyen Âge*, 2 vols (Amsterdam, 2nd ed. 1959).

S. Lane-Poole, *History of Egypt in the Middle Ages* (London, Methuen, 4th ed. 1925).

A. C. Littleton and B. S. Yamey (eds.) *Studies in the History of Accounting* (London, Sweet & Maxwell, 1956).

R. S. Lopez and I. W. Raymond, *Mediaeval Trade in the Mediterranean World*, translated documents with introduction (New York, Columbia U.P., 1955).

F. Lot, *Recherches sur la population et la superficie des cités remontant à la période gallo-romaine*, 3 vols (Paris, Champion, 1945–54).

R. Mols, *Introduction à la démographie historique des villes d'Europe du XIVe au XVIIIe siècle*, 3 vols (University of Louvain, 1954–6).

I. Origo, *The Merchant of Prato: Francesco di Marco Datini* (London, Cape, rev. ed. 1963).

H. Pirenne, *Medieval Cities: Their Origins and the Revival of Trade*, trans. F. D. Halsey (Princeton U.P., 1969).

H. Pirenne, *Economic and Social History of Medieval Europe*, trans. I. E. Clegg (London, Routledge, 1936). A revised edition of the original French text edited by H. van Werveke (1963) is especially useful for its *Annexe bibliographique et critique*.

Y. Renouard, *Les hommes d'affaires italiens au Moyen Âge* (Paris, Colin, 2nd ed. 1968).

F. Edler de Roover, 'Early examples of marine insurance', *J. of Econ. Hist.*, V (1945), 172–200.

R. de Roover, *L'évolution de la lettre de change, XIVe–XVIIIe siècles* (Paris, Colin, 1953).

R. de Roover, *The Rise and Decline of the Medici Bank 1397–1494* (London, Oxford U.P., 1963).

A. Sapori, *Le Marchand italien au Moyen Âge* (Paris, Colin, 1952).

F. Schevill, *History of Florence* (London, Constable, rev. ed. 1961).

W. Sombart, *Der moderne Kapitalismus* (Munich and Leipzig, Duncker & Humblot, 2nd ed. 1916–27).

J. Streider, *Zur Genesis des modernen Kapitalismus* (Munich & Leipzig, Duncker & Humblot, 2nd ed. 1953).

A. P. Usher, *The Early History of Deposit Banking in Mediterranean Europe* (Cambridge, Mass., Harvard U.P., 1943).

CHAPTER 7

The Cambridge Economic History, vols II and III.

The Cambridge Medieval History, vol. IV (ed. J. M. Hussey), parts I and II (Cambridge U.P., new ed. 1966–7).

H. Amman, 'Die Anfänge des Aktivhandels und der Tucheinfuhr aus Nordwesteuropa nach dem Mittelmeergebiet', *Studi in onore di Armondo Sapori*, vol. I (Milan, Cisalpino, 1957), pp. 275–310.

G. Barraclough (ed.), *Eastern and Western Europe in the Middle Ages* (London, Thames & Hudson, 1970).

R. H. Bautier, 'Les foires de Champagne', *La Foire, Recueils de la Société Jean Bodin*, V (1953), 97–147 (Brussels).

C. R. Beazley, *Prince Henry the Navigator* (London, Cass, reprint 1968 of 1923 ed.).

J. Combes, 'Les foires en Languedoc au Moyen Âge', *Annales: Économies, Sociétés, Civilisations*, XIII (1958), 231–59.

R. Doehaerd, 'Les galères génoises dans la Manche et la Mer du Nord à la fin du XIIIe et au début du XIVe siècle', *Bull. de l'Institut belge de Rome*, XIX, (1938).

P. Dollinger, *The German Hansa*, trans, D. S. Ault and S. H. Steinberg (London, Macmillan, 1970).

H. Laurent, *Un grand commerce d'exportation au Moyen Âge: la draperie des Pays-Bas en France et dans les Pays méditerranéens* (Paris, 1935).

F. Balducci Pegolotti, *La Pratica della Mercatura* (ed. A. Evans), Medieval Academy of America Publication No. 24 (Cambridge, Mass., 1936).

Marco Polo, *The Travels of Marco Polo*, trans. R. Latham (Harmondsworth, Penguin Books, 1958).

R. L. Reynolds, 'The market for northern textiles in Genoa, 1179–1200' *Revue Belge de Philologie et d'Histoire*, VIII (1929), 831–51.

R. L. Reynolds, 'Merchants of Arras and overland trade with Genoa, XIIth century', *Revue Belge de Philologie et d'Histoire*, IX (1930), 495–533.

R. de Roover, 'La balance commerciale entre les Pays-Bas et l'Italie au XVe siècle', *Revue Belge de Philologie et d' Histoire*, XXXVII (1959), 374–86.

F. Rörig, *Mittelalterliche Weltwirtschaft* (Jena, Fischer, 1933).

A. A. Ruddock, *Italian Merchants and Shipping in Southampton (1270–1600)* (Southampton, University College, 1951).

P. E. L. R. Russell, *Prince Henry the Navigator* (London, Hispanic & Luzo-Brazilian Councils, 1960).

W. Vogel, *Die Deutschen als Seefahrer* (Hamburg, Schmölders, 1949).

CHAPTER 8

M. W. Beresford, *New Towns of the Middle Ages* (London, Lutterworth, 1967).

A. V. Chayanov, *The Theory of Peasant Economy* (ed. D. Thorner, B. Kerblay and R. E. F. Smith) (Homewood, Ill., Irwin, 1966).

R. J. Chorley and P. Haggett (eds.), *Models in Geography* (London, Methuen, 1967).

A. J. Coale and E. M. Hoover, *Population Growth in Low-Income Economies* (London, Oxford U.P., 1959).

Rushton Coulborn (ed.), *Feudalism in History* (Princeton U.P., 1956).

G. Duby, *Rural Economy and Country Life in the Medieval West*, trans. C. Postan (London, Arnold, 1968).

A. Etzioni and E. Etzioni (eds.), *Social Change: Sources, Patterns and Consequences* (New York, Basic Books, 1964).

J. K. Galbraith, *Economic Development in Perspective* (Cambridge, Mass., Harvard U.P., 1964).

A.-G. Haudricourt, 'De l'origine de l'attelage moderne', *Annales d'histoire économique et sociale*, VIII (1936), 515–22.

B. F. Hoselitz (ed.), *Theories of Economic Growth* (London, Collier-Macmillan, 1965).

R. J. Lefebvre des Noëttes, *L'Attelage: Le Cheval de selle à travers les âges*, 2 vols (Paris, Picard, 1931).

E. Miller, 'The English economy in the thirteenth century: implications of recent research', *Past and Present*, XXVIII (1964), 21–40.

Talcott Parsons and N. J. Smelser, *Economy and Society* (London, Routledge, 1956).

C. Singer *et al.* (eds.) *A History of Technology*, vol. II (London, Oxford U.P., 1956).

R. W. Southern, *The Making of the Middle Ages* (London, Hutchinson, 1959).

W. Stark, 'The contained economy', *Aquinas Paper 26* (The Aquinas Society of London, 1956).

B. E. Supple (ed.), *The Experience of Economic Growth: Case Studies in Economic History* (New York, Random House, 1963).

S. L. Thrupp, 'Medieval gilds reconsidered', *J. of Econ. Hist.*, II (1942), 164–73.

L. White, Jr, *Medieval Technology and Social Change* (London, Oxford U.P., 1962).

CHAPTER 9

J. N. L. Baker, *Medieval Trade Routes*, Historical Association Pamphlet No. 111 (London, 1938).

F. W. Brooks, *The English Naval Forces, 1199–1272* (London, Pordes, reissue 1962, orig. pub. 1936).

M. Mollat (ed.), 'Le Navire et l'économie du moyen-âge au XVIIIe siècle principalmement en Mediterranée', *2e Colloque d'histoire maritime* (Paris, 1958).

O. Stolz, 'Zur Entwicklungsgeschichte des Zollwesens innerhalb des alten Deutschen Reiches', *Vierteljahrschrift für Sozial- und Wirtschaftsgeschichte*, XLI (1954), 1–41.

J. E. Tyler, *The Alpine Passes, 962–1250* (Oxford, Blackwell, 1930).

J. F. Willard, 'Inland transportation in England during the fourteenth century', *Speculum*, I (1926), 361–74.

J. F. Willard, 'The use of carts in the fourteenth century', *History*, XVII (1932), 246–50.

See also the bibliography of Chapter 8, especially the works of L. White, Lefebvre des Noëttes and Haudricourt.

CHAPTER 10

The Cambridge Medieval History, vol. IV (ed. J. M. Hussey), parts I and II (Cambridge U.P., new ed. 1966–7).

L. Torres Balbás, 'Extensión y demografía de las ciudades hispanomusulmanas', *Studia Islamica*, III (1955), 35–59.

N. H. Baynes and H. St L. B. Moss (eds.) *Byzantium* (London, Oxford U.P., 1953, paperback ed. 1961).

J. B. Bury, *History of the Later Roman Empire A.D. 395–565* (London, Constable, 1923).

K. J. Conant, *The Pelican History of Art, 13, Carolingian and Romanesque Architecture, 800–1200* (Harmondsworth, Penguin Books, 1959).

O. M. Dalton, *East Christian Art* (Oxford, Clarendon Press, 1925).

R. Krautheimer, *The Pelican History of Art, 24, Early Christian and Byzantine Architecture* (Harmondsworth, Penguin Books, 1965).

E. Lévi-Provençal, *Histoire de l'Espagne Musulmane,* 2 vols (Paris, Gustave-Paul Maisonneuve, 2nd ed. 1950).

E. Lévi-Provençal, *L'Espagne Musulmane au Xe siècle* (Paris, Larose, 1932).

R. S. Lopez, 'The silk industry in the Byzantine Empire', *Speculum,* XX (1945), 1–42.

R. S. Lopez, 'The dollar of the Middle Ages', *J. of Econ. Hist.,* XI (1951), 209–34.

G. Ostrogorski, *History of the Byzantine State,* trans. J. M. Hussey (Oxford, Blackwell, 2nd ed. 1969).

J. Vicens Vives, *Approaches to the History of Spain,* trans. J. C. Ullmann (Berkeley, California U.P., 1968).

J. Vicens Vives, *An Economic History of Spain,* trans. F. M. López-Morinas (London, Oxford U.P., 1969).

The Works of Liudprand of Cremona, trans. F. A. Wright (London, Routledge, 1930).

CHAPTER II

M. S. Briggs, *A Short History of the Building Crafts* (Oxford, Clarendon Press, 1925).

R. A. Brown, H. M. Colvin and A. J. Taylor, *The History of the King's Works, The Middle Ages,* 2 vols (London, H.M.S.O., 1963).

G. G. Coulton, *Art and the Reformation,* (Cambridge U.P., 2nd ed. 1953).

J. H. Harvey, *English Mediaeval Architects* (London, Batsford, 1954).

D. Knoop and G. P. Jones, *The Mediaeval Mason* (Manchester U.P., 2nd ed. 1967).

G. Künstler (ed.), *Romanesque Art in Europe* (London, Thames & Hudson, 1969).

L. F. Salzman, *Building in England Down to 1540* (London, Oxford U.P., 1968).

L. F. Salzman, *English Industries of the Middle Ages* (London, Pordes, reissue 1964 of 1928 ed.).

A. H. Thompson, 'Mediaeval building accounts and what we learn from them', *Somerset Archaeological Society Transactions,* LXVI (1920), 1–25.

M. Wood, *The English Mediaeval House* (London, Phoenix House, 1965).

CHAPTER 12

E. M. Carus-Wilson, *Medieval Merchant Venturers* (London, Methuen, 1954).

F. Consitt, *The London Weavers Company* (Oxford, Clarendon Press, 1933).

R. Davidsohn, 'Blüte und Niedergang der Florentiner Tuchindustrie', *Zeitschrift für die gesamte Staatswissenschaft*, LXXXV (1928), 225–55.

G. Espinas and H. Pirenne (eds.), *Recueil de documents relatifs à l'histoire de l'industrie drapière en Flandre*, 4 vols (Brussels, Commission Royale d'Histoire, 1906–24).

G. Espinas, *Les origines de l'association dans les villes de l'Artois et de la Flandre française*, 2 vols (Lille, Société d'Histoire du Droit des Pays flammands, Picards et Wallons, 1941–2).

H. L. Gray, 'The production and exportation of English woollens in the fourteenth century', *Eng. Hist. Review*, XXXIX (1924), 13–35.

H. Heaton, *The Yorkshire Woollen and Worsted Industries* (London, Oxford U.P., 2nd ed. 1966).

R. S. Lopez, *Studi sull'economia genovese nel medio evo, II: le origini dell'arte della lana* (Turin, S. Lattes, 1936).

H. E. Malden (ed.) *The Cely Papers*, Camden 3rd ser. I (London, Royal Historical Society, 1900).

H. Pirenne, *Histoire de Belgique*, vols I and II (Brussels, La Renaissance du Livre, 1948–52).

G. de Poerck, *La draperie médiévale en Flandre et en Artois* (Bruges, University of Ghent, 1951).

E. Power, *The Wool Trade in English Medieval History* (London, Oxford U.P., 1941).

N. Rodolico, *I Ciompi: Una pagina di Storia del proletariato operaio* (Florence, Sansoni, 1945).

R. de Roover, 'Labour conditions in Florence around 1400: theory, policy and reality', in N. Rubinstein (ed.), *Florentine Studies: Politics and Society in Renaissance Florence* (London, Faber, 1969).

G. Unwin, *Finance and Trade under Edward III* (London, 1918, 2nd ed. Cass, 1962).

G. Unwin, *The Guilds and Companies of London* (London, 4th ed. Cass, 1963).

F. Vercauteren, *Étude sur les civitates de la Belgique Seconde* (Brussels, Académie Royale de Belgique, 1934).

G. F. Ward, 'The early history of the merchant staplers', *Eng. Hist. Review*, XXXIII (1918), 297–319.

H. van Werveke, *Miscellania Mediaevalia* (Ghent, E. Story-Scientia, 1968).

C. Wyffels, 'De oorsprong der Ambachten in Vlaanderen en Brabant' (resumé in French), *Verhandelingen van de Koninklijke Vlaamse Academie Voor Geneeskunde van België*, XIII (1951), No. 13.

CHAPTER 13

The Cambridge Economic History, vol. II.

G. Agricola, *De Re Metallica*, trans. from the 1st Latin ed. of 1556 (London, Constable, 1912).

H. Hamilton, *The English Brass and Copper Industries to 1800* (London, Cass, 2nd ed. 1967).

J. Hatcher, *Rural Economy and Society in the Duchy of Cornwall, 1300–1500* (Cambridge U.P., 1970). Has a little on tin production.

G. R. Lewis, *The Stannaries: A Study of the Medieval Tin Miners of Cornwall and Devon* (Truro, Barton, reissue 1965 of 1908 ed.).

J. U. Nef, *The Rise of the British Coal Industry*, 2 vols (London, Cass, reissue 1966 of 1932 ed).

CHAPTER 14

The Cambridge Economic History, vol. I

H. S. Bennett, *Life on the English Manor: A study of Peasant Conditions. 1150–1400* (Cambridge U.P., 1937).

M. Bloch, *Les caractères originaux de l'histoire rurale française* (Paris, Colin, new ed. 1952).

H. C. Darby, *The Draining of the Fens* (Cambridge U.P., 2nd ed. 1956).

H. C. Darby, *The Medieval Fenland* (Cambridge U.P., 1940).

F. G. Davenport, *The Economic Development of a Norfolk Manor, 1086–1565* (London, Cass, reissue 1967).

N. Denholm-Young, *Seignorial Administration in England* (London, Cass, reissue 1963 of 1937 ed.).

R. Dion, *Histoire de la vigne et du vin en France* (Paris, Doullens, 1959).

B. Dodwell (ed.), *Feet of Fines for the County of Norfolk 1198–1202*, Pipe Roll Soc., new ser. vols 27 and 32 (London, 1952–8).

F. L. Ganshof, *Feudalism*, trans. P. Grierson (London, Longmans, 3rd ed. 1964).

L. Génicot, *L'économie rurale namuroise au bas Moyen Âge (1199–1429)*, 2 vols (Louvain, University of Louvain Recueil de travaux d'histoire et de philologie, 1943–60).

L. Génicot, 'Sur les témoinages d'accroissement de la population en Occident du XIe au XIIIe siècles', English trans. in S. L. Thrupp (ed.), *Change in Mediaeval Society* (London, Peter Owen, 1965), pp. 14–29.

H. E. Hallam, *The New Lands of Elloe: A Study of Early Reclamation in Lincolnshire*, University College of Leicester Dept of English Local History Occasional Paper No. 6 (Leicester, 1959).

P. D. A. Harvey, *A Medieval Oxfordshire Village, Cuxham, 1240–1400* (London, Oxford U.P., 1965).

R. H. Hilton, *A Medieval Society: The West Midlands at the end of the 13th Century* (London, Weidenfeld & Nicolson, 1966).

G. C. Homans, *English Villagers of the Thirteenth Century* (Cambridge, Mass., Harvard U.P., 1942, paperback ed. 1970).

E. Kosminsky, *Studies in the Agrarian History of England in the XIIIth Century*, ed. R. H. Hilton, trans. R. Kisch (Oxford, Blackwell, 1956).

R. Lennard, *Rural England 1086–1135: A Study of Social and Agrarian Conditions* (London, Oxford U.P., 1959).

E. Miller, *The Abbey and Bishopric of Ely: The Social History of an Ecclesiastical Estate from the 10th to the early 14th century* (Cambridge U.P., 1951).

R. Mols, *Introduction à la démographie historique des villes d'Europe du XIVe au XVIIIe siècle*, 3 vols (University of Louvain, 1954–6).

N. Neilson, *Customary Rents, Oxford Studies in Social and Legal History*, vol. 2 (Oxford, Clarendon Press, 1909).

Ch.-E. Perrin *et al.*, *Le domaine, Recueils de la Société Jean Bodin*, IV (1949).

M. Postan, *The Famulus: The Estate Labourer in the XIIth and XIIIth Centuries. Econ. Hist. Review* Supplement No. 2 (1954).

M. Postan, 'The chronology of labour services', *Trans. Royal Hist. Soc.*, 4th ser. XX (1937), 169–93.

J. A. Raftis, *The Estates of Ramsey Abbey: A Study in Economic Growth and Organization* (Toronto, Pontifical Institute of Medieval Studies, 1957).

J. A. Raftis, *Tenure and Mobility: Studies in the Social History of the Mediaeval English Village* (Toronto, Pontifical Institute of Medieval Studies, 1964).

J. C. Russell, *British Medieval Population* (Albuquerque, University of New Mexico Press, 1948).

J. W. Thompson, *Economic and Social History of Europe in the Later Middle Ages, 1300–1530* (London, Constable, 1931).

J. Z. Titow, *English Rural Society 1200–1350* (London, Allen & Unwin, 1969).

See also the bibliography for Chapters 2 and 3.

CHAPTER 15

B. H. Slicher van Bath, *The Agrarian History of Western Europe, A.D. 500–1850*, trans. O. Ordish (London, Arnold, 1963).

M. W. Beresford and J. K. S. St Joseph, *Medieval England: An Aerial Survey* (Cambridge U.P., 1958).

O. G. S. Crawford, *Air Survey and Archaeology* (London, Ordnance Survey Professional Papers, 2nd ed. 1928).

E. C. Curwen, *Air Photography and the Evolution of the English Cornfield* (London, Black, for the Economic History Society, 2nd ed. 1938).

G. A. J. Hodgett, *Agrarian England in the later Middle Ages*, Historical Association Pamphlet (London, 1966).

D. Oschinsky (ed.), *Walter of Henley and other Treatises on Estate Management and Accounting* (Oxford, Clarendon Press, 1971).

J. B. Passmore, *The English Plough*, Reading University Studies (London, 1930).

F. Seebohm, *The English Village Community* (London, Longmans, 1883).

R. Trow-Smith, *A History of the British Livestock Industry to 1700*, 2 vols (London, Routledge, 1957–9).

CHAPTER 16

W. Abel, *Die Wüstungen des ausgehenden Mittelalters* (Stuttgart, Fischer, 1955).

W. Abel, *Agrarkrisen und Agrarkonjunctur: Eine Geschichte der Land- und Ernährungswirtschaft Mitteleuropas seit dem hohen Mittelalter* (Hamburg and Berlin, Parey, 1966).

J. M. W. Bean, *The Estates of the Percy Family (1416–1537)* (Oxford U.P., 1958).

J. M. W. Bean, *The Decline of English Feudalism 1215–1540* (Manchester U.P., 1968).

M. W. Beresford, *The Lost Villages of England* (London, Lutterworth, 1954).

M. W. Beresford and J. G. Hurst, *Deserted Medieval Villages* (London, Lutterworth, 1971).

W. H. Beveridge, *Prices and Wages in England from the Twelfth to the Nine-teenth Century* (London, Longmans, 1939; 2nd imp. Cass, 1965).

F. R. H. du Boulay, *The Lordship of Canterbury* (London, Nelson, 1966).

R. Boutruche, 'La devastation des campagnes pendant la Guerre de Cent Ans et la reconstruction agricole de la France', Publications de la Faculté des Lettres de l'Université de Strasbourg, fasc. 106, Mélanges, *III Études historiques* (1945), 127–63.

A. R. Bridbury, *Economic Growth: England in the Later Middle Ages* (London, Allen & Unwin, 1962).

E. M. Carus-Wilson and O. Coleman, *England's Export Trade 1275–1547* (London, Oxford U.P., 1963). Contains an invaluable introduction.

P. Chaunu, *L'Expansion européenne du XIIIe au XVe siècle* (Paris, Presses Universitaires de France, 1969).

C. Dyer, 'A redistribution of incomes in XIVth century England', *Past and Present*, XXXIX (1968), 11–33.

H. L. Gray, 'The commutation of villein services in England before the Black Death', *Eng. Hist. Review*, XXIX (1914), 625–56.

E. J. Hamilton, *Money, Prices and Wages in Valencia, Aragon and Navarre, 1351–1500*, Harvard Economic Studies Vol. 51 (Cambridge, Mass., Harvard U.P., 1936).

J. Heers, *L'Occident aux XIVe et XVe siècles: aspects économiques et sociaux* (Paris, Presses Universitaires de France, 3rd ed. 1970). Contains an excellent bibliography.

R. H. Hilton, *The Economic Development of some Leicestershire Estates in the XIVth and XVth Centuries* (London, Oxford U.P., 1947).

R. H. Hilton, *The Decline of Serfdom in Medieval England* (London, Macmillan, 1969).

G. A. Holmes, *The Estates of the Higher Nobility in XIVth Century England* (Cambridge U.P., 1957).

W. G. Hoskins, *The Making of the English Landscape* (London, Hodder, 1955).

H. A. Miskimin, *The Economy of Early Renaissance Europe* (Englewood Cliffs, N. J., Prentice-Hall, 1969).

E. Power and M. Postan (eds.), *Studies in English Trade in the Fifteenth Century* (London, Routledge, 1933).

B. H. Putnam, *The Enforcement of the Statute of Labourers during the First Decade After the Black Death* (New York, Columbia U.P., 1908).

J. U. Nef, 'Silver production in central Europe (1450–1618)', *J. of Pol. Econ.*, XLIX (1941), 575–91.

J. E. Thorold Rogers, *A History of Agriculture and Prices in England, 1259–1793*, 7 vols (Oxford, Clarendon Press, 1866–1902). Still useful for statistical data.

J. C. Russell, 'Recent advances in medieval demography', *Speculum*, XL (1965), 84–101.

J. F. D. Shrewsbury, *A History of Bubonic Plague in the British Isles* (Cambridge U.P., 1970), for a view that diseases other than bubonic plague were responsible for population decline.

P. Ziegler, *The Black Death* (London, Collins, 1969).

RECENT PUBLICATIONS

The following publications have appeared since this volume went into production.

R.-H. Bautier, *The Economic Development of Medieval Europe* (London, Thames & Hudson, 1971).

C. Brooke, *The Structure of Medieval Society* (London, Thames & Hudson, 1971).

C. M. Cipolla (ed.) *The Fontana Economic History of Europe: The Middle Ages* (London, Collins, Fontana, 1972).

Index